WITHDRAWN

The Romantic Paradox

The Romantic Paradox

Love, Violence and the Uses of Romance, 1760–1830

Jacqueline M. Labbe
Senior Lecturer
University of Warwick

First published in Great Britain 2000 by
MACMILLAN PRESS LTD
Houndmills, Basingstoke, Hampshire RG21 6XS and London
Companies and representatives throughout the world

A catalogue record for this book is available from the British Library.

ISBN 0–333–76032–8

First published in the United States of America 2000 by
ST. MARTIN'S PRESS, LLC,
Scholarly and Reference Division,
175 Fifth Avenue, New York, N.Y. 10010

ISBN 0–312–23412–0

Library of Congress Cataloging-in-Publication Data
Labbe, Jacqueline M., 1965–
The romantic paradox : love, violence and the uses of romance, 1760–1830 /
Jacqueline M. Labbe.
p. cm.
Includes bibliographical references and index.
ISBN 0–312–23412–0
1. English poetry—18th century—History and criticism. 2. English poetry—19th
century—History and criticism. 3. Romanticism—Great Britain. 4. Narrative
poetry, English—History and criticism. 5. Love in literature. 6. Death in literature.
7. Della Cruscans (English writers) 8. Violence in literature. I. Title.

PR576.L7 L33 2000
821'.609145—dc21

00–023344

This book is printed on paper suitable for recycling and made from fully managed and sustained
forest sources.

10   9   8   7   6   5   4   3   2
09 08 07 06 05 04 03 02 01

Printed and bound in Great Britain by
Antony Rowe Ltd, Chippenham, Wiltshire

FOR ROD, who unleashes the violence of my affections

Contents

Preface and Acknowledgements

I began investigating the vagaries of the romance in 1993; the result was my first published article, 'A Family Romance: Mary Wollstonecraft, Mary Godwin, and Travel' (*Genre* 25 [1992], 211–28). Arguing that the romance was the unrecognised but vital structural element of Wollstonecraft's and Godwin's travel narratives started me thinking: how many other Romantic-period writings depended on the romance? And why were so many critics determined to apologise for those very romances? The more I read, the more I saw the romance: in plain sight, in the poems of Keats, Byron, Robinson and Landon; less obvious but still essential to the poems of Coleridge, Hemans, the Della Cruscans. And the more I read, the stranger the Romantic romance became: even as they relied on it, poets destroyed it. This book represents my attempt to understand the matrix of romance and violence that infiltrates Romanticism.

I have been assisted in my quest by various agencies. I am grateful to the Department of English Literature at the University of Sheffield for a research grant that allowed me to begin my research in August 1996 and for the sabbatical that allowed me to get down to serious work; to the University of Sheffield Research Fund for a grant that allowed a month's study in London in August 1997; to the British Academy Arts and Humanities Research Board for the Matching Research Leave Award that allowed me the luxury of an extra semester's leave in which to complete the book. I also thank the Editors of the *European Romantic Review* for permission to reprint those parts of Chapter 4 that appeared in Volume 10 (1999).

My greatest debts, however, are to those whose advice and assistance have made this book a stronger, more resilient work. I am most grateful to E.J. Clery, Kate Davies, Frederick De Naples and Jane Hodson, all of whom read chapters and whose comments have helped immensely. Dominic Shellard, the Labbe family, Duco van Oostrum and Lisa Vargo have been patient listeners. Most of all, Rod Jones has given me more than I can express, and this book is dedicated to him.

J.L.
Sheffield

Introduction

The romance has always had a bad press within Romanticism. As a genre, its associations with women readers and writers and assumptions of its inherent inferiority to, for instance, the epic, the ode, or even the sonnet have for many readers contained its power; as a plotline, its fabled preoccupation with love and fantasy has limited its appeal. The romance is rule-bound, immature, feminised and predictable: readers know the outcome before the story even begins. Its very familiarity underscores the fruitlessness of the reading experience – how can enlightenment reside in the heroic exploits of a lover determined against all odds to rescue and win his love, the basic plot outline of almost every romance? And how can intensity survive such an overworked storyline? Surely the value of poetry – of Romantic poetry – is its investigation of the new, the subtle, the subjective, the personal and the many other abstracts attached to critical understandings of the period. How can we reconcile the rote nature of the romance with the energy of Romanticism?

And yet such questions fail to appreciate that, as Stuart Curran points out, 'the etymological root of Romanticism ... is romance'.[1] The romance and its parts infiltrate the period under discussion in this book, about 1760–1830; readers witness not only the novel's embrace of the romance plot (that is, sensibility), but, as this book discusses, poetry's elaborate stockpiling of and investment in the romance. To quote Curran again, 'it might be argued that the term by which we retrospectively define the period simply honors the primacy of romance in British poetry during this epoch' (129); indeed, each of the Big Six – Wordsworth, Coleridge, Blake, Keats, Shelley, Byron – wrote romances or made use of the genre's constituent parts, but beyond this we see that most poets of the period did so, whether simply, through love lyrics, or more complexly, in full-blown romantic narratives. Maybe more importantly, poets affirmed the centrality of the romance by judicially selecting specific aspects to explore: the make-up of the hero and his quest, for instance, or romantic love, or chivalry. As the following chapters show, poets during the Romantic period return repeatedly to the romance, mining it, choosing particulars, eventually transforming it. And while Curran's indispensable explication of this 'poetic form' traces the boom of the romance

1

revival to the early nineteenth century, as this book will show the romance was being manipulated in poetry from at least the late 1780s onwards. Curran dates the romance revival to 'the first decade of the new century, [when] the actual romances were republished' (129), but he is too meticulous: poets had been writing new romances, updating old ones, and interrogating its values for decades. As this book maintains, the romance reveals its essential outlines both explicitly (in the work of Robinson, Keats, Byron and Landon) and more unexpectedly (in the work of Coleridge, the Della Cruscans, Hemans). For the poets of this period, the genre mapped experience, and it provided the tools for self-exploration.

The Romantic romance contains all the necessary ingredients, although not always at the same time: a love relationship central to the plot; a hero, heroine and villain; journeys, adventure and escapes; the supernatural or magical. Importantly, however, it largely dispenses with 'happily ever after'; lovers meet, love, are parted, but seldom are reunited, and if they are, it is seldom to good effect. Instead of celebrating their happiness, the Romantic romance utilises their distress; it finds in the elements of the romance justification for pursuing a changed romance. Rachel Brownstein has said that 'the paradigmatic heroine of courtly love poetry and aristocratic romance is a creature of art and idea ... she is the Ideal incarnate. Therefore, in romance the Lover seeks her'.[2] In the Romantic romance, too, the quest is organised more often around a construct than an object: the hero seeks because he is meant to, and his quest exists because it must. The heroine, however, is less the cipher Brownstein describes, at least in the poems under discussion here that are by women. Instead, she too becomes a questing subject, in search of the intangible, hampered by the ethereal. Like the hero, she must negotiate the pitfalls of genre, and like the hero, she must engage with the strictures of gender. For an interesting corollary to romancing arises from the close study of its mores and requirements this book conducts: gender, and gendering, underpin its structure and unavoidably inform its concerns. In fact, the social construction of sexualised behaviour and its attendant expectations and assumptions emerge as vital to the Romantic concept of romance. The poets under scrutiny in this study struggle with gender through what they write about and how they write it. The traditional romance is inherently deeply conservative in its gender constructions; indeed, many gender stereotypes about strong heroes and passive, beautiful heroines are directly traceable to its plot.[3] The Romantic romance throws down a challenge to the romance of gender; subverting the familiar angles of plot, the Romantic romance reveals the emptiness of generic rhetoric.

In this way, the Romantic romance disorders itself; it commits crimes against genre, impairing the cliché of plot. This is the de Manian 'violence of literary language' described by Adela Pinch: it 'tropes and disfigures what we thought we knew, a counterspirit (to borrow Wordsworth's words) that wastes and destroys'.[4] The romance is put to violent use by its Romantic practitioners, and this is signalled by the violence of the Romantic romance, by its increasingly overt reliance on violent and deathly imagery during the period under discussion. In two recent studies that have focused on different aspects of the romance, David Duff's *Romance and Revolution* and Laurie Langbauer's *Women and Romance*, violence operates peripherally: Duff defines the romance through the image of the French revolution, seeing it as a forum wherein revolutionary ideas can find voice, while Langbauer charts the emergence of the romance in the (mainly) nineteenth-century novel and links it to ideas of gender and consolation.[5] Both of these valuable works, however, invoke the romance only to relocate their critical emphases, reflecting a critical discomfort with the terms offered by the romance as a genre. In refocusing attention on the romance itself, in exploring its engagement with and exploration of violence and its culturally disruptive potential, this book forces a confrontation with the unremarked oddities of Romantic romance.

Moreover, its very status as newly resurgent in the Romantic period begs the question of why this is. One answer can be found in history: alongside the antiquarian discoveries of the 1760s and the literary endeavours of the 1780s onwards, there exists a cultural preoccupation and fascination with violence, war and death. The 1750s see war with France over America; the 1770s and 1780s see war with America; the 1790s and early 1800s see war with France. Of course, Romantic poetry has often been discussed in terms of the French Revolution, but the actual continuity of war from the 1750s is less often remarked. The consolations, to borrow Langbauer's word, offered by a genre reliant on reordering disorder, routing evil and rewarding valour are vast. The rise of the romance must be contextualised historically, and its necessary links to cultural unrest re-established. The loss figured by British defeat in the American Revolution finds play in a genre that concerns itself with military gains, and with a strongly positive national character – valorous, independent, chivalric. The challenge to British sovereignty posed by the French Revolution, fears of a class war, and the resultant government-sponsored cultural repression exists along-side the increasing popularity of a genre that promised the maintenance of certainties. The privations and unrest occasioned by war with France are counterpointed by the poetry of medieval British hardihood and nation-building. Interweaving romance and culture produces a tapestry of meaning, where genre answers a cultural need and violence mirrors the cultural valence. If it is true that 'violence and representation [are] truly interconnected' (Pinch 424) – and this book presumes that it is – then the methodology of violence combines with the representations of the romance to produce documents of cultural unease.

Under this rubric it is interesting to note that while by the 1790s the romance was re-established as a highly popular and widely used generic form, this decade also seemed unable to confront its own use of violence directly, substituting obscurity, indirectness and dream-visions for more visible forms of violence. The disturbing fervour of, and conflicting attitudes towards, the French Revolution and subsequent war with France as well as the unsettling novelties offered by the proponents of the Rights of Man and Woman and the proto-Machine Age offer one explanation. As the new century progresses, and the romance becomes ever more popular and widespread, it also gains the ability to engage directly with the violence its describes: texts become metaphorically blood-soaked as human relations disintegrate into an anti-fairy-tale world of dying unhappily every after. What begins as dream-visions progresses to nightmares and culminates in a glamorisation of literary violence and an increasingly flamboyant approach to romance.

As I have indicated, the Romantic romancers distinguish themselves by a commitment to a kind of romance that picks up on historical signals and cultural need. In their use of violence, they undercut Langbauer's 'consolations of genre', offering a competing rhetoric: violence both reflects culture and inflects it; its imagery engages with a cultural trope and challenges it. Romantic romances perform on multiple levels. They are salutes to a genre, recognisable, comforting and entertaining; they are experiments with a genre, unsettling, odd and compelling; they are subversions of a genre, rebellious, innovative and transformative. They make incursions into the territory occupied by competing genres: ballads, the novel, the Gothic. Romantic romancers specialise in rewriting and delight in generic dismemberment. They find that the elements that make up a romance are detachable and can be used outside the confines of genre; they find that elements can be privileged, overturned, or exposed. For this reason, the romances under discussion in this book are not always complete or fully formed; each chapter instead concentrates on an aspect of romance, on its use-value, and on its interactions with or celebrations of violence. Death figures frequently, but so does love: the eros/thanatos drive is gestured towards, if not fully articulated. Even as poets tear the romance to bits, they reify its prominence, its ability to speak to and of the time; its translation of cultural violence into literary representation functions as an unacknowledged legislator of Romanticism.

Readers and critics of Romantic poetry, then, find themselves haunted by a spectral genre whose outlines have appeared too flimsy to support the weight of Romanticism, and yet its continual return belies its repression.[6] Wordsworth, for instance, inserts romance into his document of personal poetic philosophy, *The Prelude*.[7] As is well-known, the romance of Julia and Vaudracour partly disguises Wordsworth's own romance with Annette Vallon; it allows him to confess without actually revealing anything at all. But besides the violence residing in his decision to literalise – that is, make literary – his personal romance and thereby mask it, this interlude also illustrates Wordsworth's involvement in Romanticising romance.[8] Wordsworth deposits his romance in Book IX, 'Residence in France', and leads up to it via images of courtly romance – maidens on palfreys, knights jousting, satyrs, imprisoned damsels, convents 'dismantled ... by violence abrupt' (IX: 472)[9] – combined with examples of the tyranny and poverty in present-day revolutionary France. His 'chivalrous delight' (IX: 503) thus bound up with political repression, Wordsworth decides to 'draw from obscurity a tragic Tale' (IX: 551) to illustrate the need for revolutionary change. The story of Julia and Vaudracour follows romantic convention, which its status as a 'Tale' emphasises: young love, stern parents, separation, reunion, final separation. This is a tragic romance, but more than its lack of a happy ending impedes its generic trajectory. Vaudracour transgresses the conventions of courtly love when, 'through effect/ Of some delirious hour' (IX: 596–7), or because of his frustration at his father's intransigence, he impregnates Julia; already the romance is being challenged. When Julia's parents send her away to hide her pregnancy, the prosaic motive of shame intervenes in the meeting of true lovers. The most fully realised romance character is Vaudracour's father, whose villainy is undiffused: he operates, *deus ex machina*, outside of Vaudracour's and Julia's romance to thwart it. The crystallising moment of violence works simultaneously to prove the father's heartlessness and Vaudracour's useless valour: set upon by his father's minions, Vaudracour kills one, 'perilously' wounds another and gives himself up to a third (IX: 675–84). After this, Vaudracour goes into romantic decline; he passively accepts his fate, fails to rescue Julia from her convent fate, fails to persuade or placate his father, fails even to protect his baby son, who, 'after a short time, by some mistake/ Or indiscretion of the Father [Vaudracour], died' (IX: 907–8). The romance thus ends, having led only to imprisonment, death and Vaudracour's 'imbecile mind' (IX: 935). Wordsworth disregards the generic requirements of romance, using the story to exemplify the pernicious effects of tyranny, but he shows clearly enough the capacity for violence offered by the genre: by linking the Tale directly with the depradations of French tyranny, by utilising murder as a turning point, by killing off the baby. On another level he does violence to the notion of romance itself: love is defined by trauma, terror, murder, imprisonment and separation. Vaudracour is revealed as an inadequate hero, unable to withstand the forces of, here, parental oppression.[10] Finally, Wordsworth operates on an extra-textual level, showing the congeniality with which the romance co-operates with authorial desires: the story of Vaudracour and Julia hides Wordsworth's personal history; it exemplifies the need to change in France; it illustrates the effects of tyranny. The bodily harm suffered by Julia, Vaudracour and the baby combine with the damage Wordsworth does to plot, with the result that the romance implodes, its meaning detached from plot yet contingent on that plot's disorder. For Wordsworth, romantic violence represents political violence.

Wordsworth conjoins the romance and violence to make a political point, but he embeds in his Tale his personal love story, itself disjointed and fragmentary. In this way he participates in the romance revival, and yet he is seldom discussed as a romancer; even Curran mentions only *The White Doe of Rylstone*, calling it a 'lyrical romance, whose central concern is not action, but the functioning of symbols' (142). Walter Scott, by contrast, is frequently discussed as a writer of romances, although his novels are the focus, along with his standing as the 'creator' of the regional novel/historical novel/national novel. Indeed, a recent article on his poetic romances emphasises Scott's status as historian, his poetry serving as historical documents.[11] This offers an interesting insight into Scott's method, but also implies that Scott's romances need tightening up – that they need, as well as exemplify, the vigour of the masculine. The use of Gothic imagery and antiquarian detail is not gender-determined, however, as the romances of Mary Robinson, Felicia Hemans and Letitia Landon show. Michael Gamer, the critic in question, mentions only in passing what is particularly telling about Scott's style of romance: the peculiarly vexed heroism of his heroes. *Marmion* especially threatens to undo the weave of romance altogether: 'Marmion threatens to subvert the poem's' – and the genre's – 'standards of chivalric warfare and courtship' (Gamer 546), while Curran notes that Marmion's lawlessness questions the romance ethos (138 *passim*). Certainly Marmion's villainy cancels out his martial prowess; Scott seems uninterested in composing a thorough hero, and his creative role-mixing injects a scepticism aimed at an unthinking ratification of chivalric values: Scott undercuts chivalry to demonstrate its liabilities. As much as he relies on the popularity of romance, and uses its tropes to establish a heroic national history for Scotland, he is uncomfortable with a total investment in its import. To convey his dissatisfaction, he rewrites chivalry by rehousing it. To balance Marmion's treachery and baseness and the general ineffectualness of his heroes, Scott offers chivalrous women: Constance, Margaret, the Ladye, Ellen, all of whom demonstrate the positive aspects of romantic chivalry: constancy, loyalty, bravery, honesty, hardihood. Scott's worlds of romance are informed by a sense of the past and a creative medievalism that functions as the early nineteenth-century version of the mid-eighteenth-century revival of the romance. The work of earlier antiquarian researchers – Hurd, Percy, Reeve – is theatrically recast: Scott's world of romance is both historically informed and ahistorically aware of its own imminent disappearance. Hence, he can write (of) the lay performed by the 'last' minstrel even though the minstrel himself is only hazily aware of his belatedness. Similarly, the romances he sings of contain the familiar elements, but infected with a sense of cynicism and self-regard: Scott's knights and heroes are strangely unable to conquer their own violent impulses, let alone slay villains and rescue fair maidens. Instead, echoing the challenges to gender thrown down by most of the poets this book discusses, Scott invests his female characters with the strength, honour and purity expected of the true Knight. It is a marker of his loss of confidence in the romantic ethos that his heroines are not protected by their honour, but are instead the victims of a blind chivalry that may follow its rules to the strict letter, but has forgotten about the spirit.

Both Wordsworth and Scott write romances; both radically alter the romance's meaning and both use violence to do so. They, and the poets whose work is the focus of this book, explore the 'dark side of romanticism ... the loneliness, dread, and ... violence of human experience that stand counter to predominant romantic assumptions about ideal beauty and human possibility'.[12] They do this at an historical epoch peculiarly inflected by war and political violence, and they do so through a genre that requires specific adaptations to suit. The romance transmogrifies from a peripheral genre, embarrassing in its shallowness, to a key to romantic-period cultural anxiety. As this book shows, the style of writing romance remains fairly stable, with some important plot deviations, but the style in which violence is portrayed changes from the indirect, metaphorical method of the 1780s and 1790s to the direct representation of 'real' violence in the 1810–20s. It is difficult to assign a reason for this change, but one may speculate: as the intensity and duration of real-life violence – war – continued unabated, violence itself may have become easier to represent – an instance of art imitating life. What was unspeakable in the 1790s had become routine a generation later. In this way, the presence of actual violence implants a receptivity to violence in literature, at first countered by reluctance, fear and a preference for masquerade, later dulled by the repetitive onslaught of actual images of violence and thus requiring increasing explicitness. For both the poet and the reader, the dose must be increased to achieve the same thrill. As Chapter 1 explains, for many theorists of the romance, it was its very propensity to encourage vicarious emotions that constituted its strength, and its threat. Once attach violence to the romance and its currency – as risk, as sop, as mirror, as protest – goes up. As this book seeks to establish, this is the romantic appeal of romance: it is flexible, open to suggestion, desirous to please, malleable. And under the handling of Romantic poets, it reveals its sociopathic nature.

Each chapter in this book focuses on one aspect of the romance and explores its manipulations and metamorphoses by representative poets. First, Chapter 1 sets the scene by reviewing the history of the romance revival. Offering an analysis of tracts purporting to define and place the 'new' romance in the late eighteenth century, this chapter investigates the allure of chivalry and its association with fantasy. David Duff, for instance, discusses the chivalric tone of several pro- and anti-Revolutionary tracts of the 1790s; his romanticised version of chivalry, however, does not take into account its dark side: that what chivalry can hide is a devotion to and glorification of war and killing. As much as chivalric values are the embodiment of virtue and order, they also represent an attempt to *impose* order;

repression and restriction shadow the purity that is associated with knightly behaviour. The myth of order is undermined by an increasing inability to maintain that order, and the rhetoric surrounding the romance, the many attempts to define and contain it, mirror this conflict. I contextualise this discussion by concentrating on tracts produced during the revolutionary years, including the American Revolution (the repercussions of which are usually ignored). This chapter sets up key sources and defines the terms and tropes that the rest of the study will approach in detail.

Chapter 2 discusses the erotic and violent world of the Della Cruscan poets. These authors knowingly exploit the elements of the romance: the Della Cruscan circle's intimacy and veiled eroticism exert a strong and abiding – even romantic – influence on its mainly female readership. By casting their poetry as versions of sexual love-letters to each other, poets such as Robert Merry (the circle's leader) and his female 'correspondents' skirt issues of propriety and social order; they establish a kind of poetical harem that defies decorum. And yet, the language of their poetry remains curiously formulaic, as if the power of sexuality can only be tapped if the flow is rendered weak. Even, then, as the Della Cruscan version of the romance creates individualised contracts of poetic passion, it also defuses the strength it invokes. Emotional violence is countered with poetical precision.

In Chapter 3, I contrast the personal romance constructed by Coleridge in his 'conversation poems' with Keats's romances from his 1820 volume. I argue that each poet can be seen to be constructing versions of the quest; where Coleridge makes himself – that is, his poetic persona – into the questing hero, Keats utilises myth and literary history as his sources. And yet both poets seem unable to imagine a successful resolution for their heroes. Coleridge's continual heroic self-armouring concludes as continually in failure and dejection, while Keats's heroes – Lycius, Lorenzo, the Knight-at-arms, even Porphyro – meet violent ends or else disappear into the past. These poems of failed quest-heroes do literary violence to the notion of the heroic romantic subject, while their different approaches reflect a changing attitude to the level of violence depictable.

Chapter 4 focuses on Mary Robinson and Felicia Hemans and their versions of the interrupted romance. Again, the contrast exists between Robinson's suggestive approach, wherein her violent disruption to romantic closure is expressed through dream-visions and allusions, and Hemans's direct representations of dying men. Where Robinson's romances fail because of the weakness of her characters,

Hemans's are often undone through their strengths: that is, masculine endurance is put to the test of disease and torture until it finally gives out. The outcome – the romance gone awry – dramatises an increasing unease with the relationships offered by the romance.

The study concludes by examining how Letitia Landon and Byron transform the romance into the violent and sensational world of the melodrama. Byron's melodramatic Eastern poems often recast the heterosexual vision of star-crossed lovers offered by the romance as a moment of homosocial masculine definition, while Landon's equally melodramatic poems of blasted love reveal the emptiness of the promise held out by the romance a generation earlier. Both authors privilege death – suicide, murder – over any more peaceful resolution, and neither can imagine a world wherein romantic relationships are viable. For both, the growing solidification of gender roles and expectations and the formation of absolutely separate spheres renders male/female relationships impossible. Although Landon's strategy is to cast the feminine sphere as destructive to masculinity and hence love, while Byron's is to construct masculinity itself as destructive to women, the work of both reveals the breakdown of the ideals of the romance and in this, the triumph of a cultural insistence on concretised sexual roles.

In 1930, when he first published *The Romantic Agony*, Mario Praz thrust violence into the discourse of Romanticism and was rewarded with twenty years of dismissive and patronising reactions.[13] Violence in literature is difficult to discuss, in part because it is only ever textual; it depends on the susceptibility of its readers for its effect, and especially when the genre is Romantic poetry, it must contend with decades of criticism divorcing subjectivity from corporeality.[14] The romance, however, actively encourages the disorder and strife that accompany violent imagery and content; and Romantic romance poetry is less queasy than its critics. The trajectory followed by the romance supplies modern readers with important insights into a cultural reliance on the unreal, a multivalent dependence mirrored in the clash between readers and works, desire and expectation, romance and reality, love and death. Despite critical willingness to underestimate its vigour, in its changing and increasingly violent world the romance figures and emblematises Romanticism itself.

1
Reviving the Romance: What's Love Got to Do with It?

What wildly-beauteous form,
  High on the Summit of yon bicrowned hill,
Lovely in horror, takes her dauntless stand?
    Tho' speeds the thunder there its deep'ning way
    Tho' round her head the lightnings play,
Undaunted she abides the storm;
      She waves her magic wand,
    The clouds retire, the storm is still;
Bright beams the sun unwonted light around,
And many a rising flower bedecks the enchanted ground.

    Romance! I know thee now,
    I know the terrors of thy brow;
I know thy awful mien, thy beaming eye;
      And lo! whilst mists arise around
      Yon car that cleaves the pregnant ground!
Two fiery dragons whirl her through the sky;
      Her milder sister loves to rove
      Amid Parnassus' laurell'd grove,
      On Helicon's harmonious side,
      To mark the gurgling streamlet glide;
Meantime, thro' wilder scenes and sterner skies,
From clime to clime the ardent genius flies.
                    . . .
Dim shadows circle round her secret seat,
Where wandering, who shall approach shall hear
      The wild wolf rend the air;
      Thro' the cloud-mantled sky

> Shall see the imps of darkness fly,
> And hear the sad scream from the grim retreat;
> Around her throne
> Ten thousand dangers lurk, most fearful, most unknown.[1]

In 1795, when the young undergraduate Robert Southey published his ode 'To Romance' under the pen-name 'Bion', the revival of the romance was fully established; since the mid-1760s scholars had been publishing defences and explications of a form that, nonetheless, refused a completely fixed definition.[2] As Southey's enthusiastic verse shows, Romance encompassed love and war, peace and violence: its female figurehead seductively offers both complete submission and exciting domination. Southey cannot decide if he wants his emblem to embrace or reject the traits assigned her gender; to get around his difficulty he provides her with a 'milder sister' who roves through softer, more appropriately pastoral landscapes, but he cannot resist the compelling nature of the 'ardent genius' who 'flies' 'thro' wilder scenes and sterner skies'. True to her gender, Romance cannot be pinned down; she refuses the softer, more genteel life her sister leads; she is not 'romantic' but unruly. Her demeanour suggests not pliability, not love, but mastery. As the poem shows, much of Romance's attraction lies, for Southey at least, in her ability to control, through a kind of stern sexiness, both the elements and her readers, here embodied by Southey's poet persona: as both reader and writer of what he reads he occupies a uniquely supervisory position, both in thrall to and in control of a genre. But Romance herself asserts an authority that compels the poet to versify her history, and in a chronology heavily indebted to Hurd, Warton, Reeve, and the other theorisers of earlier decades, he works his way from early medievalism to Rousseau, whom he names 'the guide of my life', and then abruptly ends the poem.

Southey's panegyric usefully encapsulates the themes this chapter will explore. It demonstrates the general availability of theories of the romance to the educated reader (if immature poet); it makes plain the association between women and the romance; it reveals the powerful hold of war and violence on the conventions of the genre; it echoes the turn to chivalry especially powerful in the 1790s but gaining prominence from the 1760s on, as David Duff has established.[3] Although the figure of Romance is powerful enough to stand as a Britomart thoroughly able to take care of herself, she nonetheless requires the poetic champion Southey to present her sympathetically, a critically chivalrous impulse that, as I shall discuss, informs many of the scholarly tracts dedicated to this theme. And this is vital, for, as Southey's Romance shows, as much as he wants to turn her towards love, war keeps getting in the way, and given her gender, such an emphasis is unseemly and even disruptive. Southey's allegory performs for modern readers the masquerade that this book addresses: that the romance is concerned more with violence than with peace, and that chivalry is a euphemism for repression. His poem makes plain the violence embedded in both the 'old' (medieval) and the 'new' (post-Spenser) romances: even once 'love, with innocence, assumes his reign',[4] the verse almost immediately turns to chieftains' 'deadly blows'. Clearly, Romance needs her poet to keep her in line, and she relies on his skill to make her presentable. Underpinning, then, the attractions of Romance is the trope that threatens to explode them: this chapter will trace the modifications of critical idiom in tracts devoted to the romance, starting slightly before the revolutionary period and culminating in the 1790s and that decade's explorations of chivalry. By 'revolutionary period' I mean approximately 1770 onwards; as part of my argument unpicks the knots created by the cultural affect of revolution, it is important to note that the power of the French uprising was foreshadowed, and even emblematised, by the American Revolution (1775–83). Of course, the critical commonplace is that the American War of Independence (to give it its name in British history) did not really impinge on the culture of the time, that few thinkers concerned themselves with such a distant conflict, and that it was rather more a relief than a regret when the Colonies were 'lost'. And yet, as subsequent chapters suggest a complex and deep interrelationship between the threat posed by the Revolution and war with France and the solace offered by the conventional romance, so too an initial investigation of the revival of the romance in the second half of the eighteenth century – and its critical transformation from disgusting and immoral to pleasing (though still immoral) – can be linked in profitable ways with the rumblings of the American Revolution.[5]

David Duff makes the valuable point in *Romance and Revolution* that 'the revolutionisation of the language of romance that took place in the political writing of the [French] Revolution debate, and ... the existence in the English imagination of the "revolutionary romance" of the Revolution itself' characterises the 1790s. The thrust of his argument – that political writers championed their cause through the canny deployment of language borrowed from the romance – reminds readers of the pervasive influence of the genre, despite its public guise as insipid, corrupting and debased. This, indeed, is an instance of the 'ambivalence' of the romance; as Patricia Parker says, 'its charms were indistinguishable from its snares' (163). For Duff's purposes, one charm was the seemingly dependable nature of the romance world: 'The magical narratives of romance – with their ideal heroes, transformation scenes and earthly paradises, but also their terrifying monsters, and their deceptions, temptations and errors – offered an apt and accurate metaphorical language to write about the extraordinary phenomenon that confronted them' (13). As this characterisation shows, however, the romance world did not and could not offer merely the escapist fantasy described by Northrop Frye; even as its 'charms were its snares', so too its snares were very present: although one mark of the hero/heroine may be his/her imperviousness to – or, in the case of the hero, his escape from – deception, temptation and error, still such danger awaited – indeed, invited – him/her. Duff implies but does not discuss that one reason the romance metaphor was so attractive to political writers was because the world it contained was one wherein the French Revolution and cultural upheaval were not happening. In other words, it was safe, ordered, recognisable and definable. But because, in Fredric Jameson's words, 'romance ... is that event in which the *world* in the technical sense of the transcendental horizon of my experience becomes precisely visible as something like an innerworldly object in its own right, taking on the shape of the *world* in the popular sense of nature, landscape, and so forth' (142) – that is, romance both replaces and reifies 'world' – its safety and security were compromised by its narrative reliance on tropes of violence. Duff's 'revolutionisation of the language of romance' is only possible because of what the romance allows: both violence and the rejection of it, a restabilisation of a world temporarily shaken.

Although theorists of the romance in the 1760s, 1770s and 1780s do not make overt reference to the Revolution their culture was witnessing – or refusing to watch – it is telling that a genre that emphasised military ardour and chivalric exploits was being re-examined at the same time that the Redcoats were arming, then fighting, then straggling home. The reverential tone adopted by Hurd, Percy and others towards the heroics of romance replaces real-life attention paid to their defeated army. Indeed, if one accepts Eric Auerbach's class-based analysis of the service that romance was put to, then its reviving popularity suggests that it acts as a stand-in for, as much as a mirror of, the generals and colonels in America. Auerbach's contention that the romance 'offers a very rich and pungent picture of the life of a single class', and that such a plot-line allows for the continuation of class distinction as well as a reassuring frisson for readers of being of the 'right sort', confers on those who write about it a privilege both intellectual and social.[6] Real-world soldiers are defeated and humiliated; in the world of the romance, such events, if they happen, have a meaning, and they don't happen very often. To understand the romance, then, means to make all right with the world.[7] Thus, if one chooses to discuss the romance, to deflect attention from military imprecision and class conflict to tales which maintain the *status quo*, then in one sense the disruption is not happening. The loss embodied by the lost war becomes the gain figured by the thick volumes of Percy's *Reliques* and the multiple attempts to pin down the exact nature of the romance.

Of course, a direct correlation – ignore the Revolution, concentrate on the romance – is too simple a formulation, and yet the attention paid to the unreal exploits of ages past, the turn to the comforting, knowable, ordered set of rites that is chivalry, and the desire to establish the literary heritage of the nation in the workings of a genre where right, truth and purity were rewarded betrays a desire to justify and support the courtly values of the nation.[8] Even, then, as they wrote *about* the romance, intellectuals were also recreating its world, re-establishing its importance, and reinscribing its parameters – repeatedly. For despite a general agreement about how to define the romance and its world, writers still did so again and again, citing and supporting each other without seeming to recognise that they were rewriting each other as much as re-presenting the romance. And even as volumes appeared defining the romance, differentiating it from the novel, and declaring the superiority of one or the other, they also protested the general loss of the romance and its values, as a genre and as an ideal – Burke's famous pronouncement is only the most well-known. 'Bishop Hurd, with others of his century, saw romance as a receding form, a world of fine fabling being crowded out by the advance of mind', says Parker (15). Such an elegiac attitude, however, is belied by the constant reinvocations of the romance, whether positively or negatively. Further, the apparent need to distinguish between the romance and the novel, and curious inability to do so (manifested by repeated attempts to do so) well into the nineteenth century, show that, far from being about to die out, the romance was continually resuscitated by critics who seemed anxious they might lose it. Clearly, the genre was viable and deeply significant. Why? And how?

Critical chivalry

For many critics rediscovering the romance, its worth lay in the chivalric world created by knights, ladies, castles, and courtly values. The belatedness of John Batty's 1890 study *The Spirit and Influence of Chivalry* only emphasises this point; he is lyrical, even rhapsodic in his proposal that chivalry is the basis for all virtuous human (that is, male) action: 'Oh! what would become of the human race if the spirit of self-sacrifice, which is one of the brightest gems in the crown of chivalry, became extinct?'[9] Batty's examples of modern chivalry – manning lifeboats, rescuing trapped miners, saving a drowning child – rely on a gentlemanly sense of noblesse oblige and right; writing at the end of a century that refocused attention on the medieval romance as narrative, he is fulsome in his praise of its values. Inhabiting his account of courtly behaviour, however, is a sanitised form of violence: 'The highest development of the chivalric idea gives a spiritual aspect to chivalry – in fact, makes it the exponent of Christianity ... religion put in action' (84). This religious chivalry translates into the Christian's fight for his faith:

> By sacred and allegorical writers this world has been frequently represented as a scene of spiritual warfare, the foes in the field against which the Christian has to fight being those of the world, the flesh, and the devil .... [L]ife is a constant struggle against evil ... in order to overcome it .... The weapons of this spiritual warfare are taken from the 'armoury of knighthood', and are made use of metaphorically to illustrate the doctrines and truths of Christianity. Thus St. Paul ... says 'put on the whole armour of God', 'taking the shield of faith', 'the helmet of salvation', 'the sword of the Spirit', and so on. (84–5)

Transferring chivalry from the secular to the sacred world (and intriguingly casting St Paul as a kind of apostolic de Scudery), Batty still infuses it with violence, even if the fight is, as he eventually labels it, metaphorical: Batty's romance ur-text is the Bible, wherein St Paul functions as a page to his squire, the Christian, arming him for the battle against evil. With the Bible transformed into a romance containing lessons in chivalry, the origins of both are validated and celebrated: if romance informs the Bible, Batty seems to argue, then who but the devil can contest its worth? And if violence is put to the service of good – religion – against evil – the devil – then it, too, is transformed, no longer an impulse for which to apologise, but for which to give thanks. Batty's romantic religion achieves for the 1890s what Duff's romantic revolution does for the 1790s: it displaces the tenets of chivalry, here onto an external 'Christian soldier' whose onward movement is assisted by his association with courtliness. Inheriting 150 years' worth of speculating about and defining such terms, he turns them inward, disembodies them, renders them 'metaphorical'. For Batty, the dark ages to be combated would be the previous centuries which did not recognise the fundamentally Christian nature of chivalry.

Batty's *fin-de-siècle* reappropriation insists on the presence of a Biblical chivalry, but the eighteenth-century revival was concerned less with faith than with fable. Despite laments that the Age of Reason killed the romance, Hurd's 1762 *Letters* signalled a resuscitation; as Duff notes, 'once the prejudice against the "dark ages" began to fall away, it is not surprising that the intrinsic appeal of the ideal of chivalry, and the validity of many of the ideals which the chivalric code expressed, began once more to be recognised' (30). Hurd's investigation of the romance and chivalry takes the form of didactic letters to a 'dear friend' and is determinedly intellectualised, just as Batty's will be determinedly religious: the appeal here is to the mind, and to 'curious speculation'. Even barbarous times have something to offer rational thinkers, he posits. Hurd's understanding of the romance mixes interpretation with speculation, but like Batty and Southey he clearly locates chivalry's origins in violent war: what comes to be a series of courtly rituals begins as mere self-defence in an age of gothic disorder. '*Chivalry* ... seems to have sprung immediately out of the FEUDAL CONSTITUTION .... the feudal state was, in a good degree, a state of war,' and chivalry itself a 'military institution'.[10] Hurd is careful to explain that such violent origins did not mean the institution itself was irrational: 'Chivalry was no absurd or freakish institution, but the natural and even sober effect of the feudal policy; whose turbulent genius breathed nothing but war, and was fierce and military even in its amusements' (85). Just as Batty will describe his christianised chivalry as metaphorical, here Hurd designates his version as 'sober' – *not* heady, *not* irrational, *not* uncontrolled. Because 'the barbarians' of the 'barbarous ages' had good reasons for their conduct, and because method could be discerned and behaviour labelled, Hurd's own study is justified, and although his unfolding of chivalry reveals an institution almost wholly dependent on personal and communal violation and bloodshed, his tone remains approving, even admiring, throughout. Hence knight-errantry develops from bandit-raids and the self-interested protection of one's property, which included one's woman: 'the interest, each had to protect his own, would of course introduce the point of honour in attempting by all means not only to retaliate on the enemy, but to rescue the captive sufferers out of the hands of their oppressors' (87). Courtesy is borne out of fear: 'the castles of the Barons were ... the courts of these little sovereigns, as well as their fortresses; and the resort of the vassals thither, in honour of their chiefs, *and for their own proper security*, would make that civility and politeness, which is seen in courts ... a predominant part in the character of these assemblies' (88, emphasis added). Most tellingly, chivalry's ornament, chaste courtly love and its veneration of women, arises out of resentment at the rapine of one's enemies: 'gallantry would take a refined turn ... from the inflamed sense [princes] must needs have of the frequent outrages committed, by their ... adversaries, on the honour of the Sex .... Violations of chastity being the most atrocious crimes they had to charge on their enemies, they would pride themselves in the glory of being its protectors ...' (89). Hurd's conscientiously historicised account teeters on the edge of revealing chivalry to be every bit as barbaric and selfish as its critics charged.

That the ideals of chivalry and the courtly code can be so cogently derived from bloody internal conflict and the need to contain it suggest that the sturdy apolitical tone of Hurd's letters acts as a kind of defence against the national rumblings and unrest in those distant American colonies. Uncovering the logic of what was a system designed to repress rebellion and contain violence – suggested by its origins *in* violence – and declaring the rightness, even the beauty of that system allowed this conservative clergyman to substitute a fantasy past for a potentially troublesome present. And yet the parameters of that past – its basis in bloodshed and uncontrolled violence – also necessitate a recovery of the past from itself. When Hurd comes to discuss the romance and its development from an idealised chivalry, he is able to dismiss chivalry's violence in favour of romance's version of it: 'Gothic manners of chivalry, as springing out of the feudal system, were as singular, as that system itself. So that, when that political constitution vanished out of Europe, the manners, that belonged to it, were no longer seen or understood .... people would be led of course to think and speak of them, as romantic, and unnatural' (148). Having established the reality of romantic chivalry, Hurd now consigns it to romantic fantasy, at least in the minds of those past 'people'; it has become, to use Batty's term, metaphorical. In its newly romanticised – that is, unreal and unnatural – form, gothic chivalry is divested of its rationality: and we have reached the court of Elizabeth I, whose 'inclinations for *the fancies of Chivalry* is well-known' (152, emphasis added). Now that chivalry has moved from a mode to a fancy, Hurd can only watch in dismay as the 'glowing splendour' of 'dawning' Reason puts 'the portentous spectres of the imagination' 'to flight, and allow[s] them no quarter even amongst the poets' (153). As he records the death of the chivalric ideal (and places it some centuries earlier than does Burke), Hurd takes on the very language of the form that he mourns: chivalry and the romance undergo a transformation to spectres, and are then routed by the Red Cross Knight of Reason, being denied sanctuary even by their natural protectors. This is a kind of dark romance, gone awry, where the good and noble appear tainted, and where even the poets reject the offspring of the imagination. That Hurd himself has effected a pre-transformation when he allows the violence of chivalry to be its own justification only enhances the romantic nature of his conclusion. A straight reading of Hurd's elegy would produce the conviction that he now approves of the demise of that which he has striven to resurrect: and yet it is clear that Hurd has inserted himself into the romance of his own reconstruction. He is bard, translator, sorcerer, hero, and even villain, for as much as he champions romance, he also kills it off.

Hurd's wavering between supporting and rejecting the romance results in a text wherein he takes on the very chivalric values he describes. His description of the powers of the 'Gothic enchanters' who 'shook and alarmed all nature' (110) finds its source in Hurd's own scholarship; his revival and re-enactment of chivalry and gothic romance requires a reordering of the nature of his culture's attitude to the romance. Supported by Percy, Warton and others, Hurd reorients the romance as not the Cervantes-style mindless imagining but as a historical, recognisable and valid literary form. Concerned to present it to its fullest advantage, he compares the gothic romance favourably with the Grecian: 'the boisterous passions ... are provoked and kept alive from one end of the Iliad to the other, by every imaginable scene of rage, revenge, and slaughter .... on the whole, tho' the spirit, passions, rapin, and violence of the two sets of manners were equal, yet there was a dignity, a magnificence, a variety in the feudal, which the other wanted' (109). As a Knight preserves and protects the honour of his Lady, so Hurd does with chivalric romance, with the crowning touch that 'Gothic manners and machinery ... have, by their nature and genius, the advantage of the [Classical] in producing the *sublime*' (117). The dawning age of reason may have banished the romance, but, Hurd implies, this is more a limitation of the current age than a strength; and the validity of the romance and its values are attested to by the ease with which Hurd deploys its language. Even as Percy 'laboured on the texts [in his *Reliques*], to present them in as palatable a form as possible',[11] and in this way performs his own knightly feat, so too Hurd imbues his text with a chivalric appreciation of and respect for what may be called the chastity of chivalry and the honour of romance. Poets may have forsaken the romance, he indicates, but this Bishop hasn't, and while Hurd avoids the romantic religiosity of Batty, he conveys instead a critical chivalry that champions a genre *on its behalf*. That is, as female knights were an example of 'the excesses of military fanaticism' (86), so too romance on its own presents dangerous excesses and must be mediated through the scholarly mind. In Percy's words: 'a taste for the old Romances begins to revive (not among the common Readers, where it would do hurt but) amongst our Critics and Poets'.[12] The physical violence out of which chivalry and the romance arose may safely be stowed in the past, but clearly, the romance itself still poses a threat.

Percy's attitude reflects the common conclusion that reading romances destabilised and shocked young minds, unready for its excesses; it is those excesses that fascinate and disgust Hurd, and feed his inability fully to champion the romance. However, Clara Reeve's *The Progress of Romance* (1785) sees its female speaker declare to an incredulous male listener that romances are actually 'epics in prose', hence fully respectable, and having thrown down this challenge begins her own critical recovery of a maligned form, in what may be called 'The Romance of *The Progress of Romance*'. By 1785, it has become necessary not merely to define 'romance' but to distinguish it from 'novel', and Reeve deftly separates the two by commenting that in a novel things happen that could happen, while in a romance things happen that are unlikely ever *really* to happen. The text is in two volumes, and the first deals mainly with the romance, the second mainly with the novel. But Reeve is most concerned with continuing the debate on the value and worth of the romance; even in Volume II she contextualises the shortcomings of the novel by highlighting the advantages of the romance. Reeve's study points out the quizzical, almost fairy-tale nature of defences of the romance: as often as they appear, it seems as if there must always be a fresh one, as if instead of acting cumulatively to establish an impregnable defence, they merely effect each other: that is, they act to bring the next tract into being, creating a world as insular and contained as the romance-world itself. Certainly, Reeve's takes note of what has gone before – Hurd, Percy, Susannah Dobson[13] all get their mention and are extensively quoted, in extracts the romance's advocate, Euphrasia, uses to her advantage. But the implication is that it just hasn't been done well enough yet – the romance remains vulnerable, continues to require a champion, as if the genre itself is like an imprisoned, enchanted damsel: many champions, seemingly unconquerable, will come forward, and all will fail. Reeve plots this trope into her study, for at the outset it is plain that Euphrasia – Reeve's voice in the text – sees herself as Romance's new protector, and her listeners – sceptical Hortensius, supportive Sophronia – as alternately her assistants and her foes. That Reeve creates a fictive non-fiction demonstrates her romantic commitment to her task: what better way of illustrating the respectable viability of the romance than through the writing of a version of it? Reeve employs her characters in the romance's service, showing its flexibility (her three characters play all the roles), its viability (they sustain their interest for more than 230 pages over two volumes), and its morality. Unlike Hurd, Reeve shows no ambivalence; the perfect partisan, she admits romance's faults but soon converts them into strengths. And she argues from a uniquely informed position she makes plain is contingent on her gender: she *knows* romances because, as a woman, she has *read* them. Further, as a rational being (and Reeve/Euphrasia's claim to rationality is all the more striking for her unapologetic assumption of it), she *understands* romance. *The Progress of Romance*, then, is also Euphrasia's – and her companions' – progress *through* Romance.

Euphrasia refuses the usual female roles offered by the romance, those of victim or villain, allowing Reeve immediately to begin rewriting her romantic tract. She is neither (to borrow Cixous's terms) sorceress nor hysteric, although she does make use of kinds of talismans, as any proper knight must do. To borrow yet more terminology, where Frye argues that in the romance, 'virginity is female honor, the symbol of the heroine's ... independence',[14] Euphrasia follows instead a code of (intellectual) experience: her independence of mind is gained through independent thought, and *The Progress of Romance* makes clear that this affords Euphrasia bodily protection. Viewed by her listeners as a friend, rather than as the sexualised body that is 'woman', Euphrasia's knightly demeanour relies on a courtly chastity which is self- rather then other-protected: she is her own Knight as well as Romance's. And the tournament begins immediately – almost the first words in the text are Hortensius'.

> What, Madam, do you think you can give a challenge, and go off with impunity? – I am come hither to demand an explanation of your behaviour ... and I have brought [Sophronia] with me to be a witness to our dispute – of the defeat of one of us, – or perhaps of our compromise, and reconciliation.
>
> *Sophronia.* Or that *Euphrasia* shall make a convert to her own opinion.[15]

Hortensius begins by invoking the language of gentlemen: he wants to settle their 'dispute' through a kind of verbal duel. Sophronia's contribution, however, opens the possibility that the usual gender hierarchy will not be observed in this text, furthered by Euphrasia's subsequent metaphorical arming. As the first paragraphs progress, it emerges that Euphrasia has compared romances to epic poetry, which Hortensius cannot abide, insisting on an inherent literary inequality; when Sophronia finds she is unable to 'ward off his attack' she 'engage[s] her honour' that Euphrasia can 'give Hortensius full satisfaction' (3). Reeve has plunged us deep in the language of chivalry, eighteenth-century style, but before long a more familiarly romantic version takes its place.

Throughout *The Progress of Romance* Reeve maintains her romance-derived plotting, ensuring that Euphrasia's Knight has both an adversary (in the shapes of Hortensius and received wisdom) and her necessary pages (again Hortensius and the patient Sophronia). Enlisting them, she says 'I shall depend upon your assistance, and since you have opened my mouth upon the subject, you are bound in honour to correct my redundancies, and to supply my deficiencies' (9). Juggling his roles as page and villain, Hortensius asks 'What to furnish you with weapons for my defeat?' Although the answer can only be 'yes', Euphrasia unravels Hortensius' confused identities by retorting 'Not so, but to assist me in the course of my progress through the land of Romance' (9). Euphrasia, as determined in her defence of romance as Hortensius is in his denigration, disables his villain-status and places him in her service. 'Armed with [her] papers and extracts – Artillery and fire-arms against the small sword, the tongue' (notes Hortensius [5]), she conducts her listeners and readers through romance's claims to legitimacy: by describing the plots of Virgil and Homer, she links the romance and epic worlds to romance's benefit; she argues for the inspirational effect of the romance on the court of Elizabeth I;[16] she characterises the romance as itself a guardian and guide when she declares its narrative strategy to be 'point[ing] out the difference between Virtue and Vice, to shew one rewarded and the other punished' (94). Euphrasia is less concerned to unpack the violent nature of romance than to emphasise its soothing effect on readers; and yet, even Euphrasia is anxious about the 'bad' – that is, badly formed – romances: they are 'apt to give a romantic turn to the reader's mind', they can contain 'absurdities' (79, 87 *passim*). Interestingly, it takes Euphrasia three-quarters of her narrative to admit any defects to the romance world, and it seems, further, as if this occurs not simply because they must be mentioned but because Euphrasia is growing tired. She increasingly exhibits an embattled attitude, and grows physically weaker as her defence falters; as if she and the romance are symbiotically linked, and under a spell, her weakness and that of the romance invade Reeve's text simultaneously. Indeed, towards the end a concerned Sophronia needs to coax Euphrasia outdoors and give her her arm once there.[17] Euphrasia, like her romance counterparts, finds herself at risk from the very thing she would protect; in her verbal jousting with Hortensius her energy is sapped.

As if affected against his will by the force of Euphrasia's arguments, however, Hortensius tries more than once to reposition her as a more familiar female romance character, the Enchantress. Having seen her extracts as weapons, and in this way played along with her self-characterisation as Knight, Hortensius changes his mind and begins to refer to those extracts as charms: 'She comes upon us with her extracts again, and she uses them so as to make them irresistible' (92). Embedded in Hortensius' complaint is fear: Euphrasia's skilful use of men's weapons – i.e. words, intellectual studies – is convincing him, and he must counter this by attempting to transform her and her accoutrements into something his limited knowledge of the romance understands. If she is an enchantress, then she is unnatural, and his weakness in succumbing to her is allowable, even understandable – indeed, Hortensius has become a victim at the hands of Romance, and his attitude that romances are vulgar and inferior is, perversely, borne out: not because he sees himself as in thrall, as if in a romance, but because Euphrasia has descended to such tactics. Again in reference to Euphrasia's extensive evidence, Hortensius sneers that 'From whence, and to what purpose have you conjured up such a list of uncouth names – to frighten us' (30); feeling the force of her argument,

Hortensius attempts to remove it from Reason to Fancy – words like 'conjure' and 'frighten' belong to the despised world of romance. Because Euphrasia does not play along, Hortensius keeps trying: "Whenever I think to catch you tripping, you glide away from me, and in your place I find another person, whom I am to contend with' (61). Euphrasia's shapeshifting – her use of extracts – means for Hortensius she is never really present; she 'has contrived so as to transfer [his] attack from [her]self to [men of first-rate Genius, learning, and judgment] whom [he] dare[s] not contradict' (90). In Hortensius' complicated repositioning of the object of the chivalric impulse – not women but learned men – he also gives further credence to Euphrasia's argument and to the impervious nature of her weapons. Part of Reeve's skill in *The Progress of Romance* is that, throughout the argument, she both allows Euphrasia scholarly access to her intellectual peers and allows Hortensius to expose his own bias when he complains about this. Sophronia, the mostly silent moderator, always judges in favour of Euphrasia.

And, despite her witchery, Euphrasia mounts an increasingly impressive campaign. Braving Hortensius' discomfort, she deploys her extracts to advantage. But there is one aspect of the romance that Euphrasia cannot support wholeheartedly, and it is signalled by her genderbending assumption of the Knight's role: she steadily undermines the romance's unthinking veneration of women, the very aspect that Hurd and others especially approve. Recognising that it limits rather than strengthens her Knightly valour, she refuses Hortensius' attempts at gallantry:

Hortensius. I shall pay [Romance] due respect for your sake.

Euphrasia. Not so, Hortensius, I will not accept such respect for them. – You shall pay it for the sake of those illustrious men, who imbibed their enthusiasm, and carried it into practice. (52)[18]

Insisting on reasoned argument rather than gallantry, Euphrasia incidentally presents a picture of romance-affected men, just as she will hint at when describing the Elizabethan court. Male readers, then, are as susceptible as female readers to the attractions of the romance; they too imbibe the precepts of romance, and hence its 'right' aspects. At the heart of Euphrasia's rationale is the notion of an egalitarian readership likely to benefit from reading, and in that way exploring, the purified land of the romance. Reeve relocates violence to the world outside the romance; she notes that the disorder and chaos of the real world is encouraged by a style of writing that mimics that world (this is her main criticism of the novel) and values the romance for the positive impulses it inculcates, and for the order it keeps within its highly structured world. As Euphrasia remarks, 'mankind are apt to run into extremes. We ridicule the enthusiasm of honour and glory, and run headlong into the gulph of folly and dissipation – we throw aside forms and ceremonies and sink into carelessness and negligence; – we despise decorum and preciseness, and plunge into licentiousness' (104). There is something breathless and threatened in Reeve's use of multiple dashes, and her longing for forms, ceremonies, decorum and precision (all found in the chivalric romance), and her fear of extremes, folly and licentiousness reflects a desire to calm a disordered world. In 1785, a balance-point between two revolutions, Reeve's text looks to the romance for the order it offers, the formulaic plots it delivers, the heroics it encourages. In the romance, 'heroes were patterns of courage, truth, generosity, humanity, and the most exalted of virtues, – its heroines were distinguished for modesty, delicacy, and the utmost dignity of manners' (86–7).[19]

A successful defence of romance means a successful defence of such virtues. Far from wanting to escape into this world, Euphrasia wants to import the romance into reality, to see it receive its fair due, to watch its influence reorder, even cleanse, a culture threatened by violent forces. As she progresses through the land of Romance, and as she and her partners speak the language of Romance, they demonstrate the viability of such conduct. As the questing Knight, Euphrasia seeks to disentangle the good from the bad, to put a genre in order, and to strengthen it against uninformed attacks like Hortensius' – who, as he admits, hasn't read very many romances. Her victory comes when she persuades Hortensius that a schoolboy's Classics contain more harmful material than any Romance:

Hortensius. Your sex are most concerned in my remonstrance, for they read more of these books than ours, and consequently are most hurt by them.

Euphrasia. You well then become a Knight errant, to combat with the windmills, which your imagination represents as Giants; while in the mean time you leave a side unguarded.

Hortensius. And you have found it out. – Pray tell me without metaphors, your meaning in plain English.

> *Euphrasia.* It seems to me that you are unreasonably severe upon these books, which you suppose to be appropriated to our sex, (which however is not the case): – not considering how many books of worse tendency, are put into that hands of the youth of [y]our own, without scruple. (80–1)

When it becomes clear that Euphrasia refers to the violence and 'depravity' contained in the Greek Classics and their unmediated use by schoolboys, Hortensius can only gasp 'I am astonished – admonished – and convinced!' (82). He is vanquished. Euphrasia can ridicule Hortensius with romance terminology because she is sure of victory, and she sees that his argument is based on its own form of thoughtless absurdities – he is, here, a false Knight, spreading false doctrine. Reeve's Britomart thus rescues Romance, and *The Progress of Romance* ends with a general benediction: '[I] thank you for your assistance, and the patience with which you have attended me in my progress' (100). Reeve reveals far fewer reservations than does Hurd about the value of romance, but she exposes a need: as much as chivalry originates in violence, she implies, it seems now to be what will help to contain it.

The 1790s will make extensive use of chivalric imagery; it will have a great need for its tropes. Much of what it understood about the romance it inherited from Hurd, Reeve, *et al.* The actual details of troubadours and chivalry, however, were supplied by Susannah Dobson in two thick volumes, *The Literary History of the Troubadours* (1779) and *Memoirs of Ancient Chivalry* (1784), both translated from the French of M. de Saint-Pelaie (or Palaye), but extensively annotated by Dobson. The two volumes demonstrate the more conflicted, fluid approach to the romance that will characterise the 1790s; Dobson's indecision regarding the overall benefit of chivalry to society finds its analogue in, in Duff's words, the 'fundamentally *unstable*' 'language of romance and chivalry' (133; Duff's emphasis). Even as Reeve's progress through the land of Romance is marked by her certainty of its beauties, Dobson's contemporaneous volumes mapping that same land betray a greater unease with its parameters – and its influence. Writing in 1760, Elizabeth Montagu notes that 'Histories of chivalry, instead of enervating, tend to invigorate the mind, and endeavour to raise human nature above the condition which is naturally prescribed to it'.[20] And yet for Dobson (and indeed, for readers and writers in the

1790s, as the last section of this chapter will discuss), this virtue also acts as a threat: the invigorated, enhanced mind, risen above nature, is by strict definition unnatural. Even as one celebrates the liveliness of such a mind, one also fears its quickness. Chivalric ideals may purify and ennoble, but they also de-naturalise: the world thus created is unrecognisable.[21] Akin to Beattie's assertion in 1783 that the publication of *Don Quixote* had the Prince-Charming affect of awakening its readers from the sleep of unthinking torpor ('Mankind awoke as from a dream. They laughed at themselves for having been so long imposed on by absurdity; and wondered they had not made the discovery sooner'[22]), Dobson's texts at first believe in, then debunk, then rethink, the viability and advisability of chivalry.

Dobson resembles the other writers I have discussed in that she assumes the champion's knightly role, although here her 'Lady' is not Romance itself but M. de Saint-Pelaie. In *The Literary History of the Troubadours*, Dobson situates de Saint-Pelaie as ever more strictly feminised: she praises and admires 'the immense labours' that have given birth to the original text, and she names 'the Troubadours' as 'the fathers of modern literature'.[23] De Saint-Pelaie's labours and his success in producing in coherent form the works of the fathers transform him into the works' figurative mother, while Dobson's role in preparing those texts for English readers place her most logically as the midwife. But having anchored de Saint-Pelaie's chivalric history in nature, even biology, allows Dobson to arm herself as his protector: the familial metaphor makes for the familiar – homely – character of the texts, and encourages Dobson's readers to see de Saint-Pelaie as deserving of attention, both Dobson's as his translator and the public's as his readers. When Dobson tells us that de Saint-Pelaie's work involved 'collect[ing] near four thousand compositions, and the original lives of several of the poets'; gathering together scattered fragments; and, most impressively, translating the fragments despite not knowing old Provençal 'by great pains, in comparing different words, and different passages' and showing sensitivity to idiom; then, we sense, she takes for granted our agreement of his worth as a scholar (*History*, vi–vii). 'Yet did he encounter and overcome all the dignities, inspired with the honourable motive peculiar to men of letters, the desire of acquiring and communicating knowledge' (*History*, vii): the spirit of chivalry underpins Dobson's text, as she invites us to see de Saint-Pelaie as a knight striving in aid of the Troubadours, even as she strives in aid of him. This layering of chivalric imagery underscores Dobson's trust in its transparency and its value: knights champion knights who champion bards whose lays admire the feats of knights. The 'rustic simplicity, joined with lively, and sometimes sublime images' (*History*, x) that distinguish the works she has translated point to the unique suitability of the lays to the Age of Sensibility that cohabits with the Age of Reason: Dobson's prose appeals to the feeling mind, the combination of heart and head, and suggests anew the appropriate nature of such texts and such habits as romances and chivalry.

Dobson's tone consistently allies chivalry with nobility, even as she, in her turn, acknowledges the violent origins of the code: 'chivalry introduced a career of heroism, in which some of the social virtues gave an éclat to the exploits of military life' (*History*, xiii). That is, Dobson wants to link chivalry and nobility, but in a striking passage all her best efforts seem only to reveal the questionable, if not distasteful, aspects of the system she champions. It is worth quoting in its entirety:

> There [in romances] we behold a passionate and outrageous valour, which breathed after combats as its dearest pleasures, and which drew the first laws of nature from the barbarous decisions of the sword.... [T]he prodigality of the Nobles, set up as the essential virtue of their nobility; as little delicate in acquiring the means, as in the manner of their dissipation; and not blushing to accumulate by rapine, what was to be exhibited by ruinous ostentation. There we behold that spirit of independence which fosters the disorders of anarchy; sometimes indeed with a view to interest, crouching under the pliant and humble demeanour of a courtier, but always ready to stand forth with audacity of the first favourable conjuncture. There we behold a boorish and masculine familiarity, which talks without reserves of persons and things; which censures with equal rudeness the Prince and the subject, and establishes a tyranny often greater than that which it opposes.[24] There we behold a blind superstition, feeding itself with follies and absurdities; sacrificing to its chimeras, reason, humanity, and the Divinity itself; debasing the Supreme Being by a mistaken homage, and furnishing arms to that irreligion to which it gives birth. There we behold the system of chivalry fully delineated. War, love, and religion formed the basis of this singular institution ... (*History*, xvi–xvii)

The heaping-up of negative imagery, culminating in 'boorish and masculine familiarity', suggests that, after all, Dobson is not so

comfortable with either chivalry's ideals or its prime players; her feminising of de Saint-Pelaie in her Introduction's earlier pages takes on a
greater resonance when it becomes clear that 'boorish' and 'masculine'
can be linked so evocatively. Her confusion foreshadows the ambiguity of the 1790s, and yet it seems clear that Dobson herself does not
recognise her indecision; in her concluding remarks she regards her
source material as 'useful examples to succeeding times' (*History*, 489)
of heroic behaviour, even as she fears that some readers might 'censure
them as dangerous', indeed, even as she expresses doubt about her
'ability to collect and weed them properly . . . *without injuring my own
principles* or their originality' (*History*, 489, emphasis added). The
danger experienced by the translator is hastily displaced onto the
integrity of the texts. Dobson uneasily reins in her anxieties about the
threats posed by the texts and substitutes them with the conventional
appeal to what may be called, in light of her subject, the chivalry of her
readers, when she begs their indulgence for the inevitable weaknesses
her gender will impart to the translation.[25] In the end, chivalry is a
condition of, as well as the basis for, her translation.

When she publishes her translation of de Saint-Pelaie's (now de
Saint-Palaye) *Memoirs of Ancient Chivalry* five years later, Dobson
maintains a stronger grip on her text, and her own relation to her
source material. She erects the barrier of education, stressing the moral
and instructional nature of her text, and eliminating both the enthusiastic support for and attending anxiety about the elements of
chivalry. Under this new rubric, a sensible study of chivalric romance
helps to 'rescue the mind from ignorance and superstition' even if
such works now appear 'a childish object to attend to'.[26] Dobson's
earlier excitement over the allure of chivalry has transmuted into a
kind of maternal regard for the 'prattle' that 'prognostic[ates] . . .
future perfection' (*Memoirs*, viii–ix). By reorienting the practice of
chivalry and its attendant storylines from the world of heroes to that
of children – by emphasising the immaturity and simplicity of the
romance – Dobson deflates the threat that nearly undid her in *History*.
Chivalry is now safe: 'pursued in their *just* measure [i.e. as childish],
such studies are not only innocent, but might prove useful relax-
ations' and a suitable, healthier alternative to late nights,
card-playing, and dances (*Memoirs*, xii, Dobson's emphasis). Dobson
stresses the educational value of the romances, the virtues they inspire
in young readers, and in doing so transfers the birth image the first
translation associated with de Saint-Pelaie to herself: 'I shall feel
amply rewarded for my labour' if the 'youth of both sexes' benefit

(*Memoirs*, 373). And yet, it emerges, Dobson hopes for more than this, and, further, attaches to romance the first trappings of a need that, as the last section of this chapter takes up, becomes a focus in the 1790s: she concludes her text by arguing for the advantages of a new order of chivalry, one that will keep civilisation itself in order. The neglect of chivalric values has brought France to the edge of ruin,[27] 'and it is an awful consideration, that however dissimilar in some respects, yet in this point, with all the superior knowledge we boast in this enlightened period and country, the declining age of Chivalry bears a strong resemblance to the present time' (*Memoirs*, 373). Although muted, this is apocalyptic talk; Dobson's earlier casting of chivalry as a childish, yet charming and instructive, code gives way to a concluding emphasis on its capacity to prevent social disorder and decay. Her desire for a new age of chivalry prefigures the later sanctifying of King Arthur as national emblem, once and future king, whose second coming will herald a new age. Dobson ends on a valedictory, rhapsodic, and unsettling note:

> Happy will it be, indeed, if that affectionate compact of youth and age, that discretion and modesty, and that noble hospitality of character and refinement of manners, shall revive in this nation, which, in the first years of Chivalry, were the foundations of its glory (and for which, in the good old times, the English were no less renowned); and shall join with the increase of knowledge to check the progress of dissipation, and restore those principles of morality, order, and respect, which can alone insure solid virtue, real elegance, and public peace. (*Memoirs*, 373–4)

Her percipient plotting of social chaos, to be held back only by the judicious reintroduction of chivalric values, indicates the national direction chivalry will take in the 1790s, and its loaded nature as a governing metaphor. Chivalry is both a balm and a threat; the romance both orders and disorders a familiar way of life. On the one hand features 'the importance of raising the standard [of romances] as high as possible; of exhibiting characters possessed of the most brilliant virtue, and purified as much as possible from every stain of imperfection'; on the other, 'war, religion, and love, were the pillars of this famous institution [chivalry]',[28] all of which were firmly attached to a flawed world.

The aesthetics of vicarious fear

Mary Robinson, in her 1796 novel *Hubert de Sevrac, a Romance of the Eighteenth Century*, makes plain the romance that was to be derived from the Revolution:

> The Ancient chateau of Montnoir, situated on the confines of Lombardy, was the melancholy asylum of Hubert de Sevrac and his unfortunate family. Born to an elevated rank in society, and educated amidst the splendours of a court, he shrunk from the approach of poverty, because it was accompanied by the menace of disgrace, and embraced the moment which presented an opportunity for flight, under the dreadful apprehension, that the next might conduct him to a scaffold.[29]

She begins her story in the summer of 1792, securely linking her romance, the Reign of Terror, and an exploration of an enervated, yet pitiable, aristocracy. As much as de Sevrac is admirable, he is also pathetic, allowing his 'exquisitely feeling heart, and ... dignified sense of honour' (6) to drag him and his family into poverty and misery. The danger from which de Sevrac flees is countered by his own inability to take care of himself; the aristocratic abstraction from the world that characterises him threatens his life every bit as much as the guillotine. Robinson's romance is clearly republican, and sympathetic to the aims of the Revolution; she reflects the thinking person's disillusion when she balances her description of de Sevrac's plight with her support for 'the cause of universal liberty' (7) even in its 'momentous crisis': 'in the glorious effort for the emancipation of millions, justice and humanity were for a short time unheard, or unregarded' (7). Embedded in her romance, then, is an engagement with the violence of the Terror as well as a veiled criticism of its aristocratic victims: de Sevrac is not applauded for his sensibility, which causes his family continuing trouble. Robinson thus dramatises the real experience of many for the entertainment of her readers, demonstrating the viability of a Revolutionary romance and the attraction of vicarious Terror. She also reveals the association between the romance of chivalry, class and violence that will be the focus of this final section.

Chivalry's origin in war proves the starting-point for nearly every writer who takes up this topic, as this chapter has discussed. The ground prepared so carefully by Reeve, Dobson, Hurd, and the rest proves fertile enough in the 1790s. What is also required, however, is an insistence on the unreality of romance as its main virtue: Montagu's 'Dialogue' (1760) is being facetious, but reflecting a real concern, when she has her Bookseller maintain that 'when a gentleman has spent his time in reading adventures that never occurred, exploits that never were atchieved [sic], and events that not only never did, but never can happen, it is impossible that in life or discourse he should ever apply them' (Montagu, *Novel and Romance*, 224). Montagu's Bookseller unwittingly points out the value of romance-reading to the nervous 1790s: their very unreality keeps reality at bay; their inbred fantastic-ness alleviates the temptations to take chivalry seriously, that is, to emulate the French and champion liberty. Theorising about what the romance was and from what impulses it originated was, then, accom-panied, if not overtaken, by investigations of what the romance offered, what it threatened, and, finally, what it had become.

Auerbach was not the first to discern a class-based morality in the romance. Chivalry's origin in war-games has as its necessary corollary an insistence on the impermeability of class boundaries: knights were noble, and part of the pathos as well as the humour of *Don Quixote* comes from his inability to recognise that he lacks a basic requirement for knighthood of the errant sort. The chivalric ideal is also an aristo-cratic ideal;[30] upholding the desirability of chivalric values means supporting the notion of class-based behaviour, even as it may entail certain responsibilities on that class. When, therefore, Burke bemoans the death of chivalry,[31] he is also mourning the passing of a class: knights who protect ladies and queens, ladies who deserve protection. Even as, in Duff's words, 'while recording the death of chivalry Burke gives us a singularly vivid picture of it' (20), he also appeals to linger-ing notions of who exactly was fitted to be a knight. The conservatism of Burke is here manifested in his uncomplicated association between aristocratic and chivalric values, but more than this Burke hints at the lack of such values among those who would guillotine a queen – that is, the labouring rabble who also stormed the Bastille and declared Revolution. Burke in no way echoes Robinson's pro-Revolutionary sympathies; he declares that the absence of chivalry fans the flames of Revolution, that the absence of knights allows the free 'reign' given to French violence. From Burke's point of view, what is needed is exactly the restoration of courtly values, and a court in which to practise them. Burke's rubric transfers the violence that underpins chivalry to a world singularly in need of chivalry; for him, Marie Antoinette is a symbol of a lost system, and her experience of violence reifies the troubling, even deadly lack of an ideology to hold it at bay. For Burke, chivalry works to hold back violence, but he can only uphold this definition by ignoring chivalry's own appeals to violence. By performing his own textually chivalric move, Burke allies himself with a chivalric aristocracy and against the violently unromantic mob, even as he chastises the group to which he aspires.

Burke's positive presentation of chivalry stresses that what it offers a chaotic society is order and protection, the virtues of a known code against the uncertainties of an egalitarian arrangement. The 'regular and splendid system' of chivalry 'may probably be ascribed to the great number of nobility, who, in every part of Europe, were devoted to the profession of arms' (Murray 68): in other words, a knightly disinterestedness, an abstract approach that ensured purity of purpose, and was only available to noble 'professors' of the 'art'.[32] Chivalry is as much a governing code as any constitution,[33] a fact that makes the romance into a version of political primer. As early as 1725 Eliza Haywood notes that romances are designed for '*Instruction*' as well as '*Amusement*', 'most of them containing Morals, which if well observed would be of no small Service to those that read 'em'.[34] In many ways, the moral of the conventional romance is the preservation and strengthening of the *status quo*, a task facilitated by the attractiveness and the viability of the romance metaphor. Indeed, as Duff shows, anti-Revolution rhetoric was as much indebted to the language of chivalry as pro-Revolution talk. If the Bishop of Auranches, Pierre Daniel Huet, can say in 1715 that 'Nothing conduces so much to the Forming and Advancing [of Wit] to the Approbation of the World, as the Reading of Romances',[35] then a general invocation of and reliance on chivalric romances in the 1790s appears as the logical outgrowth of their earlier social usefulness. Romance offered, even demanded, the continuation of a lifestyle where strength and goodness were rewarded, gender distinctions (mostly) upheld, men protected women, social classes were strictly observed and believed in. What current events offered was severe and threatening class instability, at home and abroad; the breaking down of old certainties, values and reward systems; anarchic worlds where the Rights of Man, Men and Woman refused to acknowledge the Right of tradition. The common tropes of the Romance, the recognisable storylines, above all the stability it offered proved, for Burke and those like him, the antidote to real-life violence and trauma. That such a stance involved the re(w)riting of the genre was less troubling than its alternative;[36] chivalry could be described as holding back violence only by ignoring its own appeal to it. Those whose version of chivalry was a tool to calm social disorder subscribe to Blair's description: romances 'furnish one of the best channels for conveying instruction, for painting human life and manners, for showing the errors into which we are betrayed by our passions, for rendering virtue amiable and vice odious'.[37] Romance and chivalry instructed their readers in virtue of a particularly non-threatening sort.

And yet, for every Burkean lamentation there is another voice raised *against* the romance, and it is in this general disagreement that the two-pronged nature of a reliance on chivalry becomes plain. Chivalry protects, but the romance can reject, social order; even Reeve acknowledged that the wrong kind of romance in the wrong hands was disastrous. Indiscriminate romance-reading led to mental disorder, a violence in the brain that, as Don Quixote, the Female Quixote, Austen's Catherine Morland, and others attest, unfits readers for the world. The danger of modern – 1790s – society is matched by the danger of retreating from it into the romance, and this forms the core of the romantic paradox: nothing maintains social order like the chivalric romance, and nothing threatens it more.[38] Murray makes it plain: 'Shall the reader be transported entirely into a new world, from which everything coarse and turbulent is excluded .... The natural effect [of this] will be, to lead a man to look for perfection in all those whom he meets .... [This] is extremely apt to terminate in discontent and misanthropy' (Murray 29). The newly emphasised escapist quality of the romance, then, is both its greatest asset and greatest danger. In lifting the mind above the troubles of the world, it unfits the mind for its return journey; the result is a naïveté transformed into a kind of idiocy. This brand of reader is too absorbed in the romance to notice current events, and so the *schadenfreude* conducive to counting one's blessings and keeping the boat steady is disabled. Barbauld notes this aspect of romance-reading in 1773, twelve years before Reeve's study; she too utilises its language, describing romance-reading as a kind of enchantment: the 'gloom', 'languor', 'toil' and 'disappointments' of ordinary life 'induce men to step aside from the rugged road of life, and wander in the fairy land of fiction; where every bank is sprinkled with flowers, and every gale loaded with perfume; where every event introduces a hero, and every cottage is inhabited by a Grace'.[39] Indeed, as George Canning elaborates (although his point of view clearly differs from Barbauld's), 'the fiction of romance is restricted by no fetters of reason, or of truth; but gives a loose to lawless imagination, and transgresses at will the bounds of time and space, of nature and possibility'.[40] The danger of romance is that it is unreal, and its fictionality, whether fairly benevolent as in Barbauld or subversive as in Canning, battles against its reassuring effect. 'Romance', says Parker, 'is simultaneously a refuge from the waking world and a dangerous evasion [of it]' (160).

In the 1790s the romance is used by both sides: it both preserves and threatens social order. Romance replaces history – 'romances are more entertaining than history itself, and ... thereby breed a dislike to that useful study' (Moore xciv) – seducing young minds away from 'all the substantive parts of knowledge[,] withdraw[ing] the attention from nature, and truth; and fill[ing] the mind with extravagant thought, and too often criminal propensities' (Beattie, *Novel and Romance*, 327). Beattie writes this in 1783, and his rhetoric endows the romance itself with Revolutionary qualities, spilling over from the one just ending and foreshadowing the one to come. Beattie's romance provides illicit pleasures, the force of which he cannot deny and yet cannot condone: if the young reader must amuse himself (Beattie's readers are male), 'if he must ... indulge himself in this way now and then, let it be sparingly, and seldom' (Beattie, *Novel and Romance*, 327). Whether arch and knowing or condemnatory, Beattie's tone sexualises romance-reading, creating an erotic zone for 'sex in the head' that necessitates self-control. The violence that reading romances does to one's mind and, presumably, morals, balanced with the social advantages offered by perpetuating the ideals of chivalry and emulating the refined world of the romance create a self-feeding loop: romance has 'given an amiable name to vice'[41] *and* it has offered an alternative to worldly expressions of vice. It both replaces and reinforces history, and in that way both supports and undermines 1790s establishment culture.

Perhaps one way to unravel this paradox is through a closer look at the aesthetics of vicarious experience. Even as one rejects the world in favour of the 'fairy land of romance', one imports into that land the expectations, and plot-line, of the world. The refining carried out by the 'good' romance depends on the existence of that which is to be refined. One of the reasons the romance is dangerous lies in its praiseworthy purity: as readers experience the romance, vicariously living the lives they read about, they experience the emotions that would accompany a real-world equivalent event, but their experience is artificial, void of real-life complications, and finite. Repeatedly undergoing such vicarious experience leads to satiation, worry many of the writers on the romance from the 1780s onwards. Barbauld most fully develops this thesis, noting too that it is not only pleasant scenes that attract readers:

> It is, indeed, no ways extraordinary that the mind should be charmed by fancy, and attracted by pleasure; but that we should listen to the groans of misery, and delight to view the exacerbations of complicated anguish, that we should chuse to chill the bosom with imaginary fears, and dim the eyes with fictitious sorrow, seems a kind of paradox of the heart, and only to be credited because it is universally felt. (Barbauld, *Novel and Romance*, 282)[42]

The Burkean sublime underpins Barbauld's reasoning here: we enjoy such scenes because we know we are safe from them. But they nonetheless arouse emotions, the satisfying of which is itself pleasurable: 'The painful sensation immediately arising from a scene of misery, is so much softened and alleviated by the reflex sense of self-approbation attending virtuous sympathy, that we find, on the whole, a very exquisite and refined pleasure remaining, which makes us desirous of again being witnesses to such scenes, instead of flying from them with disgust and horror' (Barbauld, *Novel and Romance*, 283). This in turn creates a more problematic 'paradox': 'But the apparent delight with which we dwell upon objects of pure terror, where our moral feelings are not in the least concerned, and no passion seems to be excited but the depressing one of fear, is a paradox of the heart, much more difficult of solution' (Barbauld, *Novel and Romance*, 283). The lack of moral engagement with the feeling aroused by the romance means that they cannot be *used*, only felt; the romance encourages gratuitous emotions, useless impulses. Barbauld develops a theory of vicarious suffering, of vicarious participation in the romance world, that draws readers in and keeps them coming back for more: an addiction whose high is the successful resolution of fictional traumas. Readerly satisfaction is only more fully enhanced by the attractiveness of the experience, its nature as an aesthetic object: we derive pleasure from its form and from the feelings it inspires.

> The pain of suspense, and the irresistible desire of satisfying curiosity, when once raised, will account for our eagerness to go through an adventure, though we suffer actual pain during the whole course of it. We rather chuse to suffer the smart pang of a violent emotion than the uneasy craving of an unsatisfied desire.... Hence, the more wild, fanciful, and extraordinary are the circumstances of a scene of horror, the more pleasure we receive from it.... A judicious author[, therefore,] will never attempt to raise pity by anything mean or disgusting. As we have already observed, there

must be a degree of complacence mixed with our sorrows to produce an agreeable sympathy; nothing, therefore, must be admitted which destroys the grace and dignity of suffering.... (Barbauld, *Novel and Romance*, 284, 285)

In this self-gratifying world, a kind of voyeuristic imperative is created; the satisfaction comes from experiencing the experience, from observing the adventures of others, and as with most addictions, readers become jaded: 'Romance-writers ... make great misfortunes so familiar to our ears, that we have hardly any pity to spare for the common accidents of life' (Barbauld, *Novel and Romance*, 289). And so, in exaggerated terms: by immersing oneself in the world of the romance, one both loses interest in, and lacks a susceptibility to, the events of real life. Hence, the *status quo* is preserved through a kind of general inaction – which is also the problem.

The complexities of this paradox arise from the critical inability to decide whether the romance was/is good or bad. Chivalry allows for – even encourages – a vicarious displacement, an absorption, of fear; on the other hand, by its own code it exists to repress violent impulses and maintain order. As a code, it relies on and enacts fear and repression even as it dresses up its tactics in the flowery language of the romance. The gallantry that considered female chastity its highest treasure, for instance, also enforced such chastity and regarded sexual women as temptresses – enchantresses. The chivalric code does not transcend, but rather requires, attention to order and social cohesion and homogeneity. The Green Knight stands out for his colour, which marks him a deviant; Tom Paine is marked by 'deviant' language, Mary Wollstonecraft by 'deviant' behaviour. If the romance 'is characterised primarily as a form which simultaneously quests for and postpones a particular end, objective, or object' (Parker 4), then one can see the 1790s as sanctioning a perpetual romance of postponement in its inability – or refusal – to decide whether 'romance' was the hero or the villain of the decade. The reality of Revolution, repression, social change and disintegration is countered by the fantasy of order and stasis offered by chivalry, its modern equivalents, and the romance. The genre becomes a site, or tournament, within which the inconsistencies, contradictions and disagreements joust endlessly. The strength of the myth of romance lies in its ability to write its own stories; because the attractions of chivalry and romance are strong, and very real, their provenance is glossed over. At the end of *Hubert de Sevrac*, however, Robinson indicates her personal rejection of the form on which she has based more than 300 pages by undercutting its reliance on the *status quo* of class:

> So terminated the eventful history [happily]; which exhibits a series of misfortunes, the *effects* of those CAUSES, which cannot fail to prove, that however exalted the aggressor, the hour of retribution is inevitable; that energy and philosophy will triumph over adventitious claims; and, that –
> 'Whoever 'midst the sons
> Of REASON, VALOUR, LIBERTY, or VIRTUE
> Displays distinguished MERIT, is A NOBLE
> of NATURE'S OWN CREATING!'
> THOMSON (318–19)

In this way she subverts one of chivalry's main requirements, and begins to dismantle the institution as a whole.

The central paradox of the romance, however, is its engagement with violence on a variety of textual levels; the cultural inability to decide the status of the romance thereby allows poets to rewrite and refocus its terms. As early as 1715 Huet declares that 'Love ought to be the Principal Subject of *Romance*' (Huet, *Novel and Romance*, 46). And yet, as this chapter has discussed, more than anything else the romance relies on violence. Chivalry provides a fantasy of order that disguises the imposition of order with ceremony, and sets aside the reality of revolutionary violence by promising an invariable happy ending (even Robinson provides this). But as subsequent chapters will show, this is increasingly traded for violence in the poetical romances of the 1790s onwards. The dreams, allusions, uncertainties, silences and incompleteness that distinguish 1790s romantic violence arise from a desire to relocate violence from reality to the romance, where it can be more cleanly dealt with. And yet, the suspension and indecision inhabiting theoretical tracts find their analogues in the poetry's incapacity to treat violence directly. The vicarious terror offered by this new version of romance is doubly deflected: fictionalised, and then evaded. The next chapter will discuss the intellectualised sexual violence offered by a style of poetry that freely explored erotic longing, as long as it was on paper and at a distance. As an ironic twist on Wollstonecraft's call for a 'revolution in Female Manners', Della Cruscan poetry quite bluntly trafficked in the desire that love be the principle subject of romance.

2
Sexing the Romance: the Erotic Violence of the Della Cruscans

'Abortive thoughts that right and wrong confound'[1]

William Gifford's intemperate responses to English Della Cruscanism, *The Baviad and Maeviad*, have influenced readers of this poetry ever since – or rather, non-readers, since Gifford's jeremiad has taken the place of the original for most. As Jerome McGann points out, however, Gifford's condemnation rests on a more thorough understanding of the dynamics of the poetry than its deeply negative, scurrilous, and potentially libellous tone makes enlightened modern readers comfortable acknowledging.[2] Amid Gifford's indignant reactionism, in his descriptions of poetic cuckolding, 'obscene' imagery and 'crude conception[s]', his completely accurate statement stands out: 'the two "great luminaries of the age" [Della Crusca and Anna Matilda[3]], as Mr. Bell calls them, fell desperately in love with each other' (*Baviad and Maeviad*, xii). Della Cruscan poetry, in its English incarnation, charts a romance in terminology that offends the sensibilities of sensibility: it is too physical, too open, too desiring, too expressive. Most dangerously, it allows for, even encourages, the poeticising of erotic attraction. Readers of *The World* in 1787–8 watched breathlessly as Della Crusca and Anna Matilda fell in, and then out of, love; the serialisation of their romance was then packed up and produced in book form in *The British Album*, first in 1788 but going through several editions until 1794.[4] Gifford's horror arises as much from the lasting spectacle of men and women openly declaring love and physical desire as it does from aesthetic concerns: poetry itself was being violated, its classical purity put in the service of a pornographic emphasis on the passions. Gifford's chivalric attitude towards a helpless genre provides another instance of the critical chivalry discussed in the last chapter; the *Baviad and Maeviad* resounds with outrage at the 'false glare, [and] incongruous images' (43) that deface Della Cruscan poetry. When poetry is put to the service of conveying physical desire, we infer, it is inevitably tainted, while romance loses any claim to protection once it descends to the level of sex.

Readers of *The World* and *The British Album*, however, were transfixed by the romance between Della Crusca and Anna Matilda; it offered the promise of a 'real-life' exploration of the heights and depths of fantasy – of romance. As the previous chapter discussed, the last few decades of the eighteenth century found the romance ceaselessly interesting; repeatedly, writers attempted to define and dismiss the genre, the resilience of which showed in their periodic critical returns. Consensus was found in the decision that the romance was unreal: its purity, its unworldliness, the prominence that it gave to a love which conquered all, lent it a lustre not found in 'real life'. Although, as Chapter 1 established, the romance owed more to the world than many commentators gave it credit for, nonetheless its immediate appeal was seen to be its blissful sojourning in the vales of true love. Sensibility, familiar to novel-readers in the 1780s, was romance intensified, a celebration of emotional attachment between lovers, of female endurance, and of the triumph of love over lust. For Gifford, a signal crime of Della Cruscanism was its contradictory devotion to sensibility; even as its sensual language fell foul of sensibility's celebration of virtue, its plotline depended heavily on a scenario of love deferred – a plotline eventually exploded, as I will discuss later in this chapter. Gifford's view is endorsed by McGann, who situates Della Cruscanism as exemplifying 'the poetics of sensibility'. But Gifford's visceral hatred indicates what McGann, despite his description of the erotics of the poetry, successfully elides: the romance between Della Crusca and Anna Matilda offends sensibility exactly because it is sexual, rather than sensual. The ordered and balanced purity of romance is conquered by the fiery passions and bodily desires voiced in their amatory verse.

Understanding the impact of Della Cruscan poetry, then, means confronting its physicality, its willingness to undermine the conventions of purity in the romance and to focus on the sexuality of love. What is at stake is the protection of virtue, the perpetuation of the ideology of romantic love as thoroughly uninformed by physicality. Although heroines and heroes are as much celebrated for their physical charms as for their moral beauties, for the most part readers are meant to understand that outer reflects inner – that physical beauty is

both the reward for and marker of inner worth.[5] The romance subordinated bodily responses to the lasting attractions of soulmates, and
readers understood that pants and sighs, perhaps the pressure of the
hand, functioned only as choreography, culminating in the chaste
embrace that signified the meeting of like with like rather than solely
of lip with lip. Della Cruscan poetry uses the available vocabulary of
romance; as I will discuss later in this chapter, the exchange collected
in *The British Album* follows with little deviation the plot conventions
familiar to its readers, with the signal difference that it is entirely epistolary. Della Crusca and Anna Matilda correspond through poetry, but
their exchanges convert the absence of bodies into a paradoxical presence: the corpus of their love is composed of print. And yet physicality
and bodily responses are crucial to their romance, and it is this aspect
that undoes the balanced nature of the ideology of romance, and that
provokes Gifford's charges of obscenity. English Della Cruscanism can
be compared to the proverbial still waters; its depths conceal trans-
gressions against romance itself. Its superficial simplicity, however,
and its ornate, decorative diction – even by 1793 falling from fashion
– combined with Gifford's polemic to bury it from critical notice.
Edward Bostetter's 1956 article makes only passing reference, concentrating on 'the original Della Cruscans' rather than the 'affected and
silly group of sentimental versifiers' who succeeded them. W.N.
Hargreaves-Mawdsley's 1967 book *The English Della Cruscans and Their
Time* focuses almost entirely on Robert Merry and his possible influence on the canonical Romantic poets.[6] McGann's and Judith Pascoe's
more recent studies take the poetry more seriously, and in so doing
find the poetry addresses some serious concerns: issues of genre,
gender and subjectivity all find play.

Approaching the poetry not as 'romantic' but as 'romance',
however, allows its importance to this study to emerge. The romance
of wooing that underpins the poetry of *The British Album* and its
frequent appeals to bodily desire constitute a form of generic violence
– any expectations of purity are shattered by the ecstasies of longing
in this romance. And yet outright rebellion against the strictures of
decorum does not occur. As McGann notes, 'what is absolutely crucial
to understand about this kind of writing is its extreme formality. Its
world is figured, consciously artificial .... pleasure is fraught with its
reciprocal pain ... a complex pattern of nested tensions gradually
unfolds itself' (86–7). Della Cruscan poetry both formalises the romantic relationship and submerges violent impulses in ecstatic expressions
of desire. The relationship between the control imposed by 'formality'

and the potential loss of control figured by Gifford's description of the poetry as an 'epidemic malady ... spreading from fool to fool' ('Introduction', *Baviad and Maeviad*, xii) results in Della Cruscan poetry's continual struggle against its own emotive violence, its constant appeal to general stability, and its as-constant rejection of order and control. Della Cruscan poetry projects an erotics of form, a teasing opening to the world of sexual pursuit: the barrier separating romance and pornography. When Della Crusca conjures up Anna Matilda's body and poeticises his desires concerning that body, he imports into the romance the disorder of emotional violence, of potential loss of control, and the erotic privileging of a frankly male gaze – but he wraps it in the calming package of romance. Romantic love and sexual desire are entwined, and the erotic worlds created by the poetry violently disrupt the expectations of purity and virtue associated with love poetry.

Violence, then, is not overt or bloody in Della Cruscan poetry, but rather generic; in their creation of a love poetry dependent on excitation and continually sparked desire, Della Cruscan poets provoke a confrontation between genre and representation. The natural effusions they describe – spontaneous overflows of poeticised feeling – are reined in by poetry itself; as Pascoe notes, 'Merry's poems written in the guise of Della Crusca are ... prosodically unexceptional, composed almost exclusively in rhyming couplets of iambic tetrameter' (80), while Hannah Cowley's Anna Matilda responses are equally formal, resembling the lush and elegant outpourings of her contemporary, Anna Seward.[7] The poetry is both genuine and artificial, structured and spontaneous, even as the romance is both effective and laboured, sincere and theatrical. What McGann calls 'anti-nature' (78) undergirds a style that exploits the conventions of love even as it records the progress of a romance. Readers of the original serial witnessed the growth of an affair, unfolding over many months, but its full romantic force resides in the two volumes of *The British Album*, volume one ornamented with an engraving of Della Crusca, volume two with the likeness of Anna Matilda.[8] These portraits only heighten the theatricality that Pascoe discusses, since neither Della Crusca nor Anna Matilda exist – they are romantic constructs, mere masks. But the introduction of the visual nonetheless combines with the apparent sincerity of the verse to maintain the illusion of reality: readers are offered, not the fiction of sensibility, but the irresistible allure of a 'real' romance, written with the fire of immediacy, linked to time and place in both the pages of *The World* and of *The British Album*, where

each poem is signed with the poet's Della Cruscan name and the original date of newspaper publication. Readers, then, are privy to a
private – hence true – romance, conducted by 'real' people, following
familiar rules of romance, spiced with sex. The fourth wall is simultaneously up and down: the suspension of disbelief endows the
poet-players with reality, which in turn galvanises their passion and
colours their romance with illicit lust, all very correctly, elegantly and
decoratively written.

In discussing the Della Cruscans, I mean to explore the dichotomy
between false and sincere in their declaration of love and desire, the
potential for disorder predicated by the version of a bodily, yet print-
bound romance. The dynamics of heterosexual romance embraced by
Della Crusca and Anna Matilda play a signal part, but before looking
in detail at their romance it is important to discuss the eroticism
McGann mentions but does not fully engage with. McGann's useful
description of the Della Cruscan style as based on the troubadouran
stil novisti and his characterising of the Della Crusca/Anna Matilda
romance as a 'specifically heterosexual erotic exchange' (81) imports
both love and lust, but he does not develop his insight. In particular,
associating *The British Album* poetry with that of the troubadours
introduces the element of direct address evident in so many Della
Cruscan poems: when the poets entitle their offerings 'To —' they are
signalling the private, epistolary nature of the poem even as they alert
their readers to this in a very public fashion. The first part of this
chapter, then, investigates the philosophy of feeling in Della Cruscan
poetry, where the amatory stands in for the intellectual and creates
the erotic *tenso* noted by McGann. After this, the chapter will focus on
the romance between Della Crusca and Anna Matilda, where readers
learn that the course of true love never runs smoothly, and indeed can
only end in tears. Throughout, the Della Cruscan fascination with the
imagery of physicality, its easy slide into the language of physical
suffering, and the twining of love with forms of metaphorical violence
will be evident.

The erotics of apostrophe: emotional bondage

In *The Ideology of the Aesthetic*, Terry Eagleton defines the aesthetic as

> a contradictory, double-edged concept. On the one hand, it figures
> as a genuinely emancipatory force – as a community of subjects
> now linked by sensuous impulse and fellow-feeling.... On the

other hand, the aesthetic signifies what Max Horkheimer has called a kind of 'internalised repression', inserting social power more deeply into the very bodies of those it subjugates.... To lend fresh significance to bodily pleasures and drives ... is always to risk foregrounding and intensifying them beyond one's control.[9]

Eagleton describes the binding power of a shared aesthetic in both its definitions: it both attaches, and restrains. The aesthetics of direct address that operate in Della Cruscan poetry perform a similar manoeuvre: desire is freed and the desired openly identified, which encourages displays of emotion even as it conforms to expectations of genre, the aesthetic known as 'romance'. Moreover, Eagleton highlights the tendency of the body to escape the control of language; once gestured towards, the body assumes a primacy in relations that belies the intangibility of a purely print-bound relationship. Della Cruscan poetry privileges the invisible body; it directs the reader's gaze towards the corpus that makes up the textual romance, and it encourages a voyeuristic engagement with the privacy of a love affair. The epistolary mode facilitates the contradictory public/private stance affected by the poets: even as lovers address private love-letters implicitly written only for the eyes of the beloved, they also publicise their affair. The destination of the poetry – the periodical *The World* – literalises the 'worldly' aspect of public love. The aesthetic, the body, the gaze, and lovers' vows congregate in the space reserved for declarations of desire, and in this way apostrophe ensures the visuality of romance, the specularisation of sexual desire.

As McGann notes, 'the basic structure of the verse is exactly erotic because it proceeds by acts of intercourse that are at once perfectly immediate and purely imaginative. [It is] sex in the head' (82), but it also appeals to the body, to a range of embodied emotions requiring both the stylised emotive sentiment of love poetry and the liberating raptures of textual desire. Della Cruscan apostrophe creates an aesthetics of lust disguised as love; the frequent invocations of passion translate longing into a kind of textual gratification. Even as, for instance, the sublime requires a body to react to what the mind half perceives, half creates, so too Della Cruscan love relies on a poetic embodiment to define fully its aesthetics of desire. Peter Brooks contends that 'poetics ... is the necessary grounding of aesthetics'.[10] The Della Cruscans literalise this: under their handling poetics ground aesthetics, emphasising the concrete, disarranging the purities of mind, solidifying the abstract, philosophical appreciation of beauty

into straightforward declarations of the necessity of bodily gratification. The dangers of vicarious emotion, the risk they offer to
emotional stability (described by Barbauld and discussed in the previous chapter) re-emerge in Della Cruscan exchanges. The luxuries of
woe and joy indulged in situate the readers as both the receptacle for,
and the putative object of, the poet's transports. The apostrophic
content of many of the poems invite readerly participation in the
objectification of the beloved: whether it is Melissa's lips, or Anna
Matilda's breast, or Miss Campbell's dead body, the poems concoct a
special relationship between poet, subject and reader, a *ménage-à-trois*
that capitalises on the erotics of the gaze, and the aesthetics of specularisation. As Maria Dibattista notes, 'the aesthetic originates,
biologically, in aesthesis, in the perceptions of the sensitized body'.[11]
Della Cruscan apostrophe traces the aesthetic to its source, offering
the aroused body as its site, and deconstructing the purities of visual
love, that is, romantic love based on the non-sexual visual plundering
of beauty. In fact, in Della Cruscan poetry the poetic becomes the
mode of love: poetry embodies love, and the body submits to love.
Conquest is assured as soon as writing begins, so that, even if the
poem concludes in denial, possession has always already occurred. 'If
the eyes fix themselves on a certain object, it is to immobilize it so
that the gaze can work its dark magic, project its own fantasies, enact
its own desires upon it ... Scopophilia offers the possibility of the
libidinal sublimation that takes root in the gaze; in other words, the
aesthetic' (Dibattista 172). The control promised by the gaze –
rendered poetically, in direct address – leads to an aesthetic based on
emotional extravagance and bodily indulgence: intercourse that is
textual, and emotively sexual.

Most Della Cruscan erotic apostrophe, aside from the Anna
Matilda/Della Crusca exchange,[12] emanates from the male pen:
Benedict, Arley, Della Crusca himself, the Bard; and the poems apos-
trophise female objects: public women (actresses), private 'ladies'
(daughters), and errant females. The exception, the Emma/Henry
exchange, plays in significant ways upon the poetry/body association;
the others more straightforwardly objectify their targets. They function like toasts, given over the port after the ladies have retired: they
publicise private virtue, and admire the public performance of virtue.
They romanticise their subjects even as they invite readers to consume
them visually: the pleasure gained from looking overcomes the proprieties. The lover's (or admirer's) private viewing of his beloved is
transformed into the theatrical experience of being one of many – a

member of an audience. This is especially apt in the poems Della
Crusca addresses to three leading actresses of the day: Sarah Siddons,
Kitty Wells and Mary Farren. Indeed, given Siddons' reputation as the
Queen of tragedy (or 'Pathos', in Della Crusca's words) the poem
encourages a reading – that is, viewing – of Siddons as dramatically
associated with violence itself, in many guises. Her voice frightens
'pale FEAR', *'dark-brow'd* REVENGE', *'gelid* HORROR', *'lost* DESPAIR',
and *'barefoot* MADNESS'.[13] Siddons was celebrated for the power of her
voice, and Della Crusca picks up on that, binding her textually in the
effects of her own utterances. Through its power, Della Crusca
suggests, she effectively rules the negative passions; confined in Della
Crusca's poem, she exists as 'Mrs. Siddons', Queen of Pathos, and her
identity as such is emphasised when Della Crusca relegates the softer
passions of 'Pity, and generous-minded Love' (39) to a single stanza.
Having situated Siddons at the head of the train of passion, Della
Crusca enlists the Muse in what becomes a sexual appreciation of
Siddons; from extolling her dramatic skill, Della Crusca sublimates
performance into the emotions it portrays, and from there recalibrates
Siddons' appeal as that of the desirable woman:

> Ah! let not then my fond admiring Muse
> Restrain the ardour of her song,
> In silent wonder fix'd so long,
> Nor thou! From humble hands the homage meet refuse.
>
> And I will hasten oft from short repose,
> To wake the lily, on moist bed
> Reclining meek her folded head;
> *And chase with am'rous touch the slumber of the rose.*
>
> . . . .
>   Then will I form a votive wreath
> To bind thy sacred brows, – to deprecate thy scorn.
>   (40–8, 51–2, emphasis added)

Della Crusca uses the aesthetic control offered by direct address to
transform Siddons from actress to heroine in a mini-romance starring
the poet; she moves from affector to affected, from powerful to
passive. By apostrophising her beauties, Della Crusca takes them over,
and redeploys his admiration as desire – to 'bind' Siddons in the
confines of his poem. Romance is privileged, but its privacy is severely

compromised: Siddons' public persona facilitates Della Crusca's public adoration, and justifies his public gaze.

Siddons is thus transformed from Queen of Pathos to Queen of Hearts, and resituated as a sexualised body rather than an affecting voice. In addressing Mrs Wells and Miss Farren, Della Crusca performs similar manoeuvres. Both actresses inspire poetry through their strength and skill as public figures; both are reduced to desirable bodies, open to view for any reader. In 'Ode to Simplicity: Addressed to Mrs. Wells', Wells exemplifies simplicity, and invites praise for her artlessness,[14] but even so attracts Della Crusca sexually: 'And Loveliness delights to dwell,/ Upon *thy bosom's snowy swell,*/ To bid the streamy lightnings fly,/ In *liquid peril from thine eye*' (43–6, first emphasis added). The attractiveness of simplicity – of naïve, fresh, childlike sensibility – plays up Wells's new poetic status as heroine to Della Crusca's poetic hero, while the swell of her snowy breast conveys uncomplicated desire: the reader's eyes are directed at a body part, the mind encouraged to conjure an erotic image. 'Ode to Miss Farren' goes even further; even as she gives the 'Temper' of Love (6), Farren is the object of the 'gaze' of 'happy youths' (19), her attractions thoroughly physical: 'Oh, what delight to hourly trace/ The fine expression of thy Face,/ Thy willing elegance, and ease;/ To see those teeth, of lustrous pearl,/ Thy locks profuse of many a curl,/ And hear thy voice, omnipotent to please!' (31–6). Although her voice pleases, it is subordinated to her face, hair and teeth: Farren is there to be looked at, rather than listened to. The attractions of all three women are visual: the poetry exists to paint word-pictures, while expressions of admiration soon slide into declarations of desire. Della Crusca treads a fine line in these poems; as actresses, Siddons, Wells and Farren are available to the public gaze by profession, and it is no unusual move to emphasise an actress's body or construct her as sexually desirable. However, Della Crusca simultaneously wants them to be pure romance heroines, susceptible to his heroic attentions, *and* sexually available bodies, open to a lover's advances. His love poetry thus complicates itself: it is both highly romantic and sexually charged, a complexity more evident, and more significant, in his intercourse with Anna Matilda. The apostrophised actresses – whose poems briefly interrupt the Della Crusca/Anna Matilda exchange in their printed order in *The British Album* – serve to allow Della Crusca to energise his emotions, collect his thoughts, and practise his pick-up lines.

When the object of the apostrophe is not an actress, but rather a 'private' woman – respectable, genteel – desire and violence interact more forcefully. 'General Conway's Elegy for Miss C. Campbell', 'Epitaph on Miss Campbell', and 'Marquis Townshend's Verses on Miss Gardiner' have in common the death of the their subjects – more specifically, the moment of death, again focusing on the body. In these poems, the point at which the body becomes mere clay signals deepest desirability, as in 'General Conway's Elegy':

> Ere the stern Sisters cut the vital thread,
> *I saw, and kiss'd her on the fatal bed,*
> *Just as her gentle spirit took its flight,*
> And her faint eye-lids clos'd in the endless night;
> No strong convulsions shook her parting breath;
> No tremors mark'd the cold approach of Death:
> Her heart still heav'd with vital spirit warm
> And each soft feature wore its wonted charm.
>
> (41–8, emphasis added)

Miss Campbell occupies a liminal space between life and death – warm enough to be kissed, cold enough not to respond – and General Conway bestows the opposite of the fairy-tale hero's kiss, ushering her into death instead of bringing her back to life. The scene is touchingly erotic, visually meaningful. Miss Campbell, a proper lady, simultaneously lies on her private couch and in a public bed; she is exposed to the public gaze and dies, kissed into the grave, loved to death. She will join, now, the common state of death, but will also exist forever on the verge of death, as her heaving, lifeless breast attests. 'General Conway's Elegy', like its partners, physically combines love with death, and focuses attention on the expiring female body: romance resides in the poignant combination of possession (the kiss) and loss (death).

Possession, however, can be assumed as well as granted. In Benedict's series of sonnets to Melissa, he postulates a continually deferred love; each sonnet contains a burst of desire, both sated and further tempted by the body of the continually elusive Melissa. In 'To Melissa's Lips', Benedict apostrophises only that part of his love he hopes to gain, her 'balmy lips' (1), fresher than a rose-bud, warmer than the morning sun, brighter than the blossoms of the thorn (5, 6, 7). Melissa exists *only* as lips in this sonnet, a freakish synecdoche that allows the speaker to privilege bodily desire: 'Dear lips! — permit my trembling lips to press/ Your ripen'd softness, in a tender kiss:/ And, while my throbbing heart avows the bliss,/ Will you — (dear lips!) the eager stranger bless?' (9–12). The close rhyme enhances the sense of lips – alike but different

– approaching lips, while also inducing an erotic sense of inevitability. And yet, as the earlier mention of the thorn bush foreshadows, these lips are guarded by a 'beauteous owner' (13) who reclaims her body part and flirtatiously threatens violence: '"Ah, fond request! . . . / Cease, wayward youth! — whoever touches – dies!"' (13–14). The actual death that accompanies General Conway's kiss is here made playful, but nonetheless it as effectively removes the body from further contact. Whether claimed by death, or by a 'beauteous owner', lips are not as free as they seem, and their connection with death complicates the desire inhabiting Della Cruscan poetry. Even as 'kissing lovers enter . . . the tactile body' (McGann 84), so death corrupts the tactile body, and prevents the consummation of love and desire.

Benedict accepts Melissa's rebuff, and although he continually returns to her body in subsequent sonnets, he does so at arm's length, occupying the voyeur's rather than the lover's space, and sharing with his readers the visual aesthetic of desire. In 'To Melissa' he again invokes the kiss, but this time a curiously ethereal one: 'Whene'er thy angel-form salutes my eye' (1), he begins, utilising both the visual and tactile meanings of 'salute' – 'whenever thy angel-form comes into view', and 'whenever thy angel-form kisses my vision'. This time it is Melissa who kisses, or who seems to. But again the kiss is deathly:

> What tender spasms convulse my beating heart!
> My trembling limbs but small support impart;
> My aching bosom heaves the deep-drawn sigh!
> A wild confusion overwhelms my brain —-
> My falt'ring tongue cleaves to the parching roof,
> My spirits fail!
>
> (2–7)

Benedict's physical symptoms – his pain, convulsions, discomfort – prove his love, even as they threaten to bring on his death, which he, Goethe-like, welcomes for the pity it would elicit from Melissa. Love requires physical symptoms; death itself acts as a proof of love. These are not exactly original ideas, but rather a congregation of romantic clichés remarkable more for their insistence on the convulsing body than the suggestion of lovesickness. The poem's concentration on the physical continues the Della Cruscan theme of embodied desire, and of erotic need. Benedict's sonnet 'Melissa!' makes this clear: as the exclamation point suggests, the poem encapsulates Melissa from head to heart:

Her dark-brown tresses negligently flow
In curls luxuriant, to her bending waist;
Her *darker* brows, in perfect order plac'd,
Guard her bright eyes, that mildly beam below.
The Roman elegance her nose displays —
Her cheeks soft blushing, emulate the rose,
Her witching smiles, the orient pearls disclose:
And o'er her lips, the dew of Hybla strays.
Her lib'ral mind, the gentler virtues own;
Her chasten'd wit, instructive lore impart;
Her lovely breast is soft Compassion's throne,
And Honor's temple is her glowing heart.

But I, like Patriarch Moses, praise and bless
The Canaan which I never shall possess!

Benedict's description of Melissa's perfections claims her as his virgin territory; despite the couplet's despair, the first 12 lines have effectively enclosed Melissa in verse. The first 8 lines of this sonnet, like 'To Melissa' composed in faux-Petrarchan meter (abba cddc), contain her physical essence, just as the first 8 lines of 'To Melissa' describe Benedict's physical decline; the last 6 lines of each poem use Shakespearean metre (efefgg) to convey images of the mind, of sorrow, of bodily loss. Thus form and content conspire to, on the one hand, encourage the loosing of sentiment and desire and, on the other, restrict both in correct verse form: both 'protective enclosure' and 'imprisonment'.[15]

Benedict's sonnets embody Melissa: that is, they give her a body, and allow the poet to possess it, fuelling his desire in a self-limiting strategy that both acknowledges possession and defers it. His poems 'to' Melissa bind her securely to him and revel in the luxury of continually recreating the *tenso* of erotic attachment. Melissa's beauty infuses the sonnet, which in turn neatly packages her body. For Benedict, the romance with Melissa is one-sided, voyeuristic: she never responds to his passion except in echoes of his own voice. These sonnets distil Della Cruscan desire and erotic longing; Benedict's isolation functions as a corollary to his desire for Melissa, which in turn can only be voiced within the confines of a sonnet. It is both publicised and held in strict control. By contrast, the brief exchange between Emma and Henry not only allows for the contribution of the female voice, but it also opens up the confines of form: although both write mainly in rhyming iambic tetrameter (with some excursions into pentameter), within their poems one finds variations of metre reflecting variations of mood. Moreover, where the poems already discussed focus on the body of the beloved, for Emma and Henry poetry and the body of the beloved are explicitly linked: poetry literally embodies the lover/poet, so that a poem should be as recognisable a likeness as a portrait.[16] At least, this is the expectation; as the Emma/Henry exchange shows, however, it absolutely depends upon accurate reading. Without 'correct' interpretation – that is, without the control of the deciding gaze – love itself is at risk. The ideal of the Poetry/Love link should enable the beloved to read his or her lover in any poem, but instead this association allows misreading, misdirection, and misunderstanding. Desire for the beloved overcomes the romance of love poetry: love is disordered, disarranged. Romance itself suffers a body blow.

Emma exemplifies this: disappointed in her lover for misattributing a rival's love-poem to her, in 'Henry Deceived' she reproaches both Henry, and Love itself: 'GOD OF THE BOW! How *blind* art thou!/ . . . . / . . . oh dull of eye and heart!/ Thou know'st not WHENCE Love's ardors start;/ And when stiff **'s lines appear,/ Thou whisper'st in my Henry's ear/ That they are EMMA'S!!' (1, 19–23). Emma is less jealous of a sexual rival than annoyed that inferior poetry could be thought hers. '**''s lines are 'stiff' – wooden, unnatural – and yet pose a threat: 'Thou, HENRY, ne'er can learn the wounds I felt,/ Whilst you, unconscious, such barbed Satire dealt./ . . . . / What! To be lov'd for Wit I never own'd!/ And by a STRANGER'S verse to be dethron'd!' (32–3, 36–7). For Emma, the poem itself constitutes a rival; the poetry/body link is so firmly forged that another person has become unnecessary for a love triangle to exist. Emma must consequently use poetry to re-embody herself in Henry's eyes, as well as teach him to read her Self through her poetry correctly – the one slides seamlessly into the other. Emma protests against the assumption that she would write conventional love poetry, about 'love betray'd', a 'forsaken Maid', and 'sunny rays, and misty hills,/ An[d] myrtle groves, and foamy rills' (50, 51, 64–5) – the meaningless rhymes of standard poetic diction – insisting instead that 'THYSELF – HENRY, thyself alone/ Should stand confest on love's ETERNAL THRONE;/ Round THEE the brightness of my Verse should shine,/ Round THEE my living Lays for ever, ever twine!' (66–9).[17] Henry, the subject of Emma's love, props up Emma's love poetry; Henry should be able to recognise himself in Emma's verse – indeed, he should actually *exist* in her verse, an embodiment of Love itself. Transported into poetry, Henry the Reader is Henry Read. Emma makes plain the current of Della Cruscan apostrophe – it exists to embody the beloved, to reconstruct through the loving gaze his or her physical presence. As Emma instructs Henry, 'if Love thrills not in each turn/ ..../ They are not wrote to THEE, nor are their glories MINE' (123, 126). Love, the emotion, creates love poetry.

Emma's embodied Love finds further play in Henry's response; he excuses his misreading by explaining that all his thoughts are of Emma anyway, and then restructures himself physically:

> How burst the Music on my ear!
> The only Music Henry bears to hear!
> I felt it! – each strong nerve inflame!
> Like a new soul usurp my heart,
> And rage and burn in ev'ry part!
> Ah! sure, not even Death's cold spell
> Could the fierce fury of my passion quell!
> (13–19)

Thus, in the poem answering Emma's, we again see the apostrophised body, but despite the address 'To Emma' the body is Henry's; he has taken Emma's remonstrance to heart and so he, too, only embodies himself. This both fulfils Emma's injunction that Love equals Henry, and derails it, for surely Henry's Love equals Emma. The problem lies in the importation of the erotic into the romantic. Direct address, in these poems, refocuses love into lust; it emphasises the body, which here is always unattainable, whether through death, unrequited love, or misreading. These poems use the tone of romance while pursuing the satisfactions of the body, and in each case meet with disappointment. The proprieties of love are bypassed; the private becomes public. The 'dialectic of ambiguous resistance and stimulations' figured by McGann (87) spirals around a problematic embrace of physical desire twinned with the public exposure of private feeling in the poems. This in turn reacts with the essentially false nature of the poetry – its theatrical elements evident in the fabric of assumed names and disguised identities. Apostrophe promotes a fiction of intimacy, a romance built around declarations of love and desire, but the accompanying erotic tension undoes the stability of openly declared love. The result is emotional bondage: a philosophy of love based on the control – or creation – of the beloved; the Enlightenment notion that the word equals the thing allows for the conflation of art and object.

When the poet addresses the beloved, he or she taps into a flow of romantic feeling that is both performative and theatrical: playing at love maintains the play of love, while desire is simultaneously satisfied and further stoked. Apostrophising the beloved encourages both poet and reader to visualise an Other made in the poet's own imagination, and, as we shall see with the intercourse of Anna Matilda and Della Crusca, this completes the ruin of the romance. Even as the poets declare eternal attachments, referencing the power of art – their poetry – as proof, they substitute the poem for the beloved. In recreating the desirable and obtainable physical body in their poems, they corrupt romance. Contriving an ideology of attachment based on embodied art, and hemmed in by formal regularity, Della Cruscan apostrophe both signals the textual availability of the beloved, and, in the case of Miss Campbell at least, cuts off the beloved's escape.

Epistolary romance: Della Crusca and Anna Matilda anthologised

Della Crusca and Anna Matilda conduct the most sustained and thoroughly plotted romance in *The British Album*, much of it in poems entitled 'To Anna Matilda' or 'To Della Crusca', and direct address operates for them as it does for the couples discussed in the previous section: it embodies the beloved, represents and contains desire, results in decay. What commentators have overlooked, however, is the precision with which their correspondence maps out the romance plot, and the inherent limitations to romance it exposes. Della Crusca and Anna Matilda rely on expressions of extremes: they invoke frantic passions and kindling emotions. As their affair progresses, they become increasingly overwrought: Della Crusca, especially, clings to physical imagery, importing his idealised – romanticised – female body into his effusions to Anna Matilda, even rewriting her own self-description to accord with his romantic needs. Anna Matilda, too, after some decorously modest attempts to deflect Della Crusca's attention with paeans to the feeling mind, turns to the body – her own, participating in the specularisation of the female form familiar to romance.[18] Della Crusca's and Anna Matilda's is a modern romance, replete with sexuality: readers are privy to exclamations of desire, displays of sexual jealousy, the intrusion of sexual rivals. As in the previous section, poetry and lovemaking are identical: bodily passion resides in, is communicated by, and requires poetry. The body of work takes over for the body of the beloved, and is correspondingly increas-

ingly eroticised. Since, however, Della Crusca and Anna Matilda
conduct a Romantic romance, they are deprived of the most essential
of romantic ingredients: the happy ending. As with the other romance
narratives this book discusses, the Della Cruscan variety evades
romantic closure; indeed, up to the last poem the pair conduct their
love affair entirely epistolarily. Poetry literalises love, and it also maintains it: the violence of expression for which the Della Cruscan style
is notorious, and which Gifford labelled obscene, is neutralised by a
poetic style that regularly fits desire and longing into rhyming
couplets. Thus violence exists at the levels of imagery, expression,
structure and style. The love between Anna Matilda and Della Crusca
perfectly captures Romantic romance: it is violent, poetical, critical of
the genre it invokes, and without hope. In its anthologised form, it
compresses two years of newspaper-bound experience into two
volumes, each poem dated; combined with *The British Album*'s dedication to R.B. Sheridan, it encodes its own dramatic appeal.

Della Crusca and Anna Matilda, 'ethereal pseudonyms suggesting
the timeless, slightly out-of-focus nature of romance characters'
(Pascoe 72), exist in a textual world, bound by generic convention,
and yet experimental in their own fashion. What Pascoe calls the
'feminine underpinnings of the romantic endeavor' (72) are made
overt, as Della Crusca and Anna Matilda indulge in a highly public,
and widely publicised, epistolary affair. The 'Preface' to *The British
Album* takes care to preserve the literary nature of their passion, and
with it, the proprieties: 'It ought, however, to be recorded, of the celebrated Correspondence between DELLA CRUSCA and ANNA
MATILDA, that its *genuine enthusiasm* arose entirely from poetical
sympathy; for till immediately before the publication of *The Interview*,
they were totally unacquainted with each other, and reciprocally
unknown'. This protestation is echoed in Volume II, where the
'Advertisement' notes that

> Since the printing of the first Edition of these Works, the
> Correspondence between DELLA CRUSCA and ANNA MATILDA
> has been renewed; – THE EDITOR, therefore, thinks it proper to
> continue their respective Writings up to the present time; as also to
> insert the beautiful Poems by LAURA, and the one she called forth
> from LEONARDO, etc. These later additions are necessary, on
> account of the subsequent allusions to them, and because the lines
> signed LEONARDO appear to have been produced by the pen of
> DELLA CRUSCA.[19] (123)

Besides announcing the appearance of Laura, identified in the text as Mary Robinson, this passage furthers the notion of an irresistible love conducted entirely in print, spontaneously reignited, and then reprinted for the benefit of a curious readership. Considering that 'The Interview', referred to in the 'Preface' to Volume I, actually appears in Volume II (part of the 'renewed' correspondence the 'Advertisement' publicised as commencing after 'the printing of the first Edition'), the Della Crusca/Anna Matilda romance begins to take on the confusing aura of having pre-existed its own composition. Given the knowing, romanticised plotline it follows, this is not entirely impossible: instead, the 'Preface' and the 'Advertisement' build into this love affair the paradox of being simultaneously spontaneous and scripted. On the one hand, each poem builds on its predecessor, requiring a pre-existing condition – despair, admiration, desire – against which to react; on the other, the stereotyped nature of the responses themselves militate against spontaneity. Indeed, Della Crusca and Anna Matilda seem more intent on satisfying readers' expectations than on successfully resolving their love, and yet, as I will discuss, their poems also dissect the nature of romance itself. Their intercourse, compressed into anthology, highlights the artificiality of romantic ideals, the likelihood of romantic disappointment, and the unreliability of lasting love.[20]

In the epistles of Della Crusca and Anna Matilda, 'words are not so much reified as personified';[21] that is, the words 'Della Crusca' and 'Anna Matilda' are personified as the lovers Della Crusca and Anna Matilda, mutually embodied. Della Crusca opens their dialogue with 'The Adieu and Recall to Love', in which he constructs for himself a romantic past, starring himself as the abandoned lover. This poem sets up the paradigm of Della Cruscan romance: love hurts, but its very pain is valuable, because it asserts one's power to feel – that is, to experience and exhibit Sensibility. Della Crusca first renounces Love (and Louisa), only to 'recall' the emotion: 'Go, idle Boy! I quit thy pow'r;/ Thy couch of many a thorn and flow'r/ .... / O hasten back, then, heavenly Boy,/ And with thine anguish bring thy joy!' (1–2, 39–40). This kind of love is all about feeling: Della Crusca craves sensation, which is dwelt on, created, lamented, and finally rejected in the course of the Della Crusca/Anna Matilda affair. The importance given to sensation centres the cycle of poems on the feeling body, but even as this is apparent, both Della Crusca and Anna Matilda insist on the primacy of the feeling *mind*. When Anna Matilda implores Della Crusca, in her response, to 'SEIZE again thy golden quill,/ And with its point my bosom thrill' (1–2), she invigorates the poetry/body/sensation/romance matrix; she offers her bosom, erotically, to Della Crusca's view, and invites her own penetration. At the same time, the stylised language and rhyming couplet enclose the subversive force of such lines within structure: the language of sensibility encourages erotic responses *and* guards against impropriety. In this first flurried exchange, Anna Matilda takes the unprecedented step of intruding herself on Della Crusca's notice, of initiating a romantic exchange based on poetically physical responses. Della Crusca picks up on the implicitly erotic tone, characterising Anna Matilda as his Muse, bringing him pleasure and pain: she is an 'enchanting Maid' whose abstract attractions are steadily embodied. 'O well thy form divine I know', he says; he has 'mark'd', 'seen', 'met', and 'view'd' her before ('To Anna Matilda', 1, 15, 2, 3, 4, 5). But this initial flirtation is checked when Anna Matilda refuses the place of seductive Muse: even as she directs his poetic gaze to her body, she recasts herself as older (than who is left unspecified):

> O *Time*! Since these [artistic skills] are left me still,
> Of *lesser thefts* e'en take thy fill:
> Yes, steal the lustre from my eye,
> And bid the soft carnation fly;
> My tresses sprinkle with thy snow,
> Which boasted once *the auburn glow*;
> Warp the slim form that was ador'd
> By him, so lov'd, my *bosom's* Lord —
> But leave me, when all these you steal,
> The mind to *taste*, the nerve to *feel*!
> ('To Della Crusca', 31–40)

At first it seems as if Anna Matilda wants to redirect her budding romance with Della Crusca to a reality in which she – older, faded, attached to her 'bosom's Lord' – destroys her claims to romantic availability, and attempts to forestall Della Crusca's passion. And yet she also offers her mind to Della Crusca's ardent notice.[22] Anna Matilda transfers sensation to the Mind in an effort to intellectualise her poetic response, but she does so by insisting on the physical nature of that response. In this way she accomplishes the merging of Mind and Body, and with it the full physicalisation of 'Anna Matilda' into the lover Anna Matilda. Love has been relocated to the Mind, which has been redesignated the receptor of sensation – sex is now firmly in the head.[23]

This means that when Della Crusca responds 'And art thou then, alas! like me,/ OFFSPRING *of frail mortality?*' ('To Anna Matilda', 1–2), he is accepting the mind/body merge and directing his love into the channel prescribed by Anna Matilda. Or at least, he seems to: although he closes his poem by declaring he loves her mind rather than her body ('Unknown, again thou art ador'd,/ As once by him, thy *bosom's "Lord"*' [67–8]), he opens it with exclamations of passion and, again, sensation. 'Methinks, as Passion drives along,/ As frantic grown, I *feel* thy Song' (13–14, emphasis added): frenzy and sensation combine, suggesting that while, for Anna Matilda, 'mind' is uppermost, for Della Crusca 'body' holds his attention. This impression is strengthened when, in the body of the poem, Della Crusca replaces Anna Matilda's narrative of age and experience with one of romantically sheltered feminine beauty and virtue. The epistolary nature of this love affair allows Della Crusca to write his version, while Anna Matilda writes hers: although each is inflected by passion, each also displays 'appropriate' passion, Anna Matilda's demure, Della Crusca's forceful. At this point, the affair is interrupted by Della Crusca's 'Elegy, Written on the Plain of Fontenoy', the pathos of which affects Anna Matilda, who finds herself transported there: 'Ha! what a tone was that, which floating near,/ Seem'd Harmony's full soul – *whose* is the lyre?/ Which seizing thus on my enraptur'd ear,/ Chills with its force yet melts me with its fire' ('Stanzas to Della Crusca', 5–8). Even as she 'sees' Fontenoy, however, she poeticises a romantic story of sisterly devotion and sibling death: chaste Love, intertwined with death. As she pleaded age, now she pleads poetry: she concludes her poem by advocating poetic transcendence for 'FIRM' minds over sickly sentiment; again, Mind is uppermost, as is Poetry, while the body and sexual passion are deflected to the patently non-sexual story of sisterly love. And again, Della Crusca responds erotically, describing Anna Matilda as his lady-love who inspires him to greatness, whose love saves him from despair, whose wish is his command. The very familiarity of the developing plot obscures its irregularities (Anna Matilda's independence, Della Crusca's sensibility), while Della Crusca's continual re-presentations of Anna Matilda work to transform her from poetic correspondent to lover, a player in a by-the-book romance, and adjunct to Della Crusca's hero-self.[24] Anna Matilda abruptly changes the tone and direction of their romance in her response: 'I hate the tardy Elegiac lay – / Choose me a measure jocund as the day!' ('To Della Crusca', 1–2). As much as this poem chastises Della Crusca for excessive mooning, it also rebukes him for desiring insensibility, since to love and feel are what make a Poet. Anna Matilda returns to her original ground: poetry = love = sensibility = poetry.[25] Della Crusca is stymied; *The British Album* inserts odes to Prudence and Death and an elegy by Della Crusca, and an 'Invocation to Horror' by Anna Matilda, before the romance is resumed.

Anna Matilda has made her point: love is expressed through poetry, poetry embodies sensibility, sensibility proves one is a Poet. As if pondering her message, Della Crusca remains off-stage, while Anna Matilda receives the poetic attentions of Reuben. The privacy of love has already been compromised; with the entrance of Reuben, a 'Stranger ... prompted by LOVE' ('To Anna Matilda', 1, 4), Anna Matilda's status as chaste heroine is in jeopardy. She is now publicly addressed by two suitors, each of whom visualises her embodied form both as, and through, her poetry; Reuben sees her as a 'speaking paint-ing' viewed 'as we read' (7, 8), his admiration binding her up in Poetry. Reuben wants her to be a slave to feeling; he constructs her as representative of Love, a position that teeters dangerously between private romance heroine and public woman. Anna Matilda's textual romance, based on the advertised gimmick that she and her admirers have never met, threatens to transform her from chaste poetess to open poetic target. In her response to Reuben, Anna Matilda redirects the thrust of his desire, asserting love's pain over its allure, and thereby recreating herself as Love's victim – a damsel in distress rather than a *femme fatale*. She also returns to feeling, this time investing it with violence: love is 'a tyger! – a tyrant', 'a serpent in disguise,/ And as the lynx, his piercing eyes!/ A raging fire, a deadly pain/ ... / A fever, tempest, madness he —/ Of all life's ills – a DREAD EPITOME!' ('To Reuben', 31–3, 35–6). Love becomes a monster threatening Anna Matilda's self-control, and 'to speak *more* of love' entails actual pain and torment;[26] plainly, that Reuben can so casually invoke love proves he does not truly *feel* the emotion. For Anna Matilda, love hurts; romantic love translates as physical pain: the mind may rule the body but its sensations are identical. In romance-plot terms, as well, Anna Matilda responds implicitly to Della Crusca's neglect: after her chivvying of his despairing tone, he has not written back, and indeed after she publicises her lovesickness, he still does not – at this point he offers his readers his admiration of Siddons, Wells and Farren, plus 'The Slaves, an Elegy', and 'Monody, Addressed to Mr. T.' Despite Reuben's love, Anna Matilda the romance heroine feels abandoned, forced to read Della Crusca's eulogies on the perfections of other women. The Della Crusca/Anna Matilda romance continues along the expected path: declaration, tiff, neglect.

As if jealous of Della Crusca's divided attentions, Anna Matilda's next poem craves 'Indifference'; she continues the theme of love's pain, and turns on Sensibility itself, a 'cruel imp,' an 'insidious fiend', a 'SAVAGE UNTAM'D' ('Ode to Indifference', 51, 65, 79). Indifference, she implies, will be her protector, now that Della Crusca has vanished, and will defend her from suffering: 'thou shield'st the heart from rankling pain,/ And Misery *strikes*, when blest with thee, in vain;/ Wan *Jealousy*'s empoisoning tooth,/ And *Love*, which feeds upon our youth' (31–4). Where earlier Della Crusca wallowed in suffering – proof of the depth of his emotion – now Anna Matilda exposes her grief and jealousy, claiming the spectacular, and compromising, position of abandoned heroine. Again, romance both proceeds and unravels: Anna Matilda's is a familiar generic position, but once written by herself it takes on a subjective tinge not usually available to the heroine, who is more often the object of the romance. As earlier when she 'initiated a love affair in verse' (Pascoe 68), then declared the primacy of Mind, then championed open displays of feeling, Anna Matilda complicates her romantic role. She clearly makes demands on Della Crusca, and is not content passively to await his coming: she both occupies the heroine's space and enlarges its parameters, suggesting a distrust of the usual romance plot-line. She advocates sensation but also expects a return on her investment in love, preferring to withdraw when that is not forthcoming. Anna Matilda's advertisement of her woes works: Della Crusca finally responds, to tell her that Indifference allows only 'free[dom] from pain' ('Ode to Anna Matilda', 4), which by extension means freedom from love and, unsurprisingly at this point, poetry. Emotion produces poetry, which in turn inspires emotion; Anna Matilda, however, rejects Della Crusca's overtures, and enjoins poetry to combat both Della Crusca and feeling. Retreating once again to Mind, she attempts to disentangle poetry and feeling: 'Thy light'ning Pen 'tis thus I greet,/ Fearless its subtle point I meet;[27]/ Ne'er shall its spells my sad heart move,/ From the calm state it vows to love' ('Ode to Della Crusca', 27–30). Anna Matilda and Della Crusca engage in a series of feints: she desires indifference, he points out what she will lose, she implies she has lost it anyway. He in turn seeks indifference – in the hopes of finding Anna Matilda there – but fails utterly to quell passion and its concomitant physical manifestations: 'Could I repress quick Rapture's start,/ Or hide the bursting[28] of my heart' ('To Anna Matilda', 31–2). Anna Matilda, textbook-romantic upper hand clearly visible, chastises Della Crusca for succumbing to passion, which 'tears with fangs unkind' ('To Della Crusca', 22) and compromises Taste, the only path to bliss.[29] Triumphantly, she sends Della Crusca on a quest for indifference, away from her sphere of influence, provoking Della Crusca to declare his intentions openly:

> And have I strove in vain to move
> Thy Heart, *fair Phantom* of my Love?
> And cou'dst thou think 'twas my design
> Calmly to list thy Notes Divine
> That I responsive Lays might send,
> To gain a cold *Platonic Friend*?
> ('To Anna Matilda', 1–6)

Anna Matilda uses feeling strategically: she lures Della Crusca back with displays of pain, and provokes him to plain speech with protestations of indifference. Feeling and poetry, inextricably linked, combine to forward plot: the worldly romance Anna Matilda and Della Crusca pursue rejects innocence and patience for manipulation and need. Della Crusca, having shown his hand, goes further, concentrating on his vision of Anna Matilda's physical beauty (complete with the heroine's requisite golden curls[30]) and his obstructed desire to 'lure [her] to the chaste caress' (16), although one wonders at the sincerity of 'chaste'. Calling Anna Matilda's bluff, he advertises his imminent departure, and his lament that now he and Anna Matilda will never meet: 'each to each remai[n] – *a Shadow and a Shade*' (100). Faced with his loss, Anna Matilda rushes into print: 'Oh stay, oh stay! thy rash speed check' ('To Della Crusca', 1), but it is too late; Della Crusca has gone, her sensations – still felt – are now useless, and her Muse, deprived of sustenance – feeling – deserts her: 'Expiring, still her note's the same,/ She murmurs DELLA CRUSCA's *name*! – / The SACRED WORLD – ye heard it spoke; – / *Her book is clos'd – her Lyre is broke*!' (99–102). By parting the lovers, Volume I closes the book of their correspondence: once the epistles cease, so too does the 'reality' of their relationship. Anna Matilda indicates the influence of publicity when she refers to the 'SACRED WORLD' – the poems, of course, originally appeared in *The World* newspaper.[31] From 10 July 1787 to 17 May 1788, Della Crusca and Anna Matilda fall in love, a public affair based on the reciprocity of feeling and poetry and the attractions of the romance plot. Lurking behind Della Crusca and Anna Matilda, Robert Merry and Hannah Cowley manipulate conventions of genre freely:

even as a recognisable romance plot progresses, neither Della Crusca nor Anna Matilda seems fully invested in its development, continually deferring a meeting; rather, they pursue an alternative romance, that between poetry and feeling. When Anna Matilda seeks indifference, only to be thwarted by her emotions; when Della Crusca builds up his dream girl – each does so poetically, reifying the romantic attractions of form. Once their romance is extracted from *The World* and re-presented in *The British Album*, structure and style jostle for primacy: love invaded by pain, pain constricted by poetry.

Readers, on tenterhooks – are Anna Matilda and Della Crusca truly parted? – must plough through half a volume of the adolescent sex fantasies of Arley,[32] as well as Benedict's sonnets and the Emma/Henry exchange, before they re-engage with the lovers, whose story picks up where it left off, albeit five months later (28 October 1788). By now, the Della Crusca/Anna Matilda romance is taken for granted, a settled fact: outsiders have noticed it: 'For e'en *cold Criticks* have conceiv'd,/So much alike our measures run,/ That ANNA AND THAT I WERE ONE – / *Would it were so!* – we then might prove/ The sacred settled unity of Love' ('To Anna Matilda', 49–52). Verified by critical response, the romance must be followed through; hence, Della Crusca finds it is 'vain [to] fly' Anna Matilda (1), and that, moreover, Anna Matilda needs watching. Only now, apparently, has Della Crusca learned of Reuben. Calling Anna Matilda 'faithless Anna' (39), he asks for permission to return to her: 'bi[d] me still RETURN TO POETRY – and THEE' (72). As McGann has noted, the Della Cruscan world is 'immediate, material, self-conscious, limited to language' (86). Even as Anna Matilda's exchange with Reuben counts as faithlessness to Della Crusca, so too his poem announcing his desire to return effects his return – once written, the deed is done. Della Crusca's awareness that textual intercourse with one outside the Della Crusca/Anna Matilda coupling represents infidelity leads him to disguise his own indiscretion, an exchange with Laura, whose 'desert[ion] by a FAITHLESS MATE' ('To Him who will understand it', 34) leaves her alone and vulnerable. 'Leonardo' replies, offering condolences and friendship, only to be unmasked as Della Crusca in a note to the poem. Further, Anna Matilda sees through the pseudonym; like Emma, who upbraided Henry for failing to understand that poetry is Self, Anna Matilda knows that, in the Della Cruscan world, poetic style embodies one's identity and cannot be hidden. Hence, Della Crusca's flirtation with another woman is plainly discerned: 'Hah! Didst thou hope I should not trace/ The *mental features of thy*

face?/ .... / Thou stand'st confest! – thy form is seen' ('To Della
Crusca', 35–6, 42). Della Crusca's faithlessness, crassly indulged in
even as he professes his desire to return to Anna Matilda, prompts her
simultaneously to reveal and deny her feelings for him. '*Poetic Passions*
vainly burn!/ .... / Yes, write to LAURA! speed thy sighs,/ Tell her,
DELLA CRUSCA dies/ .... / FALSE *Lover*! TRUEST *Poet*! now farewell!'
(40, 43–4, 55). The concatenation of exclamation marks and capital
letters convey Anna Matilda's emotion, while her admission that she
feels 'poetic passions', her declaration that she will not encourage
them ('vainly burn'), and her conflation of false and true, show once
more the primacy of poetry: Della Crusca's verse is true, revealing his
infidelity. Poetic faithlessness means the end of sensation, since, as
Anna Matilda predicts, his '*Golden Quill*' will never again 'with magic
passion ev'ry bosom thrill./ He may write, but ANNA 'twas alone/
Lured down his guardian Goddess from her throne' (87, 88–90). Since
Anna Matilda both is, and inspires, Della Crusca's Muse, the withdrawal of her favour means the loss of Della Crusca's poetic force – the
blunting of his golden quill, and the end of 'Della Crusca' himself.
Who he is, and what he writes, are as intermingled as Love and Poetry.

At this point Laura intervenes to reassure Anna Matilda that there
was nothing between herself and Della Crusca – all pretence of
'Leonardo' dropped – but friendship,[33] and to reinforce Anna
Matilda's status as Della Crusca's embodied Muse, his source of
passionate poetry:

> O Anna, since thy graceful song
> Can wind the cadence soft among
> The heart's fine nerves, and ravish thence
> The wond'ring Poet's captive sense;
> 'Till warm'd by thy electric fire,
> His yielding soul, with fond desire,
> Glows but for Thee – dispel thy fears.
> ('Laura to Anna Matilda', 1–7)

The ethereal – soul and sense – is infused with physical sensation, as
required by Della Cruscan passion; poetry functions as a kind of emis-
sion, dependent as ever on the stoking of sensation. Echoing Laura,
Della Crusca avers that his poetry proves his fidelity merely by being
written: 'And think'st thou, ANNA! that my love,/ Like thine, could
ever faithless prove,/ That in some female Reuben's praise,/ I the
impassion'd verse could raise;/ That I so quickly led astray,/ Could

wake the warm inconstant lay?' (53–8). Della Crusca's pointed reminder of Anna Matilda's own dalliance blends with his images of poetic arousal ('raise', 'lay') in a clear appeal to the Della Cruscan body/poetry link; it signals to Anna Matilda that passion and poetry can only be inspired by Anna Matilda, and that until she 'bidst the measure pour,/ Till then, THY DELLA CRUSCA WRITES NO MORE' ('To Anna Matilda', 109–10). Poetry *pours*; it has a shape, a physicality, and an origin in passion, in emotion. As the images build up, poetry is increasingly eroticised, presented as a response to emotional – that is, physical – excitation. Della Crusca's verse will pour forth if Anna Matilda responds poetically; what has already appeared justifies Della Crusca's faith and Anna Matilda's judgement that poetry is the man. And Della Crusca is not averse to emotional blackmail: his explicit accusation concerning Reuben causes Anna Matilda to crumble. Declaring herself unable to compete with 'favour'd Man['s]' 'sagacious ART' ('To Della Crusca', 6),[34] she portrays herself as deserted by poetry – 'Poetic ardors fly me now!' – and overcome by Laura – 'Whilst LAURA still may dress the lay/ In all the lustre of the day' (64, 93–4). Again, conventions of romance are followed: the appearance of another woman provokes jealousy and the breakdown of trust; the man protests his love; the woman requires proof. And again, convention is conveyed in an unorthodox manner: the concentration on sexualised responses and the cultivation of a physical style of poetry inevitably bring passion and desire into conflict with romance. When Anna Matilda calls on Della Crusca to rescue her from her suspicions, she invokes a body entrapped by poetry and passion: 'But shall not DELLA CRUSCA sue/ For her who to HIS MUSE is true?/ *For* ONE, who round her heart hath wreath'd/ All the rich strains he ever breath'd' (101–4). All that is left, now, is the actual encounter of bodies.

All along, the romance between Anna Matilda and Della Crusca has sustained itself on absence: each lover has created a relationship based on desire rather than knowledge, and each has followed a personalised romance plot – Anna Matilda's feeling mind, Della Crusca's desiring body – spliced together with the image of embodied, passionate poetry. It has depended entirely on a textual reality; conducted in print, it is, finally, both consummated and concluded in print. McGann says that 'the desire to establish a real equation between textual and personal erotic means in this text, disaster' (92); Pascoe notes that the romance's 'fires were cooled by a disappointing meeting between the matronly Cowley and the younger Merry' (69). Neither recognises that the only possible solution to the Della

Crusca/Anna Matilda romance is a parting – it is generically required, structurally to be expected from the trajectory their relationship has followed. Further, however, neither McGann nor Pascoe acknowledges the intensely textual nature of the poem that signals the romance's conclusion, for 'The Interview' not only describes the one meeting between Anna Matilda and Della Crusca (not, significantly, between Cowley and Merry), it also dresses it up in thoroughly romantic robes, and offers closure based on the poetic mingling that, for each, represents physical contact. That is, consummation is complexly merged with a romanticised, stylised lovers' parting.

'The Interview' plots the end of romance, its subsumation into purely physical response. It literally intertwines the poets' voices; although signed by Della Crusca, it contains passages described as from the pen of Anna Matilda. Lines and stanzas are begun by Della Crusca and finished by Anna Matilda, a technique that embodies both the artistry and the artifice of their affair. Readers are offered a purely text-bound but completely intertexted intercourse – sex on the page, which both consummates and ends the affair. Della Crusca begins: 'O WE HAVE MET' (1), and his immediate invocation of the elements' fury images the failure of their interview. In romance terms, Anna Matilda has dismissed Della Crusca; 'haughty Duty' requires her to declare that 'ANOTHER claims my heart/ .... / ANNA MATILDA NEVER CAN BE THINE!' (88, 91). Readers are reminded that in her second verse-epistle Anna Matilda had referred to her 'bosom's Lord'; indeed, readers of *The British Album* can flip back to Volume I and reread Anna Matilda's words with a new comprehension. Calling herself a 'cold Ingrate', Anna Matilda asserts that, nonetheless, 'th'impassioned verse is o'er' (96, 71).[35] Having lost his lover, Della Crusca refuses to give up his love: constancy, portrayed as a feeling superior even to the possession of Anna Matilda, takes the place of companionship; the 'loftier bliss' is 'to rave,/ Without a pow'r to aid, a chance to save' (120–1). Renunciation is figured as the marker of truest love – Della Crusca romanticises his loss into a gain, as his enduring love will furnish him with an endless subject for poetry. Even as he gives up Anna Matilda, however, Della Crusca makes one last bid for her body:

> – my adoring heart is ANNA'S OWN;
> YES, ALL HER OWN, and tho' ANOTHER claim
> Her mind's rich treasure,[36] still *I* love the same;
> And tho' ANOTHER, O how blest! Has felt
> Her soften'd soul in dear delirium melt,

While from her gaze the welcome meaning sprung,
As on her neck in frantic joy he hung,
Yet I *will* bear it, and tho' Hell deride,
My pangs shall *sooth*, my curse shall be my pride.
                                        (109–17)

Poetry creates the body, the giving of which signifies success in love.
Significantly, this fantasy of embodiment occurs after the pair have
intermingled their verse, a placement that suggests that even as Della
Crusca romanticises renunciation, he publicises consummation:
poetry, the text, having contained and sustained their affair all along,
it is the only site at which they can complete it.

As I have mentioned, then, the pair become lovers literally, sharing
textual space, cohabiting poetry. After Della Crusca signals his despair
by calling on the elements, he transports his readers to the scene, 'a
garden in Paris'. Della Crusca, the 'I', pauses 'to view the mazy dash'
of a waterfall, and muse on his love for Anna Matilda. The next stanza
begins 'Sudden I turn': the speaker hears 'sweet sounds' and 'rush[es]'
to find the source (12, 23, 25, 37). The print, however, is now italicised, and, directed by a note to the text, the reader understands that
the speaker of all the poem's italicised lines is Anna Matilda. Even,
then, as Della Crusca opens the poem and sets the scene, Anna
Matilda intrudes, inserting her subjective 'I' and placing herself as an
equal partner in this poem of loss. It is Anna Matilda who hears Della
Crusca's song and turns to find him. The moment of encounter,
however, is doubly italicised, typographically ambiguous, so that the
speaker could be Anna Matilda, Della Crusca, or both simultaneously:
'*AND THERE THE SOFT MUSICIAN CONSCIOUS STOOD*' (38). The
poets merge identities in mutual spectatorship – years of writing
visionary poetry culminate in the meeting of eyes/'I's and the
mingling of verse. Della Crusca now speaks, textualising Anna Matilda
as a '*living* Angel … ANNA's self' (43, 46) whom he leads to 'the
woven bower', a traditionally romantic lovers' space. Poeticised
romance requires poeticised closure: Anna Matilda begins to speak, at
first in Della Crusca's voice (her words are not italicised), only to inter-
vene, mid-line, with her own: '"Lean not to me, *th'impassioned verse is
o'er,*/ Which chain'd thy heart, and forc'd thee to adore:/ For O! observe
where haughty Duty stands,/ …. / Dread Goddess, I obey!"'* (71–3, 77).
This remarkable poem accomplishes typographically exactly what
duty and propriety – catchwords for convention – oppose: the lovers,
only ever textual, come together in the final poem of their affair,

bound together even as they give each other up. The dual vocality of 'The Interview' illustrates most fully the physical nature of Della Cruscan romance, and finalises the intrusion of the erotic into the romantic. Although the sharp-eyed Gifford would denounce the 'weekly cuckold[ing of] her poor spouse in rhyme' figured by the exchanges in *The World*, even he apparently missed the significance of the very public exchange of poetic fervour contained in this most commingled of Della Cruscan verse.

The romance between Anna Matilda and Della Crusca requires poetry; it is constructed by poets in disguise, each of whom masquerades as a suitably romantic figure, both of whom participate in the conventions of romance while introducing the erotics of the body into the romance paradigm. Their relationship, distilled from the pages of *The World* into the package of *The British Album*, depends on a chronological reading of their exchange, and is specifically crafted to follow a familiar plot trajectory: the compiler of *The British Album* leaves out Laura's suspicious and arch response to 'Leonardo's' overture, for instance, and changes some titles to dovetail more artistically with future developments. To this end, Anna Matilda's post-'Interview poem', dated 19 June 1789 ('The Interview' is dated 16 June 1789) and entitled 'To Della Crusca – who said, "When I am dead, write my Elegy"', becomes in the 1792 edition of *The British Album*, 'To Philander', while still footnoted as 'formerly' to Della Crusca.[37] This change can be seen to reflect Anna Matilda's subsequent knowledge of Della Crusca's final poem, dated 30 June 1791 and entitled 'To A – E B – N'. Despite 'Interview''s protestations of undying love, 'To A – E B – N' shows a Della Crusca who has not only moved on, but also changed his mind about true love's expression: 'For HE who dares *assert* his grief,/ Who *boasts* the anguish he may prove,/ Obtains, perhaps, the wish'd relief,/ BUT O! THE TRAITOR DOES NOT LOVE' (9–12). By affirming that *real* love does not reveal itself, but rather serves and suffers in silence, Della Crusca dismisses the entirety of his affair with Anna Matilda, which grew from and relied on open assertion.[38] In a poem that neatly redirects emotion and functions as his last word, Della Crusca does more violence to Romance than in any of his impassioned exchanges with Anna Matilda, and shows that the most powerful threat to Love is also the most inescapable, and mundane: the passage of time. In the next chapter, it is the hero who faces extinction.

3
Failing the Romance: Coleridge, Keats and the Wilted Hero

As discussed in the previous chapter, the romance (as genre) can merge with romance (as an emotional connection) in defiance of concrete formal boundaries; the erotic world conjured by the Della Cruscans rests on a disruption of the purities of emotional contact relied on by the romance. And as the repeated returns to definitions described in Chapter 1 show, the components of the romance troubled its readers as much as its overall force. The sexual energy characteristic of the Della Cruscan romance emphasised coupling, romantic partnerships expressed through highly stylised and emotive poetry. But elements of the romance could be detached and utilised in unusual forms and unexpected surroundings. In this chapter I will investigate the character of the hero in the poetry of Coleridge and Keats, and accompany them on their quests – doomed to failure – for heroic perfection. While Keats assumes the familiar persona of narrator and projects heroic inadequacy onto his characters, Coleridge more unusually offers himself as the hero of the text, constructing in his conversation poems a cyclical quest-romance that sees, in each poem, a problematic and ultimately fatally flawed presentation of the Poet as Hero.[1] Keats sets the trend for this book's presentation of early-nineteenth-century treatments of violence in the romance; as I will discuss, his heroes meet grisly ends in full view of the reader – or they vanish altogether, a metaphorical but nonetheless telling and visceral form of creative violence. Coleridge's romance of the self in his conversation poems shares with other 1790s romancers' texts a more indirect approach: in his familiar turns to a mystical Divine and ineffectual personal retreats, he demonstrates the paradoxical decision that an ultimate loss of self is preferable to the psychic violence threatened by confronting the self's disintegration. As with Keats, then,

Coleridge's heroic Self and its various failures function on a metaphorical level to unravel the weft of genre; both poets use a familiar trope, but neither carries it to its familiar conclusion of empowerment and fulfilment. In clear contradiction of the truism that 'man has been raised in order to function, in order to address the world like a text destined to find its readers',[2] neither Coleridge nor Keats succeeds in writing heroes who function properly. Like texts destined only to find their own dissolutions, their heroes commence quests in lands hostile to the very notion and fabric of heroism; in their failure we can read another form of violence done to the romance.

Keats and Coleridge treat the relationship between self and hero differently; for Coleridge, the lack of critical distance established by the speaker in the conversation poems contributes to their sense of an emptied personality and a vitiated exploration of Self. In his conversation poems, Coleridge incessantly returns to the Self – that is, the Self mediated through poetry – fixing the readerly gaze on his own personal attractions and shortcomings. The romance he creates centres on his desires and disabilities; self-consciously, he presents his Persona as always already on the verge of failure, yet unable to resist the challenge. Coleridge's technique allows an element of performativity to enter: that is, he takes on the character of 'Coleridge/Poet' who then enters the fray of his own poetic needs, casting them as personal and hence as necessary to the formation of masculine identity. Like the theorists discussed in Chapter 1, Coleridge becomes the hero of his own tale, but unlike those theorists his goal is not to rehabilitate or otherwise affect Romance, but to reconstitute the Romanticised self – he attempts to be his own champion. That he just as consistently fails to uphold his own honour illustrates his reliance on and vexed relationship with the tropes of Romance.

Keats's romances, however, are infused with violence: feuds, transformations, curses and murder underpin these poems. In these poems, he is no more than storyteller, a kind of bardic voice; it is his characters who are victimised. Each male protagonist takes in turns the identities of swain, villain and victim; each dies or else, in Porphyro's case, dissipates into the distant past. Keats creates situations in which his heroes lose their virility, their autonomy and their lives, and in so doing he questions the impermeability of masculinity: doing violence to gender, he romanticises the losses he forces onto his characters. The famous Keatsian suspension of desire that characterises the Odes is transformed in his Romances to a satiation of desire, a punishable offence.

Both poets, then, are interested in exploring the character and limitations of the hero; Coleridge's contemporary settings and personal identification of the Self as Speaker and hence as Hero create an unsettling intimate drama, whereas Keats's more elaborate, more conventionally formal romances examine the hero as a creative construct. Keats's romances are plot-driven by a detached, often ironic narrator; Coleridge's are character-centred, focused around the narrating voice who is bard, hero and often villain combined. Coleridge and Keats fuse a straightforward appreciation of the traditional figure of the hero with a complex reworking of his main personality traits, and in this way they also imbue their heroes with a kind of existential doubt as to the very supportability of their being. This works on the level of poetry, history and culture: the literary ideal of the hero is deconstructed through his increasingly unheroic traumas; the historical veracity of the hero is questioned through the scepticism with which the poets treat their sources, whether personal or literary; finally, the cultural dominance of the heroic persona is unbalanced by the poets' erosion of his authority, centrality and permanence. Even as the erotic scenarios of the Della Cruscans drew attention to the dynamics of the romance of heterosexuality, so too the harshness with which Keats and Coleridge treat the heroic ideal disputes the veracity of the ideal of gender presented by the hero. A model of masculinity, his textbook conformity in the romantic narrative – displays of strength, honour, skill, protectiveness, sexual dominance, for instance – ensures him the rewards of successful masculinity – respect, leadership, 'the girl'. When Keats and Coleridge find themselves unable to uphold a devotion to the protocol of the romantic hero, then, they also reveal difficulties with the plot required by masculinity. Coleridge, unlucky in love, addicted to laudanum, and Keats, emasculated by class[3] – both poets' troubles with heroes could be explained biographically, but as usual biography is only part of the story; Coleridge and Keats undermine the reliability, the viability, of the generic as well as the masculine ideal when they redirect the hero towards failure.

Even as the romance engaged critical attention during the Romantic period, so did its constituent parts. To be a 'hero' meant something specific; it required certain behaviour, and necessitated some type of quest – indeed, that one was palpably questing itself gave the glamour of the hero. Gillian Beer describes this as the withdrawal of the hero from society combined with 'a complex prolonged succession of incidents usually without a single climax'.[4] G.R. Levy positions the hero as one who, 'unforeseeing, lives through the experience[s] of loss, wandering, combats with monstrous beings, some kind of transformation, achievement, a marriage, and again loss'.[5] The hero 'differs from other men in the degree of his powers.... He awakes admiration primarily because he has in rich abundance qualities which other men have to a much lesser extent', says C.M. Bowra, who notes that eloquence, as well as strength, swiftness, endurance, or resourcefulness, is a heroic gift.[6] Walter Reed elaborates:

> The Romantic hero is not a simple being, but one involved in a set of relationships both dialectical and dynamic. The hero is first of all a figure related ... to a metaphysical ontological ground. The hero is ... as an extraordinary person is to the ordinary members of his society.... Finally, the Romantic hero is involved in a relationship to himself, that is, to his own heroic identity. He ... must live up to, or decline from, an inherited heroic ideal.... His identity is never completely fixed but is in the process of evolution or devolution.[7]

And Lloyd Bishop comments that 'the romantic hero's basic trait ... is acute self-consciousness'; he is a 'solitary hero' whose quest is 'never-ending', importing a sense of circularity and claustrophobia.[8] The quest, then, is entered on for the betterment of the hero and, ultimately, society, which may but more often may not recognise the value of its hero until the quest has been successfully completed; it involves isolation and withdrawal from home, journeys of some kind (physical, intellectual, emotional, moral), and is often characterised by continual self-regeneration. During the quest, the hero gains knowledge but can also lose it, and his quest may be valued by no one but himself; he is regarded as somehow different, and 'other' – this may mean he is celebrated but just as often leads to the isolation that engenders the quest. Importantly, he is introspective; his difference in Romantic ideology is mental, and his relationship to his society vexed. He is always awaiting, in search of, self-justification and acceptance by his society, but as his quest unfolds he learns the worth of self-reliance, self-awareness, and fortitude in the face of opposition; he learns to be a man, and returns to society a verified – tested, found and made good – leader. The heroic quest itself forms the hero, whose heroism is only ever potential before the quest's completion. While an older form of romance insisted on a visible, physical quest, the Romantic-period quest can be internalised, a mental or emotional journey through one's own makeup.

However, as the different critical accounts make clear, the Romantic hero is an unstable personality, dependent on events, on history, on expectation, and on generic fidelity. Beer notes a key difference between the medieval romance and the Romantic period's version(s): 'whereas in the medieval romance the writer is quizzically present, commenting, interpreting, offering asides to the reader, in the romantic period the poet seeks to be immersed in the same element as the imaginative forms he presents' (62). The Romantic romance hero follows an emotional path laid down according to external generic principles; he seeks immersion in form and identifies with the form and content of the world he both sees and half-creates. The allusion is not incidental, since the creative landscape traversed by the hero – the poet – is externalised in the form of art, the poem that becomes a map of the quest undertaken by the hero. The swings from external (genre) to internal (quest) to external (poem) create the reader's quest; as Beer says, 'we have to depend entirely on the narrator of the romance: he remakes the rules of what is possible, what impossible' (8). The success of our readerly quest for meaning, then, depends on the poet's own handling of his quest; the forays into an internal landscape are, perversely, often unsignposted, frustrating our desire for narrative coherency while also allowing glimpses of a personality in flux. The formation of Romantic sensibility, the achievement of full heroic capability, the creation and domination of poetic creativity – these are truisms of Romantic selfhood, itself an expression of an idealised form of masculinity.[9] The combination of a turn to an internal landscape, a reorientation of the quest towards self-illumination, and the solipsistic nature of the romance of 'I' creates the instability of the hero and the circularity of a quest defined by 'a never-ending movement toward fulfilled vision and self-comprehension, an ever-intensifying desire for what is desired'.[10]

Even, then, as the hero directs his quest inward, seeking the key to wholeness of self, vision, knowledge, creative maturity, or understanding, he is also following the path laid out by cultural norms: becoming a hero and becoming a man feed into each other. The romance of selfhood accompanies and mirrors the romance of gender, and the hero pursues the tracks of genre and gender. Where, then, is the uncharted wilderness the hero traditionally encounters? If in both literary and cultural terms the journey is always already mapped, how can the hero achieve the independent personality that guarantees his heroism – how does he demonstrate his specialness? How can he ever experience isolation? This central paradox in the development of heroic identity is routinely ignored by the questing hero, who must maintain the unique nature of his quest or risk his heroism altogether. But its presence is endemic to the failed heroes written by Coleridge and Keats; they illustrate the impossibility of ever attaining full heroic status by offering, repeatedly, inadequate heroes on self-defeating quests. Whether conducting the reader through the self-immersion of the conversation poems, as Coleridge does, or directing the reader's attention to the destruction of the scenario he has spent stanzas creating, as Keats does, both poets construct romances saturated with imbalance and loss. The hero's orderly path from youth and inexperience to full maturity and manhood is fragmented and disrupted; while it may be true that, as Reed asserts, the hero is 'an ideal structure of the Romantic imagination' (33), for Coleridge and Keats that ideal remains immaterial, insubstantial, and unable to compete with the debased and unstructured heroes on which they concentrate. And for each poet, violence enters as something experienced by or done to the hero that emblematises his failure: for Coleridge, the concentration on the self and concomitant loss of self that pervades the conversation poems effectively vitiates both heroic wholeness and the romance of 'I'; for Keats, more securely positioned as detached narrator, the actual physical violence and threats inflicted on his heroes lead to similar results. 'The bursting ardours of the heroic soul' (Bowra 131) become, quite literally, lethal.

The quest, then, takes place internally, for Keats as well as Coleridge; Keats's heroes, too, while more familiar in their dress and speech, traverse emotional landscapes. While appearing ever-new, the quest treacherously offers each candidate the customary and the old; as Ross puts it, 'the Romantic poet quests for the originating self within the self only to discover ... relation or ratio, only to discover his indebtedness to the world of his forefathers in making him capable of seeming to possess himself' (27).[11] As poets, the 'Romantics' quested for self-expression, for the ability to remake the world of Self and Art, for the appreciation that would make them legislators of the world, heroes of culture. In Ross's terms, this is doomed to failure because of the poets' inability to recognise that their novel approach is 'predetermined by the nature of the historical changes that envelope and transform the poetic vocation itself' (29). In other words, in trying to renew their culture, they fail to see that they are products of it, and that culture inevitably renews itself. Fatalistic as this viewpoint may be, Ross's description of Romantic entrappedness resonates within the poetry, for there we find exactly the pre-determined, ineffectual, blinkered quests he observes. If romance 'expresses the lost or repressed emotional forces of the imagination', and if poets 'sought to release' them through art (Beer 59–60), then it seems significant that so much about the romance during the Romantic period rests on disorder and both physical and metaphorical violence. Unrest, dissatisfaction, an uneasy embracing of the power of heroism combined with uncomfortable inklings of its hollowness and unhappy encounters with its banalities – these, more than triumph, more than victory, much more than a celebratory advance towards manliness, inform the portrayals of heroes in Coleridge and Keats, and indicate a little-noticed use of the romance for Romantic poets: to allow them to voice, however covertly or unconsciously, suspicions that romantic heroism had been infiltrated by cultural complacency and unthinking repetition. The association of masculinity and heroism is unmasked and its villainy exposed when Coleridge rigs his own contests and Keats allows nothing to stand between his heroes and their destruction.

En/gaging the hero: Coleridge

In *The Current of Romantic Passion*, Jeffrey Robinson frames the Romantic confessional poem in romance terms: 'autobiographical writing ... concretizes the notion of an essential self, fundamentally not socially disruptive and not defined through its political relations. That self is confirmed, *rescued into coherence* by benign interventions from nature ...'.[12] Implicitly, Robinson casts the Self as heroine-like, awaiting rescue by a protective, heroic Nature, even as he maintains the femininity of knightly nature – it is 'benign', and 'surrounds the self in a stream, or a cloak ... of language' (74). Bisexual Nature is both mother and father to the Self – it both protects and enables, while the passive Self accepts its ministrations. However, the Self also uses its own story, autobiography, to confirm its boundaries as a Self, independent of any Other; Nature is a corollary to this initial authorising action. This brings us back to the picture of the heroic 'I', the 'concretised' Subject who tells his own story. Like Nature, this 'I' displays contradictory characteristics: it is both Self-sufficient and in need of rescue. The fractures apparent in Robinson's notion of the 'essential self' underscore the fictionality of the quest undertaken by Coleridge in his conversation poems; autobiographical, philosophical, self-consciously poetical, as a group they follow a quest chronology surprisingly unfulfilling, the outcome of which dissipates the essential Self in favour of a voice mediated through social disruption, political relations, and a romantic fixation on Nature that confirms not coherence but fragmentation. The poems as a collection constitute a quest narrative that follows, roughly and haltingly, the prototypical hero's progress through a romance landscape; in his internalised quest-romance, however, Coleridge is both the hero and the saboteur of his own journey. In merging hero and villain in the person of the speaking 'I', Coleridge creates a hero-figure repeatedly compelled to traverse a metaphorical romance landscape: each poem functions as a step along the way. And yet the multiple failures and pullings-back, the continual turn to a higher authority, the manifested inability to control and direct his own movements represent recurring assaults against the coherence of the Self and the establishment of an autonomous heroic identity. Coleridge accepts an initial designation as hero; he sets out on a quest to find and maintain the parameters of a fully independent – a masculine – 'I', and he performs segments of the heroic script in each poem, but in each a crucial moment of evasion destabilises his heroic identity. Coleridge's conversation poems show his familiarity with the language of the coherent Self, and his doubt at its authenticity: in his ultimate refusal to become fully heroic we read his disenchantment with its ideals.

Anne Mellor describes the male poet in 'Kubla Khan' as 'a pariah about to be exorcised from the human community';[13] 'Kubla Khan', of course, stands as Coleridge's most extremely internalised poetic landscape, from its purported provenance in a dream to its common interpretation as a poem about poetic creativity. For Coleridge, romance was resolutely *within*: 'the romance expressed a world permanently within all men: the world of the imagination and of dream' (Beer 7). Turning the romance inward, Coleridge associated it with creativity and the poetic 'I', the artist who draws on imagination to colour reality, a technique that has seduced readers into understanding the poetic 'I' as the fully physical 'I': 'Coleridge was convinced he had earned the prophet's role. Perhaps nowhere else is his moral and esthetic self-deception so vividly illustrated as in the pious conclusions to *Ode to the Departing Year* and *Fears in Solitude*'.[14] Two heroic traits have emerged, one derived from poetry, the other assigned to life: withdrawal from society, and special knowledge indicating unique powers. When we read that 'the Romantics are seeking the ... integration of the psyche'[15] it is not too difficult to associate this with a Coleridgean quest for poetic wholeness, the conjoining of imagination and Self – the very pairing he sets up again and again in the conversation poems, only to derail it at the last moment. Similarly,

Coleridge's 'belie[f]' in Nature's 'power to heal, guide, and inspire',[16] evident most particularly in 'The Eolian Harp' and 'This Lime-Tree Bower my Prison', suggests that union with Nature is twinned with psychic integration as the object of his quest, but this, too, he sabotages. It is a common view of Coleridge that, in life as in poetry, his desires and his abilities to achieve those desires did not match, and that his art, in its fits and starts, reflects his life;[17] that the terminology employed so often invokes the romance is a unremarked measure of the consistency of his approach to both. In reading the conversation poems as a quest-narrative, however, we can begin to glimpse a poet who actively used genre to reflect meaning, whose simultaneous identification with and manipulations of the heroic persona indicates a knowing involvement with romance[18] that allows him to gesture towards a personal and poetic *différance,* and to shy away from it.

In his conversation poems, then, Coleridge appears as composite of the types of hero described by Peter Thorslev: he is a Child of Nature in his displays of sentiment and naïveté, his closeness to nature and his unworldly generosity; he is a Man of Feeling in his conspicuous benevolence, class position, education, physical frailty[19] and excessive sensibility; he is even part Gloomy Egoist in his 'cultivation of ... melancholy' and attraction to the Gothic.[20] In these guises he explores the limits of the hero, and through him the limits of the social ideal of manhood; between 1795 and 1798 he journeys from home and hearth, to a version of the outside world, to prison, and back home again, to rest, finally, outside himself in a hero-less realm of self-designated 'conversation' ('The Nightingale. A Conversation Poem'). Within each poem Coleridge follows a route from perplexity through to insight, and exits via deflation; this matrix is mirrored in the framework established by the six poems, which begin at 'home', progress through imprisonment, and end with the exchange of the heroic persona for that of the sidelined 'bard', a mere narrator. The romance landscape charted imaginatively by Coleridge offers the questing speaker a variety of mental adventures, from which he moves toward a development and growth that he is never able to sustain. In other words, in these poems Coleridge conducts a conversation with himself on, not the desirability, but the viability, of the heroic ideal; his conclusion is implicit in the arc of failure described by the sequence.

For instance, in 'The Eolian Harp' (1795) the hero comes to the realisation that he must leave home and heroine behind and begin his adventures, the romance hero's standard impetus. The poet Coleridge is on his honeymoon; the speaker is situated domestically beside 'our cot', the idealised domestic paradise requisite to a love union.[21] Himself on the brink of an idealised journey, Coleridge enlists Sara as his heroine, although the epithet 'pensive' already suggests the 'tension between the ideal role that Coleridge required her to play, and his sense that she was somehow less than adequate to that role' (Everest 62). However, at this point 'pensive' Sara merely signals her suitability; she is in accord with the 'saddening' clouds, and in tune with the 'soothing sweet[ness]' of the 'o'ergrown' cot (1, 7, 2, 3).[22] The opening lines establish a home that is almost cloying and unmistakably feminised; in addition, its odd combination of life (all those covering flowers and vines) and non-life (the hushed, 'stilly', silent world[23]) embeds a supernatural otherworldliness that resonates with romance. The turn to the 'lute', instrument of bards, further conveys the romantic feel. Within the second stanza the speaker draws three comparisons centred on the harp, and each corresponds to an attempt at creative escape from the overgrown cot. The first, concentrating on the sensual aspects of the harp's music, can go no further than a scenario suggested by the honeymoon cottage itself: the harp is 'caressed' by the breeze, and responds 'like some coy maid half-yielding to her lover' (14, 15).[24] It provides an imagery springboard, however, to the second comparison, rendered in the language of the romance and the fairy tale; here, the harp's song becomes a 'soft floating witchery of sound/ [Such] as twilight Elfins make' (20–1). And as if only romance can lead to philosophy, the third comparison theorises on 'the one life within us and abroad' (26). At this point, sound has become visionary, 'a light in sound' (28), and the speaker finds himself transported, separated in place and time from the cot and Sara.

In this first attempt at leaving the home, the speaker gets no further than a mysterious suspended 'noon'. The present-tense verbs ('stretch', 'behold', 'muse', 'traverse') establish that the speaker neither remembers a past experience nor forecasts a future one. This initial foray, however, allows him to experience an intellectual burst. His famous rhetorical question represents a station achieved in his quest: 'And what if all of animated nature/ Be but organic harps diversely framed,/ That tremble into thought, as o'er them sweeps/ Plastic and vast, one intellectual breeze,/ At once the Soul of each, and God of All?' (44–8). At this point Coleridge derails his line of thought by turning back to Sara and interpreting her 'serious eye' as a 'reproof' (49). While, as Stephen Bygrave summarises, most critics have thrown the blame for Coleridge's thump back to earth onto Sara, it is important to see that Coleridge himself creates the reproof; as Bygrave notes, 'Coleridge enjoins on himself finally the silence of the first section'.[25] The line reads 'But thy more serious eye a mild reproof/ Darts' (49–50), indicating not that *in* her eye darts a reproof, but rather that Coleridge sees her habitual seriousness (remember her opening pensiveness) *as* a reproof. In other words, Coleridge reproves himself, using Sara's serious eye as his tool, and in doing so he disables his own flight, aborts his own quest. From here on he deprecates his insight as 'bubbles' from an 'unregenerate mind' (56, 55), and then prostrates himself before God as 'a sinful and most miserable man' (62). The poem thus ends where it had begun, a closed circle focused on home. Within the poem's structure the speaker has made a bid for freedom, but he has sabotaged his own chances; as the first poem in the quest sequence, 'Harp' sets the scene for the breakdown of the heroic ideal and the endemic failure of the quest. The internal destruction of consistency that informs 'Harp' fans outward to characterise the sequence as a whole (Everest 208–9).

While in 'Harp' the speaker-hero aborts his journey, leaving home only to return to it, in 'Reflections on Having Left a Place of Retirement' (1795 or 1796) he has succeeded in stage one: home is now in the past, a source for memories, and the speaker attempts to engage in 'the bloodless fight' (61). However, the double-placement experimented with in 'Harp', where the 'I' located himself simultaneously at both the cot and the hill, continues, as despite having left the place of retirement, the speaker devotes 42 lines to recreating his experience there. Again, he strives for subjectivity at the same time as he inscribes his objectified self: the overgrown cot is now 'low' and 'twin'd' with jasmine,[26] and, moreover, is 'eyed' and 'gazed' at by a 'wealthy son of commerce' (16, 11). As Everest argues, 'the philosophical passages in the poetry are at once statements of belief, and attempts to register emotions at a high pitch, that is to say, they are expressive of *feeling*' (210, Everest's emphasis). The feeling engendered by being overlooked in his domestic idyll provokes the speaker to action, still in memory, but again expressive of departure: as in 'Harp', he leaves the cot to climb, this time to 'reach the top' (28; in 'Harp' he could only make 'the midway slope' [34]). Gaining the prospect view not only dismisses the son of commerce and his authority, it establishes the speaker in a position of validated masculinity, an ideal stance of heroic significance.[27] The vista opens images to the speaker that almost allow him to identify with God – the long dash follows nine lines of breathless description[28] that culminate with the exclamatory 'It seemed like Omnipresence!' (38). Displacing his active presence through the impersonal noun 'it' begins the process of retreat: first, however, the speaker uses the authority gained from the prospect to 'quit' the 'quiet dell! Dear cot, and mount sublime!' (44, 43). This is the necessary first step on the quest, although it is conveyed negatively ('constrained', 44), and leads to the declaration of heroic duty: 'I therefore go, and join head, heart, and hand,/ Active and firm, to fight the bloodless fight/ Of science, freedom, and the truth in Christ' (60–2). But the poem's final stanza, with its fragmentary, incoherent 'fond wishes', is unconvincing; the cot is both dismissed and constantly invoked, and the tone of the final four lines seems more desperate than contented: 'And I shall sigh fond wishes – sweet abode!/ Ah! – had none greater! And that all had such!/ It might be so – but the time is not yet./ Speed it, O Father! Let thy kingdom come!' (68–71). Clearly, while the speaker has succeeded in beginning his quest, he is not fully persuaded of its value. As a pair, 'Harp' and 'Reflections' waver between asserting the need to leave the domestic space and arguing for its primacy. Even as the speaker-hero begins his quest, he longs for its conclusion.

The next two poems, 'This Lime-Tree Bower my Prison' (1797) and 'Frost at Midnight' (1798), see the speaker-hero imprisoned, forced back into retirement and imposed immobility. In the romance, the hero's imprisonment is usually used for reflection, regeneration and renewal; he proves his versatility and ingenuity through his escape, and rededicates himself to his quest and its ideals. In 'Lime-Tree', the speaker-hero ostensibly achieves a peace and understanding by the poem's end that makes up for, even justifies, the imprisonment itself. But 'Lime-Tree' is also the first poem of the sequence wherein the speaker-hero attempts the integration of the 'I' that is the goal of his quest. As Reed points out, 'The Romantic hero is frequently jealous of his selfhood.... An interesting consequence of this jealous defense of selfhood is the tendency of the heroic character to free himself from the confines of plot' (16). The romance plot requires the imprisonment of the hero, as I noted above, but in 'Lime-Tree' the speaker simultaneously emphasises the frivolity of the injury that imprisons him – he 'met with an accident, which disabled him from walking'[29] – and denies the imprisonment altogether, not only accompanying his friends on their walk in his imagination, but also directing and controlling it. The walk they actually take is not the one the speaker is interested in; he instead creates for them 'that still roaring dell, of which I told' (9) and from this point their walk is his walk, conveyed in the same present tense that facilitated the speaker's doubled self-placement in the first two poems. Ignoring his imprisonment, the speaker devises a hero-proxy in 'gentle-hearted Charles' whose City toil resembles the 'bloodless fight' of 'Reflections' and foreshadows Coleridge's boyhood vision in 'Frost at Midnight'. Charles sees with the speaker's eyes and feels the speaker's exultation at once again achieving the prospect view. The incantatory rhythm of lines 32–7 further establishes the idea of the speaker's presence, but the lines also take on the darker tinge of the romance enchanter:

> Ah! Slowly sink
> Behind the western ridge, thou glorious sun!
> Shine in the slant beams of the sinking orb,
> Ye purple-hearted flowers! Richlier burn, ye clouds!
> Live in the yellow light, ye distant groves!
> And kindle, thou blue ocean!

The speaker-hero in 'Lime-Tree' is a more compromised figure – less passive, but also less pure.

That he parlays his union with Charles – temporary escape – into an acceptance of his prison means that even as Coleridge empowers his hero through a paradoxical denial of heroic destiny, exchanging the weakness of passivity for a plot-enlarging defection from prison, he collapses back into heroic failure at the climactic moment. Coleridge reverses this segment of the heroic quest-narrative, securing his hero even more closely in prison at the poem's end and ensuring that this develops from the hero's imaginative denial of imprisonment at the poem's start. The result is stasis: the speaker comes to accept his imprisonment as a good thing because of the visions he has used to escape it, and the continuation of the quest is again postponed. Indeed, in 'Lime-Tree' the speaker deserts subjectivity altogether in favour of an ending emphasis on Charles, the proxy, whose under-standing that 'no sound is dissonant which tells of Life' (76) concludes the poem.[30] Unwilling, now, to leave his prison, the speaker-hero ejects the very agency he has spent the bulk of the poem establishing: the union of Self with Nature through vision dwindles into the comfortably 'soothing' surroundings of the bower. This poem, with its reversals, contradictions, and retreats, signals the poet's weakening resolve to complete the poetic quest. It colours the sequence with a defeatism that reflects more on the nature of heroic action – after all, why should he leave the bower? – than on the ramifications of the speaker's choices.

This is adumbrated in 'Frost at Midnight', where again the hero speaks, apparently, from prison: this time a self-imposed one, where domestic duties function as the chain.[31] Paired as it is with 'Lime-Tree', the suspicion rises that this poem dramatises the situation of a hero who has accepted his lack of mobility, to whom imprisonment does not signify limitation. Even as the quest has always been internalised, this poem is itself internal, wrapped in layers of quiet, stillness, darkness and meditation. Once again, there is incantation: 'Sea, hill, and wood,/ This populous village! Sea, and hill, and wood,/ With all the numberless goings on of life/ Inaudible as dreams!' (10–13). The speaker seems settled in reflection: is this, then, the poem wherein prison functions to allow for heroic rejuvenation? Everest reads the turn to Hartley's future in stanza 3 as symbolic of the poet's new-found capacity for imagination: 'Coleridge will realise his own lost potential in the development of his son's consciousness' (267). The key, however, is the loss that Hartley embodies, rather than the futurity; the trajectory of the poem institutes the reality of failure and of retreat to an idealised vision of Hartley's childhood as a corrective to the speaker's own. The speaker-hero, instead of finding solace and strength in his memories, re-images his past as composed of the same layers of stillness and imprisonment he now experiences: describing the fire's grate as 'the bars' (25), he moves further back into memory, again situating his speaking self as simultaneously 'here' – in his cottage at midnight – and 'there' – in his childhood school – and beyond to another 'there' – his 'sweet birth-place' (28). 'Frost' allows for no form of escape, however; the memories are set down in the past tense, and the effect of the stanza is of the weakening of heroic ambition and the loss of autonomy and maturity. By continuing to focus on 'deep calm' and the 'vacancies/ And momentary pauses of ... thought' (45, 46–7), and linking these with further images of himself as 'pent' (52) in contrast to his son's freedom to 'wander like a breeze' (54), the speaker constructs himself as of the past, static, and hence capable only of 'realising his lost potential' – that is, realising he has lost his potential – in his son. As with his friends' walk in 'Lime-Tree', Coleridge maps out Hartley's future, rather than his own, while the benediction that closes the poem can be viewed either as, in heroic terms, merely the weakened gesture of a speaker drained of agency by the 'secret ministry of frost' and the cocooning effect of silence and quiet (72–4);[32] or, perhaps, as the poet's clue that concentration on the 'bloodless fight' is itself imprisoning. Certainly, the restrained mood of 'Frost', its embracing of the domestic space, undermine the masculine imperative to break free of such fetters and seek adventures. The quest continues, but its parameters are changing; as the speaker moves deeper into himself, as he reaches turning-points and draws conclusions, his dedication to the heroic ideal itself transforms from a self-focused desire for autonomy and independence to a more diffused concentration on the outer landscape.

The final pairing of 'Fears in Solitude' and 'The Nightingale' (both 1798) complete a cycle of questing and retreat; the melancholy and doubt pervading 'Fears' and the unfocused plot of 'Nightingale' shadow a comprehensive change of identity for the speaker, and with it a final renunciation /rejection/loss of the heroic role. The speaker's exchange of the 'mount sublime' for a 'green and silent spot, amid the hills,/ A small and silent dell' ('Fears', 1–2), via the prisons of the bower and the home, show a self-conscious desire not for action, but for withdrawal. The 'quiet spirit-healing nook' (12)[33] shelters a speaker who now chooses the inactive role of prophet or seer; his apocalyptic tone emphasises the drama of his 'fears', a self-consciously theatrical position that maintains the need for action but masks the inability to act. 'The dialectical tensions in which the romantic hero is involved ... produces ... a tenuous equilibrium which breaks down eventually, and leads either to the hero's self-destruction or to a paralysis of the will or heroic resolve' (Bishop 18). If 'Lime-Tree' and 'Frost' allowed for a 'tenuous equilibrium' in which the speaker-hero could juggle his heroic and anti-heroic impulses, 'Fears' marks a 'paralysis of the will' to act and the perversion of the quest into a kind of inquest on the state of England. Symbolism loses its force: 'dainty terms ... / Which we trundle smoothly o'er our tongues/ Like mere abstractions, empty sounds to which/ We join no feeling and attach no form!' (113, 114–16). Talismans lose their meaning: 'the Book of Life is made/ A superstitious instrument' (70–1). But worst of all, the heroic voice itself loses its depth; after 197 lines of doom, the speaker pulls back, first to doubt and then to a diminishment of the speaking self to a 'child' of his country rather than its saviour:

> May my fears,
> My *filial* fears, be vain! And may the vaunts
> And menace of the vengeful enemy
> Pass like the gust, that roared and died away
> In the distant tree: which heard, and only heard
> In this low dell, bowed not the delicate grass.
> (197–202, emphasis added)

Having depleted his warnings of their fervour, the speaker then returns anticlimactically to his dell, only to find that he must leave it. 'Homeward I wind my way' (210); the 'burst of prospect' (215) he happens on enlivens the mind but marks mainly his 'lowly cottage', while it is the 'green and silent dell' that remains in his thoughts (225, 228). 'Fears' ends calmly, quietly, contentedly, but its destination is little different than that the speaker started from in 'Harp': through five poems, each with its own internal circularity, the speaker can only rotate around a point of silence and inaction. The overall trajectory of the poems traces an heroic pathway, but the speaker himself cannot advance; each new attempt sees the same eventual failure.

The sequence concludes, then, with the one poem officially designated 'A Conversation Poem', and yet the speaker's conversants are either absent or incapable, themselves, of speech (the nightingales, the 'dear babe'). This poem has a strong flavour of benediction, and its final repeated 'farewells' recall the reversed narrative Coleridge plotted in 'Lime-Tree': the quest traditionally concludes with a homecoming, not a leave-taking. Again, the speaker creates a world of negatives, of silence: 'No cloud, no relique of the sunken day/ Distinguishes the West, no long thin slip/ Of sullen light, no obscure trembling hues/ .... / All is still' (1–3, 7). Everest says that a 'connective consciousness, a distinctive property of all the conversation poems, is a central theme of *The Nightingale*' (281), but the poem itself insists on detachment and mystery: the nightingale's song, the deserted castle, the gentle Maid. In 'Nightingale' the speaker forsakes his own story for the conventionally romantic tale of a lord and a maid – although the lord is absent and the maid is isolated. The abrupt interjection of romance and its immediate emptying, the hollow Gothicism of stanzas 3 and 4, affirm not the resolution of a quest, the completion of a narrative, or even a 'connective consciousness', but a disjoining, an unravelling of romantic convention and the rejection of romantic meaning.

The melancholy and self-doubt that infused the earlier poems is here converted to a dreamy passage from image to image; as Everest notes, 'Nightingale' is 'rather too discursive.... There is a lack of direction in the development of the poem, a rambling quality' (282, 283). Everest relates this to the plot's 'serenity' (283), but in romance terms it also signals a loss of focus, a literal 'lack of direction' in the quest for a unified consciousness. Coleridge's speaker-hero no longer recognises his journey, and instead of resolving his own narrative begins to tell someone else's story at just the point in the poem where his efforts to detach the nightingale from melancholy are floundering:

having protested this traditional association for 39 lines, he moves to a stanza seemingly intent on substituting the 'different lore' that 'Nature's sweet voices [are] always full of love/ And joyance!' (41–2). The difficulty is that the only example the speaker can devise contradicts this peaceful claim:

> 'Tis the merry Nightingale
> That crowds, and hurries, and precipitates
> With fast thick warble his delicious notes,
> *As he were fearful* that an April night
> Would be too short for him to utter forth
> His love-chant, and disburthen his full soul
> Of all its music!
>
> (43–9, emphasis added)

The speaker-hero's own fears of the shortness of the night (and the ending of the quest?) infiltrate the nightingale's loving and joyous song; it is hard to see merriment in the rather desperate bird the speaker conjures, his love-chant at risk of being cut off. Ironically, this is just what the speaker does to his own mixed image, ending the stanza mid-line and beginning the next with the conjunction 'and', illogical in light of the, at best, tangential connection between images:[34] 'And I know a grove/ Of large extent, hard by a castle huge,/ Which the great lord inhabits not' (49–51).[35] The speaker's transformation into storyteller heralds his final embrace of the domestic and the enclosed in the last stanza, and his designation of his quest as 'a father's tale' (106). For the speaker, the nightingale comes to symbolise others' songs; by exchanging his for, say, the maid's, he effectively pre-empts his quest, an abrupt termination that belies the efforts of continual re-arming each poem has represented. For the poet, the nightingale works to embody the speaker's inability to tell his tale: he utilises a symbol traditionally associated both with silence (the cut tongue of Philomel) and with violence (the tale of rape it sings). The poet also reappropriates a familiar feminine symbol and resexes it (the nightingale is always 'he' in the poem), as he does with the moon, here a symbol of a boy-baby's unearthly silent laughter and the 'father's tale' (106). In so doing, Coleridge does not merely co-opt the feminine; he also exposes his speaker's confusion and perplexity. The hero now chooses as his closing trophy one of the most familiar literary symbols of male villainy.

Throughout this sequence of poems, Coleridge constructs a hero-persona whose continual efforts to establish a viable Self and pursue a viable quest are as continually stymied. Instead of achieving psychic unity, the speaker suffers psychic disintegration, constructing a series of 'conversations' with no one: his interlocutors are never more than poetic constructs, at best functioning only as silent listeners to poetic monologues. By identifying his speaker with the hero, by ensuring that the six poems, broken down into three pairs, reconstruct a species of quest, Coleridge calls into question the validity of the quest-narrative itself. His speaker's repeated attempts to leave home, to escape prison, and to return home are shadowed by uncanny refusals, so that the stages of the quest are both evident and rewritten in each poem. As I have suggested, in part this allows Coleridge to reconfigure the strictures of heroism. The final emphasis on the 'father's tale' in 'Nightingale' hints at the alternative storyline the poems put forth: the substitution of the domestic for the heroic, which troubles the speaker but which the poet continually reinscribes. Coleridge's poetic intervention in the coherency of the heroic quest recalls the 'displacement' Stephen Bygraves sees as endemic to the conversation poems: 'the effects of the poems' egotism is to expose the reader to the doubts concerning and contiguous to egotism which animate their process' (133). 'Romantic egotism' is another formulation for dominant masculinity that remakes the world in its own image (the nightingale becomes a male symbol, for instance), and the relation to the ideal heroic type is self-evident: the hero dominates the telling of his own tale. Coleridge, attracted to and repelled by the pre-eminence of the hero, sets him on his quest and systematically sabotages his efforts to follow it. The violence is figurative, but instructive, for in disallowing heroic triumph, Coleridge destroys the viability of heroic subjectivity. He interacts with genre, pulls out a useful part, and exposes its shallowness. Bishop describes the 'hermeneutic distance' created in the first-person heroic narrative: 'when the romantic hero tells his own story in the first person, it is often framed by an authorial, editorial, or other narrative point of view' (17). By investing his heroic quest so overtly with doubt, melancholy, and failure, Coleridge withers the heroic ideal.

Detumescence: Keats

In his famous study *The Hoodwinking of Madeline*, Jack Stillinger argues that, having completed *Endymion*,[36] Keats feels a 'growing dissatisfaction with romance', and that this dissatisfaction finds expression 'in a tremendous vision of anti-romantic "truth"' coupled with a turn from 'detested moods' to 'new Romance'.[37] Reading 'new Romance' as '*a new Romance*', Stillinger turns to what he calls 'Keats's last large poetic failure, *Isabella*' and attempts its recuperation as 'a more complex poem than critics generally allow' (31).[38] Stillinger's account resonates with preconceptions about the romance: that it is opposed to 'truth', the proper aim of poetry; that it struggles with complexity; that it is identifiable as text – 'a romance' – rather than genre – 'romance'. Stillinger wants to prove that Keats had something more advanced in mind than a 'simple' romance, and in this way he betrays his critical prejudice against a genre frequently considered not complex enough for a mature poet to write seriously. However, Keats's phrase is clear: he searches for comfort in 'new Romance', and thereby suggests a desire to write the genre anew, to investigate its precepts and invest its storyline with novelty, what Marjorie Levinson calls the 'subversion of ... authoritarian values', 'elaborately estranged from their own materials and procedures'.[39] In other words, from *Isabella* onwards Keats subverts and rearranges old Romance. Rather than rejecting the genre, Keats reappropriates it, and more specifically he redraws the character of the romantic hero, creating scenarios in which the limits of heroic endeavour are recognised, tested, and found wanting. Levinson writes that Keats '*signifies* his alienation from his *materia poetica*' (15, Levinson's emphasis); as with her use of 'authoritarian', she gestures toward the authorly task of inscription, of signification: Keats troubles 'author-itarian values' of genre as derived from authors' use of genre, and he sign-ifies his rewrites through genre itself. Despite Stillinger's insistence on 'the inadequacies of romance' (32) and his assertion that this 'ineffectual and out of date' form is 'banished' from Keats's oeuvre – 'Though he sometimes subsequently call his poems "romances" ... Keats never again wholeheartedly embraces the *idea* of romance' (33, Stillinger's emphasis) – Keats privileges exactly 'new Romance' in his 1820 volume. Stillinger, concerned with the bad reputation of romance as, essentially, trivial, immature, artistically 'low', and feminising, attempts to regenre *Lamia*, *Isabella*, and *The Eve of St. Agnes* as 'not-romances', elevated in 'idea' if not in plot. And yet, what is significant is not, of course, Keats's 'banishing' of romance, but his reconsideration of romantic thematics, which he had supported in *Endymion*, and his replotting of the quest-narrative with its new and disimproved hero.

Coleridge turns his unease inward; he asks his Self to suffer, and in this way plots the hero's downfall through the failure of subjectivity. Keats is more circumspect: he targets conventional romance heroes, all of whom quest for love and erotic fulfilment. Where and how they love, and the consequences, are the focus of Keats's new Romance; his apparent devotion to narratives of love's potential masks his 'alienation' from their requirements, and from his source material. His approach to Boccaccio, or Chaucer, or Burton, or Chartier is creative, 'supplemental' in Levinson's terminology: 'specifically functional and overdetermined interferences with the romance narrative' (131), wherein the romance is relied on and destroyed simultaneously, the hero embodied and deconstructed simultaneously. Reed remarks that 'the Romantic hero usually experiences the evolution of his heroic substance or else its erosion' (30), but Keats's new Romance ignores such binaries, and instead concentrates on poeticising failure and inadequacy, disguised as romance and heroism. Like Coleridge, Keats is interested in the expectations attendant on the hero, and he interrogates the heroic ideal with his portrayals of the cunning and wily Porphyro, naïve Lorenzo, possessive Lycius, and bitter Knight-at-arms, whose first appearance (as a 'wretched wight') in the *Indicator* of May 1820 shadows and to a certain extent provides the template for the other three. None fulfil heroic duty, yet all are recognisable as romance heroes. If, as Hermann Fischer affirms, the romance hero experiences 'a human fate in such a way that the reader can identify with it',[40] then he begins to function on the level of an example, and his connection to a kind of ideal behaviour – masculinity – is again suggested. Like Coleridge, Keats explores the idea of the hero as an exemplar and, in subjecting him to varying forms of violence, signals his dissatisfaction with its parameters. The common argument that Keats inhabits the feminine subject-position, rehearsed from the earliest accusations of 'effeminacy' to contemporary critical discussions of what Mellor calls his 'ideological cross-dressing'[41] does not, however, fully explain Keats's complex position; instead, it is important to see Keats's poetical approach not as masking a perennial lack of confidence, or dramatising an immature or 'regressive' (Stillinger 37) style, or signifying an anxious establishment of 'a space where the poet can preserve a recognisable masculinity' (Mellor 181), but as the technique of a poet who manipulates images of genre and, through this, of gender. Keats challenges the viability of the very masculinity he has been seen, variously, to champion or to yearn for; he poeticises an uncomfortable, perhaps unacknowledged awareness of its weaknesses.

In this way he, like Coleridge, takes on the mantle of *differance* that he has been so often denigrated or excused for embodying. This suggests a poet skilful enough to use genre rather than being overwhelmed by it. Keats's well-known axiom that Poetry 'should strike the Reader as a wording of his own highest thoughts, and appear almost as Remembrance.... If Poetry comes not as naturally as the Leaves to a tree it had better not come at all'[42] indicates his feeling that poetry should reflect the natural processes of budding and memory; it should, therefore, reflect and confirm nature in its content and structure as well as its composition. What, then, of the denatured hero? It is not what happens to him that is disruptive of the natural skein of experience, but rather who he is, an embodiment of heroic masculinity constantly stymied by his own creator. It is common to read death or injury in literary texts as punishment for a character's innate wrongness and offence against the moral values of the world the text reflects or creates. Keats, says Richard Woodhouse in 1819, asserts that 'he does not want ladies to read his poetry: that he writes for men' (Spencer Hill 60); Stillinger notes that Keats 'never lost touch with reality' (93). What this somewhat unfair yoking of responses to the romances brings out is the intriguing notion that the romances can be seen as instructional, as cautionary tales on the psychological inadequacies of heroic masculinity. Each hero is shepherded to his individual doom by a narrator more or less blithe and detached, who tells the tale, offers critique, but does not get involved.[43] This aloof narrator provokes an understanding of the romances as fables, and of the poet as social commentator. Keats rewrites his heroes to convey something to his (male) readers; he injures, even kills off romantic masculinity once it has been sexualised. He pushes it away into allegory, or he drains it. What has been labelled effeminacy, immaturity, or a male poet's version of feminine Romanticism acts, instead, as a narrative of conviction, questioning gender: like Coleridge, Keats exposes the weaknesses of the heroic ideal. His heroes, enervated, either cannot survive their own stories, or find their futures consumed wholesale, a fate intimated in Dorothy van Ghent's study *Keats: The Myth of the Hero*.[44] In associating Keats's heroes with mythic season-gods, she underwrites his romances with archetype; the romances themselves offer the archetype of gender and the deconstruction of the masculine hero altogether. Keats trades the adolescent moonings of *Endymion* for the maturity of the unromance and its reflections on the heroic ideal. Hazlitt's critique of Keats's 'deficiency [of] masculine energy of style ... [and] want of strength and substance' (1822;

Spencer Hill 48) unwittingly points to the crux of the 1820 romances: his poetry follows a strategy of evasion and rejection of standard forms of heroic masculinity.

'La Belle Dame Sans Merci' condenses Keats's discomfort with heroic values into 48 lines; this poem outlines the parameters of his technique that he will explore more fully in the 1820 volume. The poem's competing versions agree on the violence done to the Knight/wight, however, and concur as well in the suggestion that the Knight/wight has been less than honourable in his approaches to the Dame.[45] The popular readings of the poem – that it describes the fatal attraction of a wanton woman, or of Poetry, or of the Imagination[46] – all overlook the main thrust: 'Dame' sketches out a romance plot, centring particularly on the hero's 'disastrous mistake'. Bowra links this with the 'disastrous choice', and says of the 'mistake' that it figures 'a decision ... made wrongly through some miscalculation or defect of character. The result is always some catastrophe which might otherwise have been averted' (122). The Knight/wight both proves his hero-status and compromises his heroic value when he 'control[s]' and bind[s]' the Dame 'with lovely chains', enacting the 'thematics of containment' that Karen Swann sees as endemic to the romance.[47] In fact, the Knight/wight behaves in a decidedly unchivalrous manner, forgetting his pledge to protect women and instead giving in to his own perception of the Dame as 'light' and 'wild' and therefore sexually available.[48] Perhaps it is this quickness to judge that is the Knight/wight's character defect; certainly, it allows him to set into motion the catastrophe that will end with his lonely, pale loitering 'on the cold hill's side' (44). Although most discussions of the poem tend to focus on the Dame, on her grot, on her effect on the hero, on her personality, the poem also insists on the centrality of the hero, and the ramifications of his deed: the initial speaker is concerned only with the Knight/wight's unheroic loitering, while the Knight/wight himself is keen to excuse and justify his conduct. The poet – Keats – writes into his romance plot a supplementary preoccupation with the hero's inadequacies, expressed through the Knight/wight's dismissal of chivalric values.[49]

As van Ghent notes, Keats's romances concentrate on the 'increasingly somber and violent picture of what happens when the ideal love-maiden allows herself to be loved' (88), although she too finds the heroine responsible; in her formulation the hero is punished because of the heroine's sexual surrender. However, the poems do not follow an entirely conventional plot: the Dame is compelled to 'surrender' but Isabella, for instance, is an equal participant. It is more fruitful to note that the violence the heroes suffer is traceable to the narrative itself, and from there to the poet, rather than to (or on account of) the heroine; Keats invests the familiar trope of blaming the woman with a complexity that turns our attention back to the man. This is what Levinson calls his 'meta-allegory', the 'double-signi- fication [that] prevents a discursive meltdown into expressive, mimetic, and generic authenticity' (133). In the 'authentic' romance, the Knight/wight's disastrous mistake would lead to greater under- standing, increased awareness, and eventual victory, but in Keats's new Romance the mistake serves to authenticate only the hero's essential hollowness. The Knight/wight seeks to impose his power of Self on the Dame – he desires to overwhelm her mysterious feminin- ity with his strength of masculinity. As Robinson says, 'sight [is] the sense of masculine power .... [but] it fails as an agent of power' (143). Keats follows this when he makes sight the indicator both of the Knight/wight's attempts to overpower and his inability to do so: 'And there *I shut* her wild wild eyes/ With kisses four' (31–2, emphasis added). The *Indicator* version is more telling: 'She took me to her elfin grot/ And there *she gaz'd* and sighed deep,/ And there *I shut* her wild sad eyes – /So kiss'd to sleep' (29–32, emphasis added). Once the Dame tries to claim the symbol of masculine power – vision – she is hastily prevented by the Knight/wight, whose action establishes his grab for power and authority but also hints at his loss of both. The hero's 'latest dream' (last, final, or most recent) substitutes the vision of drained and disempowered heroes ('pale kings and princes too,/ Pale warriors, death-pale were they all', 37–8) who attempt to blame the Dame for their plight but, as Wasserman and Enscoe agree, the poem has not offered any other evidence of the Dame's balefulness: '[Wasserman] rightly observes that "there is nothing in Keats's ballad even suggesting the frequent interpretation that the fairy's child is responsible for the knight's expulsion from the elfin grot; only his inherent attribute of being mortal causes his magic withdrawal". The knight, being mortal, aspired to the condition of immortality; but having reached this immortal world, "the elfin grot", he must leave again'.[50] If we read 'manhood' or 'masculinity' for 'mortality' – the Knight/wight's definition of self-actuality – then the situation clears. The hero's mistake has been to act on his sexual impulses, seize the Dame, attempt to impose control; he has betrayed that his heroism is based on a questionable code of conduct, itself commensurate with the masculine ideal; he has emerged vitiated, drained and withered.

Keats's familiar tale of chivalry thus rests on the understanding that chivalry presupposes heroes who conform to a suspected ideal. Swann concludes her excellent reading by asserting that 'the Knight's romantic tale, knowingly deployed by the artful poet, encodes ... doom in a way that distributes its effects unequally, with all benefits accruing to the masculine subject' (91). And yet this does not recognise the real violence done to the Knight/wight by the constructor of the romance, the poet – Keats himself. Keats is not really interested in the Dame (a point of view Swann would probably agree with); she is a device by which he can expose the Knight/wight's inadequacies, his red-blooded masculine heroism, and his viciousness. The hero, reduced to parroting the first speaker's words, exists in a closed circle of failure, his companions reflections of his loss of heroic viability. Instead of accruing benefits to masculinity, Keats narrates its culpability, its debits; he artfully – that is, through art – supplements the romantic ballad with a vitality-draining condemnation of the Knight/wight's heroic impulses.[51] In his longer romances, he continues to rewrite the heroic ideal.[52] The hero is rewarded sensually; the body of the beloved is gained, and consummation signals the successful resolution of the love strand of the romance. However, in Keats's poetry the satisfying of desire is never an uncomplicated blessing, as the presence of the famous Odes in the same volume as the romances attests. 'Happy, happy love' is most happy – most fortunate, and fortuitous – when it is 'still unravish'd', 'for ever panting, and forever young' ('Ode on a Grecian Urn', 25, 1, 27). In the Odes, Keats pictures a perfection of suspension, an acknowledgement that desire exists paired with a refusal to indulge it;[53] he constructs a romance of deferral that insists on its own virtue. *Lamia*, however, opens the volume with the infinitely desirable picture of a 'virgin purest lipp'd, yet in the lore/ Of love deep learned to the red heart's core' (I:189–90) – the archetypal experienced virgin, designed to stimulate Lycius' desires and occupying a curious mixed position of heroine and, to many critics, villain.

And yet this poem, like 'Dame', is really about the 'hero', Lycius, and his struggle with Apollonius. Lamia is the catalyst whereby the hero attempts independence: Lycius moves from abstract thought (the world of Apollonius) to erotic fulfilment (the world of Lamia), a journey that involves risks, the imposition of the supernatural, and eventually a battle. Charles Lamb in an 1820 review noted that *Lamia* 'is of as gorgeous stuff as ever romance was composed of' and calls Lycius 'beautiful' (Spencer Hill 66), an interestingly feminising epithet in light of the poem's insistence on Lamia's beauty; when van Ghent notes that in *Lamia* 'the bride steals the hero' (113) and Stillinger asserts that Lycius is unable to face reality (56 *passim*), they too construct Lycius as the subordinate partner in the love triangle. Keats gives Lycius both the heroic traits of mastery and irresistibility and the more problematic passivity that encourages Apollonius to see him as Lamia's 'prey'. Indeed, from his first entrance Lycius compromises his heroic role:[54]

> Lamia beheld [Lycius] coming, near, more near –
> Close to her passing, in indifference drear,
> His silent sandals swept the mossy green;
> So neighbor'd to him, and yet so unseen
> She stood: he pass'd, shut up in mysteries,
> His mind wrapp'd like his mantle, while her eyes
> Follow'd his steps[55] ....
>
> (I:237–43)

Far from realising his good fortune, Lycius does not even see Lamia, requiring the near-farce of Lamia calling after him. Initially, he is the opposite of the Knight/wight, who has only to see the Dame to take her; Lycius needs prompting, even though a few lines earlier the narrator has implied that Lamia comes in answer to his desire: 'Jove heard his vows, and better'd his desire;/ *For* by some freakful chance [Lycius] made retire/ From his companions' and instead takes the path that leads him to Lamia (I:229–31, emphasis added). That he then nearly misses Lamia underscores his abstraction, his absorption in thought that threatens to disable heroic action. Thanks to Lamia's quick thinking, however, he is brought to heed his heroic duty, and falls prostrate with love.

While the plotline of *Lamia* follows that of the romance, the narrator inflects his narrative with what Keats might have considered 'smokeability'. Robert Gittings defines this as 'open to sarcastic comment',[56] and throughout *Lamia* Lycius is subjected to the intensive gaze of a doubting narrator. Not only does he need help even to see Lamia, and then help to bear physically the pressure of his passion – he 'swoon[s]', heroine-like (I:289) – and then help to reach Corinth,[57] he also flinches from encountering Apollonius: 'Lycius shrank closer, as they met and past [Apollonius],/ Into his mantle, adding wings to haste' (I:366–7). Instead of heroically meeting the challenge, Lycius avoids it, as he attempts to do again when he does not invite Apollonius to his wedding. In all clashes, Lycius 'shrinks'[58] from conflict; despite his plot-role as hero, he prefers the safer, more passive stance of lover in a palace. Keats establishes this dispute between necessity and desire in the last lines of Part I: 'And but the flitter-winged verse must tell,/ For truth's sake, what woe afterwards befel,/ 'Twould humour many a heart to leave them thus,/ Shut from the busy world of more incredulous' (I:394–7). *Lamia* is obligated to tell the 'truth' rather than sugar-coated wish-fulfilment; new Romance must destroy the narrative of old Romance. Hence Part II opens with its ironic demystifying of love and its straightforward revelation: 'Had Lycius liv'd to hand his story down' (II:7).[59] Importantly, Keats pushes Lycius through stages of disempowerment; even as he forewarns us of Lycius' death, the poet continues to disentangle Lycius from his heroic duty, first allowing him the erotic play of sexual tyranny: 'he took delight/ Luxurious in her sorrows, soft and new./ His passion, cruel grown, took on a hue/ Fierce and sanguineous as 'twas possible/ In one whose brow had no dark veins to swell' (II:73–7).[60] This, with its overtones of 'Dame'-ish unknightly dominance, allows the narrator to continue to question Lycius' heroism, but the moment of true disclosure is reserved for the wedding, where first Lycius is unable to prevent Apollonius's entry – indeed, can only 'blus[h], and le[a]d the old man through' (II:169–70) – and then proves thoroughly inadequate to the heroic duty of protecting his beloved. Instead, he 'beseech[es]' Apollonius and then merely (hysterically?) shouts at him: 'Shut, shut those juggling eyes, thou ruthless man!/ Turn them aside, wretch! .../ ..../ Corinthians! Look upon that grey-bearded wretch!/ Mark how, possess'd, his lashless eyelids stretch/ Around his demon eyes! Corinthians, see!/ My sweet bride withers at their potency' (II:277–8, 287–90). At the moment of battle, Lycius can only raise his voice, and draw attention to Apollonius's power of vision; the villain succeeds in his most villainous duty of penetrating the heroine. Hovering around this crisis is another kind of villainy and another kind of desire: the narrative's attack on Lycius' character, and then his body; the romance's need for a hero and its need to destroy him. 'Lycius's arms were empty of delight,/ As were his limbs of life, from that same night./ On the high couch he lay! – his friends came round – / Supported him – no pulse, nor breath they found,/ And, in its marriage robe, the heavy body wound' (II: 307–11). Implicit in the last line is the key to Lycius' fate: Keats puns on 'wound', allowing it to represent both the harmless act of winding and the vicious act of wounding. Lycius wears his marriage robe as his shroud, while simultaneously the guests wound him with the marriage robe itself. The hero can survive neither his encounter with love, nor with villainy.

By concentrating the romance on a vapid and ineffectual hero, Keats offers a critique of his value; the problem is not Lamia's perfidy but Lycius' weakness. Despite Stillinger's contention that 'Lamia is still basically an evil character, a snake-woman' (57), she is more Apollonius's victim than Lycius is hers. Apollonius is self-convicted of sophistry and flawed vision. His reasoning – 'from every ill/ Of life have I preserv'd thee to this day,/ And shall I see made a serpent's prey?' (II:296–8) – rests on the incorrect assumption of Lamia's invidiousness: as she herself had said to Hermes (and the narrator had not contested) 'I was a woman once' (I:117). Gerald Enscoe states it plainly: 'Lamia is not really a serpent. By those who read the poem simply, this central fact seem to have been ignored' (151). Similarly, Apollonius is not a clear-eyed philosopher but exactly the cold-eyed sophist the narrator condemns him as. Despite the tragedy of Lamia's loss, the poem concentrates itself around Lycius and his limitations: Lamia's visibility is at least partly due to Apollonius's obsession with her and critical sympathy with his judgement on her. *Lamia* represents the hero as drained of autonomy, functioning as an accessory to Lamia or Apollonius. In this, Keats under-writes his character: he is both coy with details and submerges in Lycius a critique on the heroic ideal. But Lycius escapes with a quick death; *Isabella*, contrastingly, revolves around a 'vision of the horrors of physical annihilation' (van Ghent 129) that once again suggests the incapacity of the hero: Lorenzo, lucky in love, nevertheless cannot survive his own romance narrative.

Keats begins by naturalising the romance: Isabella and Lorenzo 'could not but' love each other, a reflex action arising from proximity, youth and a poetic attention to the demands of genre. At this point a passive narrator, the speaker presents his readers with hero and heroine in love, but prevented by Lorenzo's hesitation from declaring it; however, although the 'timid quest' for love is assigned to Isabella (55), the power to proclaim it is reserved for Lorenzo: 'but, alas,/ Honeyless days and days did he let pass' (31–2). In his inability to speak we see the first indication of Lorenzo's heroic unfitness – he requires proof of Isabella's love before he can enunciate his own, which not only undermines his heroic agency but compromises Isabella's 'heroinic' purity. Isabella, like Lamia, takes on some of the heroic traits the 'hero' cannot manage: instead of waiting, she quests; instead of listening, she speaks. Keats is already instituting his supplementary narrative, hinting at Lorenzo's tendency to inaction, his impulse to allow Isabella to enact, or energise, his role. Although Lorenzo speaks for twelve lines once encouraged by Isabella's tender lisp, Keats draws our attention to his 'erstwhile timid lips' (69), emphasising this aspect of Lorenzo's personality over his lover-status. A 'strangely-alienated reflexiveness' (Levinson 19) is encyphered in the poem, a double voice commenting on its own speaking status, ill-at-ease with the love-narrative and determined to infiltrate its conventions. The inevitability of the love-story is shadowed by doubts about Lorenzo's fitness; nature gives way before the culture of suspicion and hiddenness. The masculine power of vision that haunted 'Dame' and betrayed *Lamia* is here perverted further by Isabella's brothers, who penetrate the 'bower of hyacinth and musk' (85) representing the physical nature of Lorenzo's and Isabella's love. Keats asks 'how was it these same ledger-men could spy/ Fair Isabella in her downy nest?/ How could they find out in Lorenzo's eye/ A straying from his toil?' (137–40). The next stanza's turn to Boccaccio ostensibly provides the answer by gesturing to the poem's source, an already-written romance with an already-plotted tragedy. However, the narrator's apologetic tone, his acknowledgement that he somehow replots Boccaccio 'in English tongue' (159), shows that Keats is not willing to scapegoat Boccaccio, and that he has moved away from reportage to the supplementation that undergirds *Isabella*. The brothers find out the lovers because the poet directs them to do so; he allows their vision the required Apollonian sharpness, and he puts Lorenzo into their power. The naturalness of the poem's opening lines has transformed into the artifice of the brothers' perspicacity.

That Lorenzo fails to perceive their anger indicates that he has already been deprived of his vision; his 'courteous' naïveté and matter-of-fact declaration to Isabella that 'we'll gain/ Out of the amorous dark what day doth borrow' (205–6) illustrates that he virtually embraces his fate. The narrator encourages this by naming him a 'murder'd man' (209) proleptically, and by describing the 'forest' as 'quiet for the slaughter' (216), anticipatory and complicit. Lorenzo's fatal lack of foresight combined with the ease with which he is killed – 'There was Lorenzo slain and buried' (217) – demonstrate Keats's hostility to the possibility of his survival. He is not even allowed a fair fight, but is simply eliminated. His reappearance as a ghost merely allows the narrator to dwell on his physical decay: 'the forest tomb/ Had marr'd his glossy hair ... / ... *and* put cold doom/ Upon his lips, *and* taken the soft lute/ From his lorn vice, *and* past his loamed ears/ Had made a miry channel for his tears' (275–80, emphasis added), and to re-emphasise his passive death: 'without any word, from stabs he fell' (296). Moreover, once Isabella, again on a quest, begins to dig Lorenzo up, the narrator relishes the gory details of Lorenzo's disinterment; as Stillinger has outlined, Keats 'chooses to emphasize corruption' (39) in his rewrite. Not only is an entire stanza given over to Isabella's attempts to prettify the 'horrid thing' that is Lorenzo's head,[61] but the decapitation itself 'forgo[es]' the 'surgical tidiness' (Stillinger 40) of Keats's source, Boccaccio, in favour of an uncontextualised hacking: 'With duller steel than the Persean sword/ They cut away' Lorenzo's head (393–4).[62] Isabella seems devoted in the deranged sense of the word; her eagerness to cut up Lorenzo reflects Keats's desire to sever heroism from its idealised mystique. In this light the narrator's plaintive 'O for the gentleness of old Romance,/ The simple plaining of a minstrel's song!' (297–8) rings false; *Isabella* is 'new Romance' pointedly and deliberately. While the narrator seems genuinely taken aback at the turn the romance has taken – all along he has tried to spin a story of love, of hero and heroine united – plot supersedes this desire, instituting a morbid tale of obsession and decay centred on the broken body of a weedy hero. By the time we, with the brothers, are given a peek at 'the thing . . . vile with green and livid spot' (475), the supplementary discourse is surfacing; *Isabella* is concerned not with young love, or thwarted love, or even Isabella, but rather with the decomposition of the hero and his demotion to fertiliser. Lorenzo proves able only to nourish sweet basil. His heroic pretensions, suggested by the genre in which he appears, are undercut by Keats until they, too, rot and decay. Lorenzo, like Lycius before him, is both the necessary centre of the poem and negligible in his actual force of character, but by keeping us consistently focused on his absence Keats demonstrates the ease with which he is dispatched – Lorenzo never even sees it coming.

The precedent Keats sets of violently finishing off his heroes is rendered more metaphorical in *The Eve of St Agnes*. On the face of it, Porphyro is a thoroughly successful hero: he achieves his physical desire, wins Madeline's emotional commitment, and escapes the threat posed by the demonized 'barbarian hordes' and 'hyena foemen' (85, 86). The narrative plays up the savage nature of Madeline's kin and plays down (although it does not omit) Porphyro's ignominious recourse to 'stratagem' to ensnare Madeline and fulfil his desire. Porphyro's less-than-honourable conduct with Madeline in itself begs the question of his heroic nature: in his eagerness to melt into Madeline's dream, Porphyro displays a preoccupation with his own desires that is consonant with social masculinity (and rather Lycius-like) but not necessarily admirable.[63] Indeed, Porphyro's trickery serves to emphasise what is already suggested by his name, with its echoes of 'porphyry': even as porphyry is a type of rock distinguished by its 'homogeneous base in which crystals of one or more minerals are disseminated',[64] so too Porphyro is a mixed hero, honourable and base, respectful and opportunistic. But it is in his 'escape' that Porphyro suffers violence. Van Ghent calls the 'elfin-storm from faery land' seen by Porphyro as a 'boon' (343, 344) 'the dream-region of demonic power' (103), which begins to suggest its danger, but what is most brutal about the elimination of Porphyro (and Madeline) is that, after having encouraged his readers to see Porphyro and Madeline as young and vibrant lovers, Keats ends the poem in the far past, with images of death and insubstantiality: '*They glide, like phantoms*, into the wide hall;/ *Like phantoms*, to the iron porch, *they glide*/ .... / And they are gone: aye, *ages long ago*/ These lovers fled away into the storm' (361–2, 370–1, emphasis added). Keats simply disseminates his hero, forcing him into the past, a ghostly, disembodied revenant. Supplementing Porphyro's romance is a casual throwing-off of Porphyro's viability; once sent into the past, he is merely a memory, and in this way *Eve* deals a body-blow to the hero's meaningfulness. In this 'new Romance', Keats hollows out the old romance, withers heroic potency and signals his impatience with the standards represented by the hero.

Levinson suggests that 'in Keats's Romantic romance, meaning is something imposed by the author, badly derived from his precursors, and fissuring rather than fusing essences and appearances. Meaning is not a complement to being but an attack' (142). When Keats compels Lycius, Lorenzo, the Knight/wight, even Porphyro to suffer varieties of pain, indignity and outright violence, he encodes meaning in his attacks. Long denigrated or apologised for, his romances represent not poetic immaturity, 'failure', an embracing of the feminine, nor even (entirely) a seamless 'life of allegory', but instead subvert common assumptions about gender and genre. Keats secretes in his romances an instructional narrative, a new Romance for his male readers, that carries intimations of the uselessness, even the punishability, of adherence to the heroic ideal of manhood. He expresses *différance* by infusing the courtly romance with the unsettling question: why should they be so fatal to heroes? For some time Keats's targeted audience closed ranks and blamed the *femme fatale*, the incapacity of genre, Keats's embarrassing predilection for luxury and sensuality in verse. No longer tenable, these explanations emphasise the difficulty of challenging gender, not least in Keats himself, whose equivocations over the smokeability of his romances are well-known. But in disallowing his heroes their traditional rewards and happy endings, in subjecting their bodies to decay, their motives to suspicion, and their narratives to deconstruction, Keats infuses his romances with unease, with a lack of conviction in the value and viability of the hero. He fulfils the promise of Coleridge's conversation poems, that heroism is incompatible with subjectivity, and that, more subtly, masculinity itself is an unsuitable pursuit. 'The grip of romance can be that ... of nightmare' (Beer 9): the quest is revealed as a false trail. In the next chapter, the hero is destroyed altogether.

4
Interrupting the Romance: Robinson, Hemans and Dead Men

In discussing the romance it is to be expected that romantic love would be prominent – and yet, while this book has without hesitation explored sex and violence, it has so far delayed confronting the defining relationship of the genre, the love match. Partly this is due to the surprising dearth of successfully resolved love-relationships in the romance poetry of the period; as previous chapters have shown, the poetry itself shies away from traditional romantic conclusions. Partly, as well, I have left love to the penultimate chapter as a reflection of the strategy of one of the poets to be discussed. Mary Robinson, like Felicia Hemans, makes love central to her poetry,[1] and yet neither appears comfortable with a reassuring 'happy ever after'. Instead, both create romances wherein death, not love, is the resolution; where poetry itself sabotages the romantic relationship. For Robinson, genre works against itself: she infiltrates her romances with a tactical obfuscation, imaged through horrific dreams, narrative delay, or banality in place of climax. Leading her readers through a world of romance heavily tinged with the Gothic, she, to paraphrase E.J. Clery, 'recognises that the [romance] is bound by the metaphysics of appearance, that [its metaphorics are] of necessity given over to superstition'.[2] In Robinson, the romance is taken over from within by the supernatural, superstition and unexplained Gothicisms that belie and eventually explode its 'appearance'. Some thirty years on, writing in a changed cultural atmosphere from a very different social position, Hemans too recognises the essential emptiness of the romance, dramatising its inadequacies by allowing, then destroying, the emotionally charged love-relationship. Unlike Robinson, Hemans dwells on her images of failure; indeed, her romances rely on exactly their own destruction. Where Robinson uses dreams, Hemans poeticises reality; where

Robinson manipulates delay and expectation, Hemans glories in the immediate experience of violent loss. Both poets, however, structure their most forceful romances around the spectacle of the weakened, dying or dead man, and for both, this in itself constitutes violence. If, as I shall discuss, representation can function as an expression of desire, then Robinson's and Hemans's interruptions of the romance can be read as disguised expressions of desire, as if for a woman writing the only outlet for female desire is through violence. Neither poet can imagine a securely-resolved romance, but both poets focus resolutely on desire and its consequences. Romantic love, in its very failure, figures and emblematises its own emptiness.

Desire is fundamental to the romance, and where previous chapters have explored its sexual and performative guises, here it returns to love, its cultural haven. Love provides, or perhaps necessitates, a safe outlet for desire, allowing lust, greed, need, and other less attractive impulses to be repackaged as the dream solution – the ideal and idealised relationship of the love match that justifies social require-ments of family, property and government. As many social historians – most notably Lawrence Stone – have made clear, in the late eigh-teenth century there was a shift towards love as the basis of marriage and family, rather than social duty.[3] Indeed, to love *becomes* a duty in the nineteenth century. In the 1790s, however, the novelistic romance relies on true love to enable its lot; fed by sensibility, the romance, including its Gothic manifestations, is as much about girl-gets-boy as boy-slays-villain. In countertone to the thwarted heroes of Keats and Coleridge, for instance, heroines become the focus, and in the poetical romances of Robinson they also function as the instiga-tors, whether passively as in 'Golfre' and 'The Murdered Maid', or more creatively as in 'The Lady of the Black Tower'. However, the romance does not transform into a vehicle for female empowerment; on the contrary, Robinson and Hemans both seem to use violence constructively: that is, in disallowing romantic resolution, in filtering desire through violence, they demonstrate the weakness, the exclu-sions, figured by love, and they do so by associating it explicitly with violence. Niklas Luhmann speaks of 'incommunicability' and its entrenchment during the late eighteenth century; for him, it is a symptom of the inability of the late-Enlightenment world to cope with its own emphasis on differentiation: 'categorical barriers to communication began to emerge. It was not the failure of skilfulness that is the problem, but the lack of a capacity for sincerity. ... The old distinction between *sincere* and *insincere* love was also abrogated, to be replaced by a *new sort of difference of conscious and unconscious, proclivities, drives and aims.* ... All behaviour remained ambivalent ... And this in turn meant nothing other than incommunicability'.[4]

Luhmann's theoretics of love work to show that in the late eighteenth century something happened to change the way romance – that is, love – is represented; his formulation of 'incommunicability' is one way of saying that relations were breaking down. The turn to violence is another. Penelope Harvey and Peter Gow, in their introduction to a collection of essays entitled *Sex and Violence*, define violence as 'legislated, controlled, and studied outside or beyond normal, constructive human practice. Violence is by definition unacceptable, out of control, beyond reason. Furthermore, it is transgressive; transgressive of our sense of bodily integrity and the spirit enclosed therein which enables the notion of violation to apply to more than physical hurt'.[5] For them, violence is the unspoken, omnipresent Other against which we define 'culture' – that which is contained, restrained, representative, 'civilised'. Robinson and Hemans, however, do not relegate violence to the margins as unacceptable; neither do they highlight it as an unnatural intrusion into the social order. Instead, each locates violence squarely within the realm of normal human contact by associating it intimately with love, the emotion that facilitates contact. For each, the link with desire is inescapable.

Moreover, Robinson especially responds to cultural pressure by openly representing that which is simultaneously authorised and suppressed: irrationality. The efforts made in the 1790s to repress transgression resulted in a black market in transgression, not to mention a kind of cultural romantic hysteria:[6] curbs on free speech were matched by increased outbursts of public disorder; an increasing reliance on propriety found its evil twin in racy newspaper cartoons and knowing, arch gossip over the public figures of the demi-monde.[7] If, as Harvey and Gow assert, 'sexuality is ... associated in Anglo-American cultures with the transgressive individual, that aspect of self that emerges through lack of control, that exists and finds expression against reason' (2), then love and desire in the romance and their collusion with violence reify the insecurities and repressions of a frightened and anxious culture. Escape to romance means only the reintroduction of transgression in another form: even as chivalry promises order but promotes oppression, so too romantic love promises union but enacts disintegration. As Harvey and Gow point out, the 'substantive categories of violence ... include [the] less visible

categories of broken contract and the notion of threat' (12). Even as
the reader of Robinson's violent romances is met with unexpected
denouements and the loss of love – one form of broken contract – and
threatened with Gothic apparatus and plots driven by superstition, so
too Robinson herself disables conclusions based on Gothic rewritings
of romance: 'sublimity and violence are native to obscurity', says
Clery, echoing Burke (79), and Robinson sees to it that obscurity most
forcibly characterises her romances. In this way, she demonstrates the
contradictions of the decade: expression and repression, desire and
deflation, violence and banality cohabit, producing poetic scenarios
wherein the only certainty *is* obscurity. Robinson does not avoid
violence, but neither does she engage with it directly; her deliberately
violent spectacles are undermined, not through evasion, but through
a withering of the power her images insist on only to a point. Aware
that 'the objectification of highly-charged emotional events [is] itself
a form of violence' (Harvey and Gow 2), Robinson writes Gothicised
poetry that, somehow, always concludes at the moment of transition
from forceful to limp.

Desire, then, provides the site on which romance and violence build
their poetical edifice. 'Acting freely on sexual desire is transgressive,
and to act freely on sexual desire is to unleash the sexual master in
oneself':[8] feeling desire may be passive and harmless (heroines of
sensibility often feel desire), but acting on it is self-authorising and
potentially harmful (as so many heroes and villains demonstrate).
Parenthetically, desire has its gendered versions; in the poetical
romance, however, desire infiltrates and overturns gendered boundaries. While Cameron and Frazer can only see sexual violence as a
'masculine' activity, Robinson's and Hemans's poetry interestingly
imports femininity into violence;[9] although muted, their 'unleashing'
of female desire results in the violent elimination of the male player.[10]
Cameron and Frazer also connect sexual violence with an 'urge to
authorship' that they associate with 'Enlightenment individualism –
the construction of self as a narrative persona, as the hero of a text'
(162). In their readings of twentieth-century sex crimes, they refer to
eighteenth-century definitions of subjectivity, even citizenship, using
language that continues to tie together sex, violence and masculine
desire. However, Robinson's and Hemans's poetry feature the 'urge to
authorship' and 'the construction of self' that distinguish sexual
violence – not, indeed, figured by the authors themselves, but by their
heroines and their plots. Robinson's 'Golfre' revolves around an
unfinished folk tale about a noble girl-baby switched at birth with a

peasant's still-born daughter; 'The Lady of the Black Tower' is the hero of the text; Hemans's *Records of Woman* seek specifically to poeticise romance-laden moments in the lives of real and fictional women. And these poems of romance maintain narrative trajectories punctuated by violence dependent on, even arising from, moments of romantically charged desire.

Cameron and Frazer argue that sexual violence is an expression of immediately repressed desire, that Enlightenment individuality and freedom lead to 'subjection [by] social forces' and that this pressure eventually results in an ideology that glorifies transgression as 'erotic and beautiful', developed by 'the Romantics' into a 'full-blown aesthetics' (160). Leaving aside the vast and flattening generalities that inform this understanding of literary history, it does suggest a useful matrix, for romance abounds with repressed heroines. If one opens Cameron's and Frazer's formulation to allow for the possibility of female desire, something interesting happens: violence becomes, not the destroyer of romance, but its enabler. If the objects of desire seize the subject-position, not only feel but express their desire for a romantic partner – for Robinson and Hemans, a man[11] – what results is a topsy-turvy world: men become sexual objects, women become desiring subjects, and violence becomes the only possible form of expression. Desire is manifested through its own violent repression. Complicated by the romance's *dramatis personae* of hero (active, male), villain (active, male), and heroine (passive, female), this scenario transforms not so much roles as performance – desire, necessary yet taboo, filtered through love, reliant on romance, and dependent on 'correct' gender placements, functions as its own extinguisher. It both causes violence and is destroyed by it. 'The gendered and sexualised nature of violence' (Cameron and Frazer 156) in the romances of Robinson and Hemans is intimately and of necessity linked to their female characters' ability to feel deeply but only enunciate those feelings obliquely. Because of this, then, the many dead men in their poetic romances function as markers of female desire. And that desire, like the violence that infects and circumscribes it, is enclosed in the insular world of the romance and takes on the form allowed by genre: it presents itself romantically, the love of a maid for her swain, in danger of being foiled by a villain. The romantic landscapes of Robinson and Hemans are peopled by familiar figures who nonetheless perform their allotted roles with variations. Robinson's – 'Gothic', supernatural, interlinked – play with a metaphorics of dreams and allusion, while Hemans's build on proto-Victorian ideals of duty, endurance and morality, and do not flinch from representing inhumanity. For both poets, however, resolution is garbed not in wedding-clothes, but a shroud.

Deflected violence and dream-visions: Mary Robinson

According to Luhmann, 'Romanticism's response to [romantic instability and incommunicability], in which the semantics of love came into conflict with demands that the personal world be endowed with permanent meaning, was to take flight into exaggeration' (144). Certainly, Robinson's Gothic romances construct a poetics of exaggeration; emotions, events, personalities are heightened and sensationalised. What Curran calls her 'pathetic poetry' finds its meaning in loss, despair and disruption: 'this is a sad world, one that witnesses constant abuses of power, where armies do no one any good, where class conflict is systemic and cannot be wished away by liberal compromise, and where not perspectivism but insanity or stark alienation seem the logical end of interiorizing social conditions'.[12] Curran does not mention romantic love, but by implication it is as hopeless as the rest: exaggerating the risks and dangers of romance, Robinson inflects desire – for love, for happiness, for fulfilment – with perversion and sensationalism. At the same time, she imports to desire a centrality that rationalises its dangerous effects; for Robinson, desire disguised as love and love infected with desire undermine and eventually destroy romantic union. There is an easy reason for this: Robinson's readers were fully aware of her own failed romances with, in the 1780s, the Prince of Wales, and in the 1790s, Banastre Tarleton.[13] Cartoonists and newspaper satirists routinely reported on her liaisons, her public appearances, her efforts to support herself, and frequently the tone was itself accented with violence, as in the Gilray print 'The Thunderer'. This foregrounds Tarleton and a feather-headed Prince of Wales as the suitors for Robinson's favours; Tarleton brandishes a phallic sword while the Prince can manage only a thin and wilting riding-crop. But the real violence is saved for Robinson, spread-eagled in miniature on a pole that advertises 'Alamode Beef, hot every Night' and features a grinning face looking up her hiked skirt.[14] Robinson's public persona of abandoned, victimised, sexually suspect woman, linked with her own periodic self-refashionings, indicate her awareness of the associations her readers made between the writer and the work, which in turn suggests her utilisation of a convenient marketing tool.[15] The 'real contradictions and dangers which every gentlewoman of the period potentially faced' (Clery 74) – dangers of personal and financial loss and violation – were well-known to Robinson: she lived them. To infer, then, some personal meaning in the poetry of a writer whose *Memoirs* were left unfinished at her death is merely to allow in Robinson the ability to exploit her personal experience.

However, Robinson's romances go beyond pallid self-justification or morbid self-mining or even veiled autobiography. Her Gothicism is extreme, and both psychologically and physically based. Her characters love and lose with an emphasis on criminality and mental imbalance that both reveals and relies on the violent 'objectification of highly charged emotional events' (Harvey and Gow 2). It is tempting to see this as a backlash against the Della Cruscan eroticism that, for many of her readers, firmly fixed her as a figure of emotional excess and abandonment:[16] the Gothic poetry persistently disallows and deflates the expected romantic denouement. Clery speaks of the 'therapeutics of romance' which necessitate the happy ending (80), but Robinson stubbornly refuses this prescription: for her, the happy ending is neither guaranteed or even poetically desirable. It is this last that is most telling in Robinson's world of romance, moreover, for she does not reject outright the happy ending, as 'The Lady of the Black Tower', or even 'Golfre', for instance, shows. Instead, she twists it: she provides an ending both 'happy' and empty, unfulfilling, or untenable, narratively and creatively. Her romantically Gothic poems show their readers two options: one is the straightforwardly shocking, lurid, unhappy ending; the other a placid, credulous, happy ending that suffers from debilitating structural weakness. In the first, violence is done to characters; in the second, to the poetry itself. In both, the violence is conveyed, ultimately, indirectly: Robinson veils her violent poetry and in this way contributes to the *fin-de-siècle* dread of directness.

This is not to say that Robinson's poems evade the representation of violence altogether. Indeed, as the Gothic scenarios of poems such as 'Golfre' and 'The Hermit of Mont Blanc' make plain, Robinson can be liberal in her sprinklings of blood and gore. However, even as she laces her poetic narratives with spectres, ghouls, bodies and suicides, she also inserts directive tags that turn the attention, ultimately defusing the horror that, paradoxically, she seems unhesitatingly to pursue. In this, she elides the force of her violent scenes and transforms the potentially terrifying into the merely moral; this is especially true of 'Golfre. A Gothic Swiss Tale'. In this poem, Robinson rewrites scenes familiar to its readers: we are confronted with the well-known machinery of nature's force, but the beaches, mountains and forests here function not to reveal the nobility and dignity of the mind infused by nature, but to foreshadow and accompany, in their more well-known guise of the pathetic fallacy, the turbulent emotions and farcical efforts of characters at the mercy of their emotions, and plagued by villainous, human, forces; Robinson builds into her poetic romances denunciations of the terrors man inflicts on, not man, but woman. The Gothic-romantic 'Golfre', for instance, relies for its full effect on a combination of madness, violence, and a concluding turn towards bathos that is reminiscent of the strangely unaffecting moralising offered by Coleridge at the end of 'The Rime of the Ancient Mariner'.[17]

Robinson keenly invokes, and disarms, a cauldron of violent poetic Gothicism. The characters of the romance – knight, lady, villain – and its themes – love, loss, reunion, for instance – are remapped onto a landscape uncomfortable with its own defining landmarks. Curran identifies 'the common theme of Robinson's pathetic poetry' as being 'a sudden and total displacement of the stabilities on which existences depend' (31); one of the stabilities of genre is the familiarities of 'happily ever after', and this is the assumption that Robinson most consistently displaces. 'Golfre' on the one hand presupposes its audience's familiarity with a certain style of writing; subtitled 'A Gothic Swiss Tale', it announces its place as one of the *Lyrical Tales* of the collection in which it appears.[18] As a 'Gothic' tale, it contains the requisite supernatural, spooky elements of a mysterious death, disembodied voices, bloody murder and so on (though without the Radcliffian turn to the commonsensical explanation of the inexplicable). Robinson, in setting the tale in Switzerland, also makes use of religious convention, dotting the poem with monks and crucifixes. In this way she prepares her readers for the romance to follow, itself almost a pastiche of romantic convention, albeit with a subversive tinge. Robinson uses her first stanzas to set the scene, waiting until stanza 5 to introduce the Baron Golfre, but the revelation of his true character is further delayed. At first, he is represented as monklike, 'to solitude devoted', spending his nights in prayer. Only in the next stanzas does Robinson complicate this picture, and allow the simultaneous entry of both violence and the supernatural:

> And yet his pray'r was little mark'd
>   With pure and calm devotion;
> For oft, upon the pavement bare,

> He'd dash his limbs, and rend his hair,
>   With terrible emotion!
>
> And sometimes he, at midnight hour,
>   Would howl, like wolves wide-prowling;
> And pale the lamps would glimmer round—
> And deep the self-mov'd bell would sound,
>   A knell prophetic tolling!
>
> (I: 26–35)

Two stanzas later, she also introduces the romantic element:

> Beneath the steep, a maiden dwelt,
>   The dove-ey'd Zorietto;
> A damsel bless'd with ev'ry grace—
> And springing from as old a race,
>   As lady of Loretto!
>
> (I: 46–50)

Zorietto lives peacefully with her 'aged sire', yet her existence is characterised by 'fear' of the mysterious castle of the Baron, with its unearthly sounds and ghostly lamps, and by the 'dismal tale' her sire 'oft ... was telling'. To emphasise the point, Robinson repeats the line 'A dismal tale was telling' four times in as many stanzas with only small variations, giving the impression that this is all he ever tells, and the reader plainly sees that the tale is Zorietto's own:

> He told a long and dismal tale,
>   How a fair lady perish'd;
> How her sweet baby, doom'd to be
> The partner of her destiny,
>   Was by a peasant cherish'd!
>
> He told a long and dismal tale,
>   How, from a flinty tow'r,
> A lady wailing loud was seen,
> The lofty grated bars between,
>   At daylight's purple hour!
>
> He told a tale of bitter woe,
>   His heart with pity swelling,

How the fair lady pin'd and died,
And how her ghost, at Christmas-tide—
Would wander – near her dwelling.

He told her, how a lowly dame
The lady, lorn, befriended—
Who chang'd her own dear baby, dead,
And took the lady's in its stead—
And then – 'Forgive her, heav'n', he said;
And so his story ended.

(I: 71–90)

Zorietto hears but does not recognise her own story of origin, just as later she remains blind to the Baron's intentions – for sure enough, to see her is to love her, and after appearing at her door with pale face, wild eyes, and a bloody poniard, crazy with terror, Golfre 'gaz'd, admir'd!/ The peasant girl his fancy fir'd,/ And set his senses madding!' (II: 73–5).

Curran writes that Robinson, 'herself a deeply victimized woman', is 'attuned … to endemic injustice and abuse of power' (30), and in 'Golfre' she explores the scenario of a woman victimised by the aristocratic abuse of sexual power. Instead of courting Zorietto, Golfre claims her, taking along a retinue of soldiers to guard the door, and when Zorietto enters, he 'dart[s] forth,/ His trembling victim seizing', the violent imagery underlining Golfre's role as ravisher, rather than lover. And yet Robinson is not merely playing with stereotypes: unlike the ravisher of Gothic convention, Golfre honestly intends marriage: and by merging lover-hero and ravisher-villain, Robinson suggests not merely the abuse of power, but further, the abuse of romanticised concepts of love and desire. In 'Golfre', love itself becomes a Gothic construct, since even when confronted with a disembodied 'snowy hand … moving round the chamber' carrying a 'clasp of pearl … fix'd to a zone of amber' and the sudden appearance of 'such horrors as attend the dead' in Zorietto's cottage, the Baron responds only by invoking 'Jesu' and drawing his dagger (III: 61–2, 64–5, 74, 76). Sensible Zorietto calls on heaven to save her, to which Golfre replies 'Yes, heav'n will save thee … to be my bride!' (III: 81–2). Supremely indifferent to supernatural machinery, Golfre relies on strength of arms and a matter-of-fact twisting of Zorietto's pleas to heaven to his advantage. But then, Zorietto herself underreacts; only the old goatherd sees the phenomena as omens against the marriage, and as a reminder of the death of the Baron's first wife (who died in the 'black tower' [III: 94], thus linking 'Golfre' to 'The Lady of the Black Tower' in site if not in subject-matter). After all this, Zorietto refuses Golfre only on the romantic grounds that 'she loved another' (III: IV: 2); and, the ghostly doings forgotten, Golfre merely frames her sire in a set-up Robinson herself has complied with. At the end of Part 2, when Golfre first came to the little cottage, we were told of 'a sword of gold,/ Which poverty might well behold/ With eyes wide stretch'd and greedy!' (II: 88–90). Now, in Part 4, we learn that 'his sword was gone; the goatherd swain/ Seem'd guilty, past recalling' and so, in true romance style, Zorietto trades herself for her sire, and 'the marriage day was fix'd' (IV: 6–7, 26).

Robinson salts 'Golfre' liberally with romance and violence: for the Baron, the two are interchangeable, and Robinson continually plays one off the other. In a single stanza, for instance, Golfre gets rid of his rival: 'he seiz'd the youth, and madly strew'd/ The white cliff with his streaming blood,/ Then hurl'd him down its side', then merely puts about a story centring on a hungry wolf (IV: 43–5, 46 *passim*).[19] The wedding immediately follows; the clasp of pearl and zone of amber again make their appearance, only to stream with blood upon touching Zorietto, and her identity as Golfre's daughter is suggested, although not declared, by the bursting of the pearl clasp, the exposure of Zorietto's 'beating side', and the revelation of 'three crimson spots', borne also by Golfre's first wife and 'the baby, who had early died' (IV:89, 91, 98). One would think that this would be the poem's climactic moment, but we are only in Part 4 of a five-part poem, and Robinson subverts her own subversive turn to the sensationalism of incest by allowing the wedding, apparently, to proceed, and Zorietto to become Golfre's 'bride'. Curran describes the *Lyrical Tales* as containing 'poems of grotesque, even extreme alienation' (32), and 'Golfre' exemplifies this description: at each moment of Gothic horror the poem merely moves on without pause; climax becomes anti-climax, the characters themselves seeming not to notice the oddity of their Gothicised lives, while the piling up of violent and bloody conflicts begins, through repetition, to lose its force. Partly because no one in the poem reacts to the horrors, partly because Robinson, or her narrator, moves on so swiftly from each small explosion, the violence comes to seem cartoonish. Robinson's animation frames are stanzas: no sooner does a sensation emerge, punctuated by the obligatory exclamation mark, than we move on – hence stanza 20 (96–100) of Part 4:

And now remembrance brought to view,
(For heav'n the truth discloses,)
The baby, who had early died,
Bore, tinted on its little side,
Three spots – as red as roses!

which glides smoothly to stanza 21 (101–5):

Now, ere the wedding-day had past,
Stern Golfre and his bride
Walk'd forth to taste the evening breeze,
Soft sighing mid the sombre trees,
That drest the mountain's side.

Part 4 then ends quietly with a vision of two angelic figures ascending to heaven, while Part 5 begins with a sudden storm, showing that, while sensation may repair itself seamlessly within the poem, peace is equally prone to sudden rupture.

Finally, we have reached the poem's climax, centred not on, the violent and rapacious style of love characterised by Golfre, nor even the mystery of the dead Lady of the Tower and her baby, but on the marginalised love of Zorietto and her sweetheart: the storm wakens Zorietto's constitutional fear and provokes Golfre to ask 'what did she fear?' (V: 36). Zorietto fears 'the wolf which did my lover slay'; her maddened outburst draws from him an oblique confession – 'I see thy vengeful eyeballs roll – / Thou com'st to claim my guilty soul', he cries to no one in particular (V: 41, 53–4). Such is the blackness of Golfre's soul that he could be calling out to the lover we have seen him murder or the wife he has probably murdered – the dead mother whose voice has 'utter'd' '"hear me!"' periodically throughout the poem. Climax builds on climax now: the black tower sprouts angel's wings, Golfre confesses to murder (in suitably violent terms – "Twas I who tore the quiv'ring wound,/ Pluck'd forth the heart, and scatter'd round/ The lifestream of thy lover' [V: 78–80]), and the narrator suddenly calls Zorietto 'his daughter' (V: 69). Golfre is revealed at dawn as 'a dreadful sight,/ Black, wither'd, smear'd with gore!' and his remains are hung on a gibbet (V: 89–90).

After all this turmoil, it seems faintly ridiculous to end the poem with a familiar and comfortable religious moral, and yet, as Coleridge does with 'Rime', so too Robinson:

> For charity and pity kind,
>   To gentle souls are giv'n;
> And mercy is the sainted pow'r
> Which beams thro' mis'ry's darkest hour,
> And lights the way – to heav'n.
>   (V: 101–5)

Suddenly, Gothic violence and disrupted, murderous romance are revealed to be in the service of a tidy, rather unimaginative moralist. Robinson achieves closure not through the logic of plot, or through a reflective turn to a deeper philosophy, but through a facile religiosity that has not figured at all in the preceding 109 stanzas (547 lines), that, moreover, praises virtues not at all in evidence in the poem. While the flurried reader might gain some comfort from this ending, the tale itself is let down; far from resolving its violence, this final stanza denies its existence, ignores the pagan Gothicism that has created the poem's conflicts, and even defuses the subversive eroticism that has permitted a father to marry his daughter without repercussion (the disaster that followed was rooted in Golfre's murders rather than his incestuous desires). This constitutes another form of violence: structural damage to a poem dependent for its force on burst after burst of sensationalism. Robinson leads her readers straight up to the sight of a torn body disintegrating on a gibbet and then, without ceremony, transforms this deathly image into an uncontestable, unconvincing, violet-scented and very weak banality. However, this bathos indicates Robinson's skill in dramatically de-poeticising her poem: this is the conclusion one might expect, say, from Hannah More, whose student Robinson had been as a girl. It also dramatises Robinson's characteristic pull back from a devoted engagement with the violence she has, up to this point, seemed to glory in.

'Golfre''s turn to banality frustrates the otherwise saturated nature of the poem's violence; it means that even at the moment of confrontation Robinson can pull back to platitudes, whitewash the gibbet, and turn the readers' attention to what is, in context, empty moralising. Incest[20] and forced marriage, the perversions of romance, are bloodily intercut with murder and imprisonment, yet readers are left pondering charity, pity and mercy. Robinson deflects violence in this poem, protecting her readers from a confrontation with exaggerated and extreme wrong-doing, even as she also spices the romance with more than the usual protracted love affair or scary castle. In 'The Hermit of Mont-Blanc', she follows an alternate route. In this poem, the romance is shunted to the past:

... In early youth,
Cross'd in the fond[21] affections of his soul
By false Ambition, from his parent home
He, solitary, wander'd;[22] while the Maid
Whose peerless beauty won his yielding heart
Pined in monastic horrors! ...
...
His Orisons he pour'd, for her, whose hours
Were wasted in oblivion ...
...
... For, still, Love
A dark, though unpolluted altar, rear'd
On the white waste of wonders!
                              (12–17, 21–2, 24–6)

Again, Robinson sets a familiar scene: love opposed, lovers parted, woman holed up in 'monastic horrors', man leading a life of contemplation, prayer and regret.[23] Interestingly, the hermit seems uncertain about his object of worship: although he sets up a cross, he 'pours' orisons 'for her', not for God. 'Orisons' are, strictly speaking, merely prayers, but in common parlance are for the benefit of God; the hermit's ambiguous prayers provide the first instance of error, the first hint of disorder (the separation of the lovers, while unpleasant, is also standard). Robinson places the hermit in a landscape noted for its grandeur and sublimity – even before Shelley and Coleridge, Mont Blanc's poetic potential had been tapped, most notably by Georgiana Cavendish – but to the hermit, nature is characterised by violence: he gathers his food on summits that 'rock' the 'giddy brain' with 'fear'; he is awakened at night by howling wolves and destructive storms that send rocks 'plunging'; he views 'jutting block[s] of now-encrusted ice' and 'shudders'; even in summer his 'pensive gaze/ Trac'd the swift storm advancing whose broad wing/ Blacken'd the rushy dome of his lone hut' (65, 70, 71–2, 78–80). Although Robinson superficially celebrates the hermit's sensibility, his generosity ('nothing loath by pity or by pray'r/ Was he, to save the wretched', 51–2), and his fidelity, she also endows him with a fearfulness that sees only the 'terrible' in nature and that has inspired him to flee society when his love is forbidden, rather than work for its allowance. 'Hermit' thus sets up a romantic scenario on several levels – star-crossed lovers, affective landscape – only to embed in the poem's first 102 lines a suggestion of the hermit's weakness rather than strength, defeatism rather than valour.

Line 103 introduces the Gothic 'dreary night' in winter that changes the hermit's life forever: for a full stanza (21 lines), she dwells on his sudden, unexplained surrender to fear.

> Sudden, the HERMIT started from his couch
> Fear-struck and trembling! Ev'ry limb was shook
> With painful agitation. On his cheek
> The blanch'd interpreter of horror mute
> Sat terribly impressive! In his breast
> The ruddy fount of life convulsive flow'd
> And his broad eyes, fix'd motionless as death,
> Gaz'd vacantly aghast!
> ...
> And Silence, like a fearful centinel [*sic*]
> Marking the peril which awaited near,[24]
> Conspir'd with sullen Night, to wrap the scene
> In tenfold horrors. Thrice he rose; and thrice
> His feet recoil'd; and still the livid flame
> Lengthen'd and quiver'd as the moaning wind
> Pass'd thro' the rushy crevice, while his heart
> Beat, like the death-watch, in his shudd'ring breast.
>   (106–13, 116–23)

As with 'Golfre', the Gothicism is unexplained: like Zorietto, the hermit seems simply to Fear – an object for his fear is unimportant. He is suddenly, irrationally, superstitiously Afraid, an endemic emotion, as natural to him as 'shudd'ring'. Robinson begins to make plain what she has intimated before: the hermit inhabits a romantic landscape and has lived a romantic plotline, but he lacks a romantic personality – he is not a hero, although his actions may sometimes appear heroic. As Robinson notes, 'fear/ Will sometimes take the shape of fortitude,/ And force men into bravery' (128–30). The hermit's display of enforced bravery consists of rushing to the window and unfastening the bolt; the wind blows out his candle, 'and again/ His soul was thrill'd with terror' (133–4). 'Thrill'd' connotes a certain enjoyment of his fear, a physical pleasure gained, not from love or the presence of his beloved, but from self-induced fear of natural elements – storm, wind – that he must have experienced before in his five years on the mountain. Since this is in part a Gothic poem, Robinson allows the fear also to act as a premonition: disaster is imminent, but she no sooner introduces it than she pulls back. The hermit has suddenly begun to rush down the hill towards a 'stream of light' 'when a shriek of death/ Re-echoed to the valley' (144, 148–9); this impels him to 'fl[y]/ ... / Half hoping, half despairing, to the scene/ Of wonder-waking anguish', only for the lights to go out, the darkness and wind to 'increas[e] the Hermit's fears', and for 'four freezing hours' of prayer to ensue (149, 151–2, 156). Robinson builds ambiguity on uncertainty: she gives the hermit no motivation for his flight other than fear, she does not make it clear if he runs from or towards the shriek of death; indeed, she moves so swiftly past this moment of violence that, at this point, it seems less contributory to the hermit's fear than does 'the hollow tongues/ Of cavern'd winds' (154–5). That the hermit then settles down to pray for four hours – conveniently, the length of time needed for the sun to rise – serves to delay the moment of confrontation as well as reinforce the timidity of the hermit.

At dawn, the hermit thanks God he has not fallen down a chasm, and then catches sight of bloody tracks that, he assumes, 'mar[k] the fate/ Of some night traveller, whose bleeding form/ Had toppled from the Summit' (172–4). The reality is worse, and, considering the nature of the poem's genre, not entirely unexpected:

> ... lifeless, ghastly, paler than the snow
> On which her cheek repos'd, his darling Maid
> Slept in the dream of Death! Frantic and wild
> He clasp'd her stiff'ning form, and bath'd with tears
> The lilies of her bosom, – icy cold—
> Yet beautiful and spotless.
>
> (177–82)

The hermit apparently does not, while the reader cannot help but, remember the shriek of death: Robinson inserts 30 lines between its sound and the discovery of the body, but from here to the poem's end – only another 23 lines – the hermit's fate is sealed. Ten lines from the finding of the body the hermit discovers the murderer, a ruffian soldier whose hands are still bloody from the deed and whose guilt is made plain by the victim's golden cross he wears. Robinson goes one step further, and adds rape to the maid's violent experience: 'ANCHORET!/ Thy VESTAL Saint, by his unhallow'd hands/ Torn from RELIGION'S Altar, has been made/ The sport of a dark Fiend, whose recreant Soul/ Had sham'd the cause of Valour!' (194–8). The direct address to the hermit – 'ANCHORET!' – and the accusatory tone in which the narrator reveals the maid's horror suggest a built-in failure on the hermit's part: his love raped and murdered, the villain before him, his heroic/romantic duty is clear, but this poem has maintained, not the hermit's heroism, but his fear, from the start. 'Hermit' reinforces Robinson's ethic of evasion: the hermit, completely inadequate to the task of protecting his beloved from violence, can only listen, paralysed with terror, to her shrieks of death, and once confronted with, in quick succession, her 'bleeding form' and her bloodied killer, reacts by running away, 'and after three lone weeks, of pain and pray'r/ Shrunk from the scene of Solitude – and DIED!' (200–1). Instead of revenging the maid's death, the hermit can only wait for his own; the poem deflates its Gothic and romantic force by using violence to reveal the hero's weakness. Desire, perverted through violence into violation, provides the *raison d'être* for the hermit's exposure as more of a villain than the soldier. Again switching or merging roles, as in 'Golfre', Robinson writes for her readers a poem wherein the heroine is murdered, the hero pines away, and the villain gets away with his crime. Violence is done, not only to character, but to genre: the romance is exploded from within.

Robinson's representation of violent death – the maid's murder – is superseded in the poem, however, by the hermit's withering away, a far more passive and indirect expiration. By concluding the poem with the hermit's weakness, she goes some way towards defusing the violence of the rape and murder. She also builds into the poem's structure delay and evasion that, like the 30 lines of atmosphere that pad the poem between the shriek of death and finding the body, functions to drain suspense and redirect the reader's attention. The poem is 201 lines long; the dark and stormy night begins on line 103. This structural imbalance contributes to a sense of delay that weakens the poem's violence: we enter the crucial night *just past* the half-way point, and the hermit manages to die *just past* an even 200 lines. This unevenness draws out events unnaturally, inorganically; the poem's lack of symmetry informs both its refusal to conform to romantic convention and its refusal to portray its violence even-handedly. Robinson goes further: when 'Hermit' is republished in her collected works, she has stressed the poem's violence, retitling it 'The Murdered Maid' and thus shifting the emphasis from the weak non-hero to the martyred, victimised heroine. However, she has also removed its most shocking lines, the direct address to the hermit that make the rape plain, thus highlighting the erotic picture of the dead maid while maintaining that body's virginity – and going some way towards excusing the hermit's inaction.[25]

Robinson's complex strategy of infesting the romance with violence yet simultaneously avoiding its full force combines with a psychological approach in 'The Lady of the Black Tower'. Here, she exchanges indirectness, moralising, banality, and weakness – markers of deflated violence – for a proto-Freudian climax that more effectively eliminates the violence than her other techniques combined. For Freud, 'a dream is a (disguised) fulfillment of a (suppressed or repressed) wish'; Didier Anzieu elaborates that 'to understand dreams … is to repress [the] lost body [of the mother]', 'the primal place where infantile wishes are fulfilled'.[26] Eighteenth-century dream-analysis was less abstract; Erasmus Darwin, following Andrew Baxter, concluded that 'in dreams the power of volition is suspended, we can recollect and compare our present ideas with none of our acquired knowledge, and are hence incapable of observing any absurdities in them'.[27] For Freud, those very absurdities are expressions of desires, disguised or coded; in Anzieu's explanation, the attempt to rationalise, to observe the absurdities, results in the repression of desires and of wish-fulfilment – in other words, a species of loss. In this way one can see dreams as enacting or representing desire, and their interpretation – even the acknowledgement of a dream as a dream – provoking the disappearance or loss of desire. As I have tried to establish, for Robinson (and Hemans to follow), desire and violence are linked through their representation in romance. When dreams also enter, another layer is added: the dreamed vision becomes both literal and figurative, both an expression of desire and a negation of it, both representation and erasure. The 'narrative … of female powerlessness and of male deceit' that Ty notes is one of Robinson's favourite plots (417) is exaggerated and rejected in 'Black Tower''s dream-vision, and overtaken by the conventional romance when the dream ends.

'Black Tower' opens with a mysterious voice, never identified, which intones the death of romance:

> 'Watch no more the twinkling stars;
> 　　Watch no more the chalky bourne;
> Lady! from the holy wars
> 　　Never will thy love return!
> 　　Cease to watch, and cease to mourn,
> 　　Thy lover never will return!'
>
> 　　　　　　　　(1–6)

From the start, the Lady inhabits a world defined by Gothic mystery and the loss of love; she is 'disconsolate in mind' (35) and finds her appropriate setting in the 'lofty tower ... ivy clad' (37), enlivened only by 'the midnight bell ... toiling for a soul's repose!' (39–40). In a stanza of 12 lines – twice the length of most of the poem's – Robinson introduces the poem's first horror, suitably garlanded by mystery and fear:

> The lofty tower was ivy clad;
>> And round a dreary forest rose;
> The midnight bell was tolling sad –
>> 'Twas toiling for a soul's repose!
>>> The lady heard the gates unclose,
>>> And from her seat in terror rose.
> The summer moon shone bright and clear;
>> She saw the castle gates unclose;
> And now she saw four monks appear,
>> Loud chanting for a soul's repose.
>>> Forbear, oh, lady! look no more –
>>> They pass'd – a livid corpse they bore.
>>>> (37–48)

Robinson's repetition of the 'ose' rhyme – rose, repose, unclose, rose, unclose, repose – embeds a circularity in the stanza, and by extension the poem itself; interspersed by three individually rhyming couplets, the repeated words ring with the central mystery: whose soul? which door? whose corpse? At this point, only seven stanzas in, the Lady is already trapped in threads of rhyme, a model for a later Lady in a Tower, similarly caught up in threads. The interwoven rhymes, the achievement of order and balance through repetition rather than novelty, allow Robinson to indicate the internal, inward-looking nature of the Lady's fears, for the four monks later deny carrying any corpse at all: '"Oh, lady! question us no more:/ No corpse did we bear down the dale!"/ The Lady sunk upon the floor,/ Her quivering lip was deathly pale./ The bare-foot monks now whisper'd, sad,/ "God grant our lady be not mad"' (73–8). While the Lady's castle seems as Gothic as Golfre's, the monks' whispered concern points to the beginning of a signal difference: 'Golfre''s Gothic events were accepted unquestioningly, while the first one readers witness in 'Black Tower' inspires suspicions of a hallucinating Lady and the search for a 'rational' explanation of an irrational and supernatural happening.

For the Lady, however, the vision (as it seems to have been)[28] acts to foreshadow coming horrors: having left the Tower to question the monks, the Lady is now in the chapel and at its altar. Suddenly, we hear once again the disembodied voice, repeating its earlier caution – '"Lady, all that live must die"' – and bidding her to 'watch no more from yonder tower' since '"thy lover will no more return!"' (90, 91, 96). Robinson's narrator makes no attempt to explain the voice's provenance; indeed, a few lines earlier the narrator has herself participated in the suspense-building, apostrophising 'Ah, lady! Thou wilt pray ere long/ To sleep those lonely aisles among!' (65–6). At this point, however, the narrator retreats to passive description, so that the reader shares the Lady's alarm and fear when there suddenly appears a 'youthful knight' 'clad in a doublet gold and green', who frowns and repeats mournfully 'all that lives must die' (99, 98, 102). All this time the Lady has been at the altar, but, with a heart full of 'love and fear', has been unable to pray: the chapel, empty of monks and the religion they represent, now houses ghosts and unearthly voices, trading one belief-system,[29] and one vision, for another. The ghostly youth transforms into a 'giant spectre', whose appearance cues the presentation of five stanzas of ghastly description, centred on the wasting of flesh and the exchange of youth and love for death and decay:

> His flowing robe was long and clear,
>   His ribs were white as drifted snow:
> The lady's heart was chill'd with fear;
>   She rose, but scarce had power to go:
> The spectre grinn'd a dreadful smile,
> And walk'd beside her down the aisle.
>   (109–14)

In a clear parody of marriage, the spectre and the Lady walk together down the aisle away from the altar, their union sanctioned by the Gothic atmosphere and cemented when, at the chapel's door, the spectre conjures up the youth, this time spotted with blood and with a bloody sword. The summer day darkens, the flesh 'waste[s] away' from the spectre's cheek, and the monks return, once again to deny having seen or heard anything strange, and Part One concludes.

Robinson seems to be putting the Gothic to clear romantic use: the Lady's ceaseless watching for her lover prompts the spirit world to send her signs both of his love and his demise, so that she may give up her hopeless waiting. The romance is undermined, however, by the suggestion that watching and waiting – the romance heroine's traditional duty – are both useless and harmful. While the mysterious voice drives home the utilitarian message that all that lives must die, it has also enjoined the Lady to '"cease to watch, and cease to mourn ... Lady, lady, cheerful be"' (11, 30). This opening exhortation blithely ignores some basic requirements of traditional romance – the happy ending and the heroine's obligation to love and to mourn lost love – and instead encourages forgetfulness and cheerfulness. Robinson combines the unearthly and the commonsensical in another struc-tural challenge to the very genre she invokes from the start. Yet that genre competes with Robinson's innovations: the voice, ghost and spectre are all, as far as we can tell, 'real', even if only to the Lady, but the Gothic has never required the verification by independent witnesses of its truth. Throughout Part One, the Lady experiences visions that simultaneously assert the foolishness of watching and waiting and require ever-more-attentive watching and waiting; the parodic 'marriage' that unites the Lady and the spectre functions, as in 'Golfre', to bind together those who, by nature and culture, are unsuitably matched, even as the poem's structure both offers and rejects romantic convention.

It is no surprise, then, that the Lady is back on the 'lofty tower', watching and waiting, as Part Two opens. Once again, she sees some-thing: this time the far less ghastly sight of a ship. Part One had moved from night to day; Part Two begins in day and moves to the twilight hour, a traditional Gothic between-time. Again, there is a voice, 'airy' this time and with a slightly changed message: '"Watch no more the evening star;/ Watch no more the billowy sea;/ Lady, from the holy war/ Thy lover hastes to comfort thee:/ Lady, lady, cease to mourn;/ Soon thy lover will return"' (175–80). The portents of Part One forgotten, the Lady 'hastens to the bay', and, met by 'smiling sailors' who tell her (ominously) 'trust us', she sets sail for 'the holy land/ Never to return again' (181, 183, 185, 201–2). Since in Part One we learned that the Lady's lover has been at the 'holy wars', it makes sense that she journeys to 'the holy land',[30] but the smiling sailors have other plans: again a voice, 'low' this time, speaks, and describes the boat filling with water and beginning to sink; the Lady again sees the knight in gold and green, but this time 'from the sockets of his eyes,/ A pale and streaming light she spies!/ And now his form trans-parent stood,/ Smiling with a ghastly mien/ ... / ... "Deeper, deeper," sang the crew' (215–18, 222). Despite the waves and the crew's song, the boat lands on 'holy land', significant in its loss of the definite article: '*the* holy land' denotes a country, while 'holy land' intimates something more local – a church, or a crypt. The castle the Lady is conducted to belongs to a 'lord' in gold and green, who leads her to a scene of Gothic horror and implied violence, and needs quoting in full:

> He led her through the Gothic hall,
> With bones and skulls encircled round;
> 'Oh, let not this thy soul appal!'
> He cried, 'for this is holy ground.'[31]
>   He led her through the chambers lone,
>   'Mid many a shriek and many a groan.
>
> Now to the banquet-room they came:
> Around a table of black stone
> She mark'd a faint and vapoury flame;
> Upon the horrid feast it shone –
>   And there, to close the maddening sight,
>   Unnumber'd spectres met the light.
>
> Their teeth were like the brilliant, bright;
> Their eyes were blue as sapphire clear;
> Their bones were of a polish'd white;
> Gigantic did their ribs appear!
>   And now the knight the lady led,
>   And placed her at the table's head!
>
> (241–58)

Whereas Robinson's other Gothic romances have portrayed violent acts, 'Black Tower' illustrates a more metaphorical violence: disorder, madness, the natural progression of life, death and decay reversed. The Lady follows a path from love, through desire, to horror and insanity; her place at the head of the table of death signifies both the satisfaction, and the monstrousness, of her desires. By ignoring the first voice's unconventional direction to forget and be happy, by maintaining her heroine's stance and in this way displaying her unbending desire for her lover's return, the Lady finds herself rewarded by marriage with Death.

Horrific as the scene is, the image of the Lady and Death does not close the poem; Robinson pulls back from the moment of direct engagement with the violence of horror, to reveal that it had all been a dream: 'Just now the lady woke: – for she/ Had slept upon the lofty tower' (259–60). The entire poem – voices, corpses, monks, ghosts, the journey – has been the Lady's dream, caused, it is implied, by sleeping in the open, under the moon: by tradition (again), moonlight and strange dreams are associated. Moreover, the Lady now hears a '*real* voice', Robinson's emphasis serving to establish the unreality of the previous 41 stanzas, and finds that her lover *has* returned: 'for he,/ To calm her bosom's rending fears,/ That night had cross'd the stormy sea:/ "I come," said he, "from Palestine,/ To prove myself, sweet lady, thine"' (266–70). A thoroughly romantic ending undermines the quiddities that have made up the poem's body; as Clery phrases it, 'the previous meltdown or reification by fear is superseded by moral hypostasis' (82). The outrageous Gothicism of the poem, its challenges to convention and to representation, are checkmated by the final two stanzas, as reality and nature reassert themselves. Once again, Robinson deflates her own violent force.

And yet, remembering the significance of dreams, their connection to unspoken, even unspeakable desires, and their tendencies to hide meaning once threatened with interpretation, 'Black Tower' offers more than simply a self-defeating mechanism of retreat. The Lady's dream fulfils Darwin's and Baxter's directives that in dreams the comparative ability is lost: the Lady finds nothing strange about her dream while she is dreaming it.[32] Further, it illustrates desire on several levels: desire for her lover; for autonomy; for freedom of choice; even, in her place at the table's head, for power and mastery. None of these are allowed expression in the standard romance; all point to Robinson's own desire to represent, give voice to, her Lady's thoughts, since the mysterious voices, as well as the horrific images, must all emanate from the Lady's psyche. The monks' whispered hope that their Lady is not mad is also the Lady's own; as if subtextually aware of the unnaturalness, the irrationality, of her impulses in the world of the romance, she clothes the expression of those impulses – those desires – in supernatural, Gothic, violent garb. She locates the fulfilment of her desires in the tomb, the holy land that welcomes and imprisons her desiring self. Significantly, she also kills off her lover in her dream, indicating his peripheral unimportance. The dream can only enact the Lady's desires, however, as long as we do not know it is a dream; Robinson postpones this revelation and this allows the force of the Lady's visions to reveal the force of her desires. Once the visions are acknowledged as a dream, the force dissipates in the banality of its own resolution, and we re-enter the world of the romance, dominated by the happy ending, the substitution of the hero's voice, the declaration of the hero's desires. The dream is shown up *as* a dream – unreal, imagined, transient, the natural order is reaffirmed, and the dream's significance vanishes, repressed, along with the Lady. Of Robinson's Gothic poetic romances, 'Black Tower' is the only one to maintain the happy ending,[33] and yet it presents the most unease with the needs and requirements of the romance.

Love with death: Felicia Hemans

In 'An Hour of Romance', one of the 'Miscellaneous Pieces' from her 1828 collection *Records of Woman*, Hemans describes the 'magic page wherein I read/ Of royal chivalry and old renown': the speaker, having retreated to an isolated bower, seizes a chance moment to enslave herself willingly to 'the spell/ Breathing from that high gorgeous tale'.[34] Romance is deliberately textualised in the poem; the speaker reads, and loses herself in the visions imaged by the text. Interestingly, however, the romance thus enjoyed is not one of love – the suitable text, one would think, for the poet of the domestic affec- tions[35] – but rather one of war, a 'tale of Palestine'. The speaker loses herself in the sights and sounds of battle: trumpets, lances and spears, the Saracen's tent, the harps of English bards. The fantasy is broken only by 'a voice of happy childhood' that pulls her back to 'life's worn track', and, lest the reader question the propriety of the reading matter or, indeed, the workaday imagery of life ('worn': tired, old, used, drab, unexciting; 'track': homely, isolated, rough), the speaker ends the poem by asserting 'yet might I scarce bewail the splendours gone,/ My heart so leap'd to that sweet laughter's tone' (43–4). Romance is rele- gated to the imagination, while reality is invested with a sweetness no book can ever hold. A straightforward reading of 'An Hour of Romance' confirms the poet's conservative, domestic ideology: escape is limited to an hour, to a book; it is only marginally permissible; the duties of caring for children carry joys of which the imagination is barren. In fact, the speaker celebrates her interruption, proving as it does her overwhelming attachment to 'life's worn track' and to women's 'proper and natural business [–] the practical regulation of private life, in all its bearings, affections, and concerns'.[36] Romance nurtures an attachment to the domestic by providing an opportunity to re-enter – gladly – domestic affections.

And yet, the romance scenario that has stolen even an hour of the speaker's attention is not, as I noted above, itself a reification of domestic ideology. The speaker thrills to a scene of violence, or at least its preparations; the romance thus indulged is that which relies on death even as its removal to the distant past allows for the enjoyment of its martial energy. This reader, feminised in location (a bower), by association (with Hemans) and by occupation (a childminder), finds her soul 'chain'd' by a tale of high chivalry as violent as any anathematised by the anxious readers of the 1780s and 1790s. Even if only temporarily, Hemans trades her reality of femininity for a fantasy of masculinity, at least in the observation, and she displays, briefly, a complicated relationship with the romance that, by 1828, results in the concoction of murder, suicide, betrayal and abandonment that makes up *Records of Woman*. Hemans's 'remarkable fondness for ... warlike pomp and knightly pageantry'[37] finds play in her repeated visitations to the land of romance, her superficial complicity in its generic and gendered requirements, and her Robinsonian predilection for denouements resplendent with violence and the death of men. As Paula Feldman notes, '*Records of Woman* is a strong feminist work, [but] its ironies and subversions were subtle, for Hemans literally could not afford to alienate any major segment of her buying public'.[38] However, as an intelligent and imaginative poet who desired to write 'important' poetry – that is, 'high' rather than 'popular' art – she constructs her romances around situations in which loss and disruption were inevitable; as critics have noted, her continual replay of the destruction of domestic affections 'reminds us of the fragility of the very domestic ideology [her poetry] endorses' (Mellor 124). But while readers of Hemans have variously praised and condemned her for her allegiance to, or exposure of, the limitations of domestic ideology, none have discussed her strategies in the context of the genre she discreetly, but knowingly, parodies – the romance. Her manipulations of its requirements of duty, fidelity, honour and love in *Records of Woman* result in a collection of poems that, far from displaying a 'total absorption ... by values that appear ... patently hostile to women's individual identity and destructive of any intrinsic significance their lives may have' (Harding 140), instead reconstruct romance so that the violence it does is revealed in the violence she poeticises, and individuality is repeatedly shown to be the point, rather than the sacrifice, of her vignettes.

Hemans, like Robinson, distrusts romantic convention, and her *Records* violently overthrow its dominance in her characters' lives. Unlike Robinson, however, Hemans writes not the Gothic, but 'records'; that is, she imports an authority, a reality based on documentation and history, that replaces Robinson's dramas of spectres, prophecies and dreams. Again unlike Robinson, Hemans poeticises scenes of violence and torture without flinching and without a self-imposed avoidance, if also without the Gothicised horror of buckets of blood. Hemans's 'pageantry' of women's experiences focuses on moments of highly romanticised, occasionally even theatrical, desire and loss; she documents crises of love and betrayal. Presenting 'the Spirit of romance and chivalry ... in a female form',[39] she seems to glorify feminine self-sacrifice and allegiance to love above all, but her very fluency in such uncomplicated roles, her 'articulation of the value system' (Wolfson 130) masks her translation of stability into flux, of romance into its obverse. Writing in decades with increasingly rigid expectations of what a woman could, and should, write, Hemans shows her understanding of her textual parameters in the methods by which 'her poetry ... destabilizes, darkens, or even contests the social structures' of domestic and romantic values (Wolfson 130).[40] Instead of disguising her violent distortions of romance, as Robinson does, she openly portrays its destruction, performing a sleight-of-hand man- oeuvre that seems to maintain the existence of that it has just exploded. Indeed, rather than passively reflecting early Victorian ideology with 'women characters [who] are no longer ambitious or powerful' (Eubanks 354), Hemans rejects such characterisation, using the disruption of romance to signify another form of desire: for female autonomy and freedom from the trappings of the ideology of romance.

Records of Woman thus functions as a protest demurely clothed in the affections promoted by the domestic, an hour wherein the romance of convention is subtly exchanged for a competing version of femaleness. It is part of Hemans's strategy of concealment that her version of domesticity 'inexorably demands violence and death as its perfect tribute' (Harding 139), not in the service of effacement as Harding contends, but literally as its inevitable corollary. 'Death virtually becomes a kind of guarantee of the significance of a life' (Harding 138) not because death functions as the ultimate form of self-sacrifice, but because, in its various violent forms, it acts to free Hemans's women from the constraints of conventional romance. Death enables the expression of desires; its frequent deployment in *Records of Woman* illustrates Hemans's dissatisfaction with the roles and relationships mandated by the romance. And this goes beyond a dramatisation of the fragilities of domestic ideology that Mellor describes; it involves an exploration, and rejection, of the politics of romance, the genre most deeply implicated in the establishment and maintenance of the domestic ideology. Hemans poeticises, and in so doing extends Robinson's vision of, the impossibility of romantic love; her vehicle is death.

Records of Woman devises a number of permutations on the themes of Love and Death, liberally sprinkled with 'wo'. Luhmann's 'incommunicability' finds play in Hemans's repeated scenarios of disrupted love, interrupted love, rejected love, and thwarted love – as Mellor notes, 'in *Records of Woman*, almost all of Hemans's heroines are either *separated* from those they love, or express a love that is *unrequited*' (132, Mellor's emphasis). Love and romance, while on the one hand the necessary conditions for life, on the other symbolise the loss of life, the triumph of death. Hemans was sometimes celebrated, sometimes criticised for her poetic preoccupation with melancholy, for 'dwelling on what was painful and depressing';[41] as with Robinson, the circumstances of her life provided 'reasons' for her poetic subject-matter for her readers.[42] An expectation that her poetry will concern itself with loss and sadness, however, does not prepare a reader for *Records of Woman*, 'awash with blood', as Norma Clarke describes it (79). 'Marriage [or the decision to marry] [is always] followed by death' (Clarke 79): the romantic solution provides ample opportunities for the violent expulsion of romance. 'Where love is fractured by violence and subjectivity is an unstable and threatening arena, a keen and painful listening to the conflicting pasts and languages which constitute Woman seems an obvious and difficult imperative', writes Kadiatu Kanneh.[43] Hemans's *Records of Woman* concerns itself exclusively with the 'pasts and languages which constitute Woman'; her poems dramatise moments of crisis and instability wherein subjectivity is tested and re-evaluated. Structured around familiar, conventional love scenarios, Hemans writes into her *Records* a retelling of the romance in which she alerts her readers not merely to the 'fragility' of a domestic ideology based on love and romance (Mellor 124), but to its undesirability, even to its impossibility. In her poems, she records romances that fail, that end baldly, that reject their own generic codes, and that, finally, collapse altogether to reform around the reassuring and boundless love of a mother for her daughter. This rewriting depends on – indeed, presupposes – the death or absence of the man, whose heroism is fatally compromised by his inability to survive the demands of the romance. As Clarke notices, *Records of Woman* is 'eloquently empty of adequate men' (76); what she and other critics of Hemans fail to remark are the ensuing cracks and fissures in the believability, the reliability, of the romance. Its structural move from rupture to resolution is reversed, as one after another Hemans's women are confronted with the bleeding corpse of their Beloved.

However, Hemans opens *Records of Woman* gently; 'Arabella Stuart', accomplished in its rendering of the psychological disintegration of a heroine imprisoned, both metaphorically and literally, by love, records the failure of romance through scenes singularly devoid of violence. Instead, Arabella records her fears and insecurities about the enduring power of love – not her own, but Seymour's, her husband. Married before the poem opens, and thus already in a state of romantic fulfilment, Arabella learns that true love does not conquer all; in fact, she begins to doubt the truth of love itself, and it is in this fear that the violence of 'Arabella Stuart' is most transgressive. After an unsuccessful escape attempt, in which Seymour misses her boat but ensures his own freedom, Arabella, back in prison, begins to play out the course of love in a series of apostrophes to Seymour: at first she rejoices that '*thou* hast rent the heavy chain that bound thee;/ And this shall be my strength/ ... /Thy bonds are broken,/ And unto me, I know, thy true love's token/ Shall one day be deliverance' (117–18, 122–4). Constrained by the situation to watch and wait, Arabella has no disembodied voice to encourage her to reject such passivity; indeed, Hemans's commitment to historic veracity allows her to solidify Arabella's constricting belief in romantic rescue into an actual jail. However, even as the voice in 'Black Tower' proved to originate in the Lady herself, so too Hemans allows Arabella a muted but increasingly angry interrogation of the absent Seymour, and with it a subtle dismantling of the framework of romantic fulfilment. 'My friend, my friend! Where art thou? Day by day/ Gliding, like some dark mournful stream, away,/ My silent youth flows from me' (126–8), she laments, comparing herself to a stricken deer.[44] Arabella voices a dawning distrust of Seymour's honesty as hero, disguised as despair at her loss of the attributes of the heroine – youth, and by extension, beauty. Once the romance fractures, however, it quickly breaks: 'Dost thou forget me, Seymour? I am prov'd/ So long, so sternly! Seymour, my belov'd!/ There are such tales of holy marvels done/ By strong affection, of deliverance won/ Thro' its prevailing power/ ... / ... / Dost thou forget me in my hope's decay?' (160–4, 167). Invoking romantic precedent, Arabella simultaneously questions Seymour's commitment to his romantic duty even as she asserts her own, and yet, in describing her 'hope's decay', she begins also to inscribe her disillusionment with the trappings of genre.

From this point to the poem's end, Arabella advances through stages of anger, accusation, and a form of madness that sees her call on heaven with 'the voice of blood'[45] and declare the utter failure of romantic love:

Thou hast forsaken me! I feel, I know,
There would be rescue if this were not so.
Thou'rt at the chase, thou'rt at the festive board,
Thou'rt where the red wine free and high is pour'd,
Thou'rt where the dancers meet! — A magic glass
Is set within my soul, and proud shapes pass,
Flushing it o'er with pomp from bower and hall; –
I see one shadow, stateliest there of all, –
Thine! — What dost *thou* amidst the bright and fair,
Whispering light words, and mocking my despair?
It is not well of thee! — my love was more
Than fiery song may breathe, deep thought explore;
And there thou smilest while my heart is dying,
With all its blighted hopes around it lying;
Ev'n thou, on whom they hung their last green leaf –
Yet smile, smile on! Too bright art thou for grief.

(184–99)

Arabella renounces all faith in romantic convention, and the next
lines conjure up Death as the only substitute lover. A violent reaction
against love, her representation of Seymour's perfidy relies on a
romantic construction of the world, where heroism automatically
results in the rescue of a fair maid. Finding herself still imprisoned,
Arabella can only explain this by recasting Seymour as villain, as false
hero, but even as she does this she demonstrates the limitations of
romance. Arabella is a romance heroine in situation and in self-regard,
but she is also an historical figure whose 'romantic' imprisonment
references political strategy. Although Arabella can only see herself in
romantic terms, Hemans writes into the failure of her romance the
failure of Romance to sustain female desire – in this poem, as much for
Liberty as for Love. That Seymour is entirely absent except in
Arabella's thoughts emphasises his place on the periphery; while
Arabella relies on a romanticised view of her own 'wo' that 'may one
day flow/ To thy heart's holy place' (256, 257–8), thereby allowing a
reunion beyond the grave, Seymour is totally removed from participation in this vision.

By illustrating Arabella's dependence on romance even unto death,
Hemans begins to deconstruct its hold on life; 'Costanza' reinforces
both Hemans's discomfort with female self-sacrifice and disbelief in
the possibility of male endurance. Contrary to Mellor's assertion that
'Hemans idealizes the woman who is committed above all to an

enduring love' (131), this poem establishes Hemans's unease with idealising female endurance. Costanza, rejected in love, dedicates her life to prayer and to indulging in 'wo'; her 'blighted years,/ And wasted love, and vainly bitter tears' are confided in 'heaven alone' (15–16). Costanza, whose name resonates with 'constancy',[46] personifies a single-minded dedication to lost love, an adoration of romance that threatens to destabilise her reputation as a 'gentle saint' (l. 18).[47] It is due to that reputation that the dying participant in a battle that has left 'blood on the grass' (l. 46) is brought to her hut; Hemans devotes some lines to a lingering appraisal of the injured male body: its 'raven locks ... Steep'd in bloody showers', shuttered eyes, parted lips, 'white hue', and 'scarr'd forehead' (66, 68, 73, 75). Again, Hemans pays lip service to the romance while undermining its tenets, for unsurprisingly the warrior is discovered to be the same who deserted Costanza for 'hollow splendour' (100),[48] and his desire to be forgiven is answered by Costanza's unveiling of both her face and her heart: 'I live/ To say my heart hath bled, *and* can forgive' (111–12, emphasis added). The substitution of 'and' for a more grammatically expected 'but' entails forgiveness as conditional on a bleeding heart: the woman must suffer in order to fulfil what should be 'natural' to her. Moreover, her years of waiting bring her neither peace nor reward:

> But o'er his frame
> Too fast the strong tide rush'd — the sudden shame,
> The joy, th'amaze! — he bow'd his head — it fell
> On the wrong'd bosom which had lov'd so well;
> And love still perfect, gave him refuge there, –
> His last faint breath just wav'd her floating hair.
> (115–20)

Far from idealising Costanza's endurance, Hemans portrays it as deadly, fatal to the man and harmful to Costanza. She is not rewarded for her constancy, unless we read the poem against itself and see her reward take the form of revenge – such an interpretation satisfies the requirements of the anti-romance and of 'dark' Hemans. The similar climax of 'The Peasant Girl of the Rhone', where years of constancy to a dead hero result in nothing other than the girl's agony, again illuminates the emptiness of romance.

Hemans moves from failed romances to violently ruptured ones in 'Imelda' and 'The Bride of the Greek Isle'. In both these poems, the man is swiftly and bloodily dispatched in scenes reminiscent of 'The

Doublet of Grey' and 'Golfre'. The Bride celebrates her wedding-day with torrents of tears, first at leaving the parental home, and then at losing her new husband to brigands' violence:

> She saw but Ianthis before her lie,
> With the blood from his breast in a gushing flow,
> Like a child's large tears in its hour of wo[49]
> . . .
> She knelt down beside him, her arms she wound,
> Like tendrils, his drooping neck around,
> As if the passion of that fond grasp
> Might chain in life with its ivy-clasp
> . . .
> So clos'd the triumph of youth and love!
>
>   (140–2, 145–8, 154)

Again, youth and love are overpowered by violence, and again Hemans's ambivalence expresses itself in her less-than-idealising description of Eudora's clinging tendril-clasp: she simultaneously portrays Eudora as fighting against Ianthis's death and contributing towards it, the gentle yet inexorable violence of her ivy-clasp threatening in itself. Captured and taken aboard the brigands' ship, Eudora finds her revenge in arson, setting fire to the ship and herself in what Tricia Lootens calls 'an evocation of suttee' that also sees the bride 'stand as a torch to marital misery, an embodiment of pre-emptive self-sacrifice'.[50] Hemans destroys the romance from within; as 'night gathers o'er youth and love' (l. 226) readers are reminded forcibly of the hero's failure to protect his heroine, or even to survive, and the heroine's deadly dedication to romantic ideals of self-sacrifice. Hemans writes this self-sacrifice as itself heroic, a 'battle against the spiritual death of man's inadequacy' (Clarke 80), but cannot reward Eudora[51] – the romance climaxes in the violent destruction of its players, a theme she returns to in 'Imelda'. Opening with a Romeo and Juliet scenario of lovers defying their families' mutual hatred, 'Imelda' abruptly terminates its initial romantic storyline with a long dash and the narrator's apostrophe: ' — What reck'd *their* souls of strife/ Between their fathers?' (21–2). Interrupted by 'the footstep of her brother's wrath' (31), Imelda hurries away, pausing briefly at the sound of 'the clash of swords' (34). As in 'The Doublet of Grey', 'Golfre', or indeed Keats's 'Isabella', Imelda's romantic attachment serves only to enrage her male relatives and, thus, to prefigure its own elimination. Imelda returns to the fountain-side to find bloodied water and her lover, Azzo, 'graceful' even in death (78). As in 'Costanza', Hemans invites the objectification of the dead man, dwelling on the details of his 'blood ... cold cheek ... [and] moveless lip' (81, 82). Imelda no sooner sees Death than she sees its instrument, her brother's sword, with its 'venom'd point' (94). Proving that 'love is strong' even in 'wo', Imelda 'press[es]/ Her lips of glowing life to Azzo's breast,/ Drawing the poison forth', and dies (95, 99–101).[52] The morning finds 'two fair forms laid/ Like sculptured sleepers' (107–8). Their long kiss goodnight has been sanctified by poison, and the potential illegitimacy of their premarital shared bed obviated by death. Romance sustains itself only at the expense of its players; Hemans uses blood to bind her lovers, and in so doing fuses love and death.

 'Imelda' closes with the ambiguous epithet that 'Love with true heart had striven – but Death had won' (l. 124). We are invited to read 'love', 'true heart', and 'death' all as adversaries, which raises the possibility that Death functions not to prolong Love, but to terminate it. In 'Gertrude' and to a lesser extent 'Juana', Hemans continues to prop her romance on the body of a dead man, but in these poems she leaves the woman's fate open. Juana, the 'neglected wife' of Philip the Handsome, cannot accept his death and so watches over the corpse, waiting for it to awake and return her love:

But when thou wak'st, my prince, my lord! And hear'st how I have kept
A lonely vigil by thy side, and o'er thee pray'd and wept;
How in one long, deep dream of thee my nights and days have past,
Surely that humble, patient love *must* win back love at last!

(29–32)

Juana, like Arabella, like Costanza, relies on a romantic construct that presupposes the rewards of virtue; she believes in love to the point of denying death. Her vigil lasts 'until the shadows of the grave had swept o'er every grace,/ Left midst the awfulness of death on the princely form and face' (47–8). Faced with the decomposing body of her husband, Juana exchanges its decay for the 'lone despair' of a 'broken heart' (52). While this certainly dramatises 'the lasting commitment of a woman to her chosen mate', does it 'celebrate' such endurance (Mellor 124)? Juana's commitment to a decaying corpse exposes her as less a dutiful wife than a maniac one, her need for requited love such that she would rather be companion to such horrors than husbandless. This seems less a celebration than a critique

of Juana's single-minded loyalty, a critique based on the decomposition and devaluation of romantic ideology and the devolution of
domestic affections. Again, love and death coexist, since it is only
Philip's death that allows Juana to express her love. Not even love,
however, can retard the processes of death. In her total commitment
to her duties and identity as 'wife', Juana exposes unwittingly the
ghastly limitations of an ideology based on love. Hemans, in writing
'Juana', begins to map out an escape route from Romance itself.

In 'Gertrude' we find what seems to be the purest expression of
romantic love and commitment in *Records of Woman*. Subtitled
'Fidelity till Death', it opens with an epigraph from Joanna Baillie:

> Dark lowers our fate,
> And terrible the storm that gathers o'er us;
> But nothing, till that latest agony
> Which severs thee from nature, shall unloose
> This fix'd and sacred hold. In thy dark prison-house,
> In the terrific face of armed law,
> Yea, on the scaffold, if it needs must be,
> I never will forsake thee.

'Gertrude' dramatises wifely duty: Gertrude 'will not leave' (16) her
husband in his final hour, and forsakes the domestic space for a spectacular position at the foot of the wheel on which her husband is
bound. In what is by now a familiar scene in *Records of Woman*,
Rudolph, the husband, is physically weakened and, soon to die, is
tangential to the romance; Gertrude, attending him 'with the most
heroic devotedness' (*Records of Woman* 55, headnote to 'Gertrude'), is
both heroine and hero. Gertrude proves her wifely devotion by
staying with Rudolph until 'his worn spirit pass'd'; content with 'her
meed — one smile in death –', Gertrude embodies 'Love and Faith,/
Enduring to the last!' (52, 51, 49–50). In 'Gertrude', love and death
again meet, troped by the man's dead body; like Juana, Gertrude
survives past the romantic disaster of the death of love, and neatly,
almost patly, exemplifies 'fidelity'. But it is in the poem's subtitle and
epigraph that romantic fissures appear. Gertrude, like Juana, apparently has no existence after the death of her husband; the poem ends
as she thanks God for the strength that allowed her to brave the public
eye. If traditional romance is meant to end with 'happily ever after',
however, what comes next? Built into the poem's framework is the
suggestion that Gertrude has performed a duty that has a specific

ending point: 'fidelity *till* death', not 'past' or 'beyond' death. The Baillie epigraph reinforces this: 'nothing, *till that latest agony,/ Which severs thee from nature*, shall unloose this fix'd and sacred hold'.[53] Both subtitle and epigraph posit a limitation on fidelity and love; both identify death as the moment which sees the evaporation, the loosing of romanticised concepts of constancy. In 'Gertrude', love and duty merge: Gertrude's duty to Rudolph *is* her love, but it is a love and duty dependent on circumstance, a condition of Gertrude's identity as wife and Rudolph's presence as her husband. Only death can disengage the fixed and sacred hold of dutiful 'earthly love' (8), but equally powerful is the implicit suggestion that only life can maintain that fixed hold. Hemans thus underpins her romantic vignettes with unsettling rejections of its codes and with repeated assaults on its probity.[54] In 'paus[ing] over the seemingly inescapable social fate of women to suffer and endure' (Wolfson 140), and in binding this fate so tightly to failed romances, Hemans shades her public allegiance to the domestic affections with a stubborn disbelief in their viability and a disinclination to retreat to its comforts. Yet, always remembering that she wrote for money and hence had to please her reading audience, Hemans is discreet in her attacks and subtle in her exposés; her romances with their contradictory market-appeal correlate with W.M. Rossetti's description of Hemans as 'odd' because she 'wore a veil on her head, like no one else' (in Eubanks 356). *Records of Woman*, too, wears a veil.

However, *Records* does not reject romance entirely. Indeed, it becomes plain that Hemans primarily reserves violence and death for her male characters; of the poems I have discussed so far, only Seymour in 'Arabella Stuart' escapes with his life, mainly because he is never present to start with. In killing off so many men, Hemans conveys her disillusionment with a romance based on romantic love. 'Madeline', however, interestingly repositions romantic roles to allow for a 'happy ever after' conclusion even though the man has, as usual, been killed off, this time through succumbing to fever. Opening with another Baillie epigraph that identifies 'mother' as the one reliable figure in a world of sickness and wretchedness, the poem gives its first 24 lines to Madeline's mother: 'My child, my child, thou leav'st me!' (1). Madeline, like Eudora, leaves her maternal home to take up her duties as a wife in 'the youthful world' (43) – that is, the new world, America, but also the world of youth. The mother's blessing foreshadows Madeline's experience; lines 14–15 call on 'Love' to 'guard' Madeline, 'and the exile's wo/ From thy young heart be far!' (14–15). Almost as if the mother's blessing has been a curse in disguise, Madeline no sooner reaches the new world than the narrator interjects doom:

> – Alas! We trace
> The map of our own paths, and long ere years
> With their dull steps the brilliant lines efface,
> On sweeps the storm, and blots them out with tears.
> That home was darken'd soon: the summer breeze
> Welcom'd with death the wanderers from the seas,
> Death unto one, and anguish – how forlorn!
> To her, that widow'd sat in her marriage-morn...
>   (47–54)

The husband has proved his incapability; Madeline's physical strength secures her health. Left alone, however, her emotional fragility leads to literal homesickness: 'at last she lay/ On her lone couch of sickness, lost in dreams/ Of the gay vineyards and blue-rushing streams/ In her own sunny land, and murmuring oft/ Familiar names' (70–4). Madeline pines away, lost in her desires for, not husband, but the childhood home where safety, security and love were supplied by the mother, and Hemans obliges by sending that mother to the rescue: 'had *she* come,/ Thus in life's evening, from her distant home,/ To save her child? – Ev'n so' (91–3, Hemans's emphasis). Madeline's mother performs the hero's part, rescuing the damsel in distress from her own memories and frustrated desires, and Madeline recovers, exclaiming 'Take back thy wanderer from this fatal shore,/ Peace shall be ours beneath our vines once more' (101–2). *Records of Woman* has at last furnished a happy ending, but can only do so by realigning romantic love and recasting its players as mother and daughter. That Madeline calls herself a 'wanderer' confirms the poem's ethos that to leave the maternal home, even for the marital one, is to stray – it is and always was going to be a misdirected journey.

Hemans's own love for her mother, and her sense of loss and deprivation when her mother died in 1827 (the year before *Records of Woman* was published) is well-documented and was a feature of her public femininity; Mellor calls it a 'passionate love' (230, n. 37), while Rossetti remarked that, for Hemans, the 'affections of mother and daughter were more dominant and vivid ... than conjugal love' (in Wolfson 139). *Records of Woman* celebrates the intensity of the mother–daughter bond in other poems, although without the same successful resolution: 'The Memorial Pillar' sanctifies the moment of parting but ends hopefully with the lines 'Mother & child! – Your tears are past – / Surely your hearts have met at least!' (60–1). 'Pauline' is like 'Madeline' in that the mother, Pauline, goes to the rescue of her daughter when their manor catches fire, but unlike 'Madeline' the attempt is unsuccessful; both die, and the only memorial is the miniature of Bertha, the daughter, worn by Pauline – a romantically tragic ending.[55] In 'Madeline', however, Hemans constructs a familiar love triangle and shows her allegiance in whom she allows to win Madeline; in what Wolfson calls 'a fantasy of restoration' (139) the primacy of mother–daughter love is established, assisted by the weakness and insubstantiality of the male hero. Indeed, considering Madeline's plea to be re-received into the maternal sphere, the hero almost comes to seem the villain of the piece, he who tempted Madeline away and then deserted her. Despite Harding's claim that 'the whole point of this "domestic tale" is that individuality is sacrificed to the mother–daughter relationship' (140), 'Madeline' actually encourages its readers to substitute a family romance, guaranteed to succeed, for the fraught, violent, and death-plagued male–female romance that, in *Records of Woman*, inevitably leads to 'wo'. Hemans sacrifices, not female individuality, but the male body, rewriting the romance as hero-less, exposing its inadequacies, and advocating a return to 'domestic' love. In writing of Mary Wollstonecraft, Laurie Langbauer says that 'the mother is double. She is both outside and inside romance'.[56] *Records of Woman* asserts a similar line: while 'mother' may be outside traditional romantic conclusions, she is nonetheless vital to successful romantic conclusions. The romance of home is most potent of all, and the only one that assures happiness. The 'subtle ideologies of the romance plot',[57] as manipulated by Hemans, are reversed; sexual union is displaced, and woman's ultimate happiness and fulfilment can only be found if the romance is unclosed, or rather, re-opened, rewritten, and re-sexed. Mellor argues that 'Hemans's poetry subtly and painfully explore[s] the ways in which [the social] construction of gender finally collapses upon itself, bringing nothing but suffering, and the void of nothingness, to both women and men' (142). *Records of Woman* reveals the collapse of romance as well, but also offers a solution: return romance to the maternal home and avoid 'the mysteries of . . . wo' ('Pauline', 90).

The discomfort and unease – even horror – that underpin the romances of both Robinson and Hemans suggest that neither could be said to support or uphold a romantic ideology which bound together women and men with promises based on desire rather than experience. That neither poet was 'successful' in romantic love might be put forward as the reason – after all, Robinson was frequently publicly humiliated by love, and Hemans found security not with her husband but with her mother. It would not be difficult to cast both poets as heroines of their own romantic visions; Robinson could even participate in such identifications, taking the role of heroine implicitly (as in her *Memoirs*) and explicitly (as Perdita to the Prince of Wales's Florizel). Indeed, for Robinson romance could only culminate in loss and, at the least, violence to her reputation. It is possible to read her Gothic poems as mini revenge-dramas, where hero merges with villain and is suitably punished. Similarly, Hemans's could be read as advertisements for the rejection of marriage by the abandoned wife, leading as they all do to sorrow and loss. But this approach gets us only so far; neither poet is a one-dimensional 'woman scorned', and for both, poetry flourishes outside the realms of biographical wish-fulfilment. Instead, Robinson and Hemans write romances in which romance itself – as an ideology, as a lifestyle – is shown to be corrupt, where reliance on romantic love leads only to catastrophe, and where the violence suffered, by women and men, reveals the emptiness of behavioural stereotypes. True love does not conquer all; the prince will never come, no matter how many 'somedays' there are; hero and villain are not so easy to distinguish; the hero will not protect you; self-sacrifice is all too often literal. Robinson's violence is expressed though fantasy, Hemans's through historicised scenes of 'wo', but for each the violence masks desire which is itself masked. The many dead men do not evince a desire to kill men, but a desire to kill off stereotypes of behaviour that harm both sexes; mainly, the violence figures the desire to destroy romance. For both poets, the romance is itself synonymous with violence, and by destroying, defying, avoiding and rewriting it they communicate their dissatisfaction with a genre thought most appealing to women as writers and as readers. By interrupting the romantic trajectory, Robinson and Hemans redirect its energies, and the resulting storm of emotions can only be voiced violently. Yet, although the romances of Robinson and Hemans are explosive and revelatory, they are also sterile: if male–female congress can never be successful, if the only true romance is found with the mother, then 'ever after' stops here. As long as the romance is false, it will destroy its own meaning. The final chapter explores the violence that infuses gendered relations when the only alternative to romance is murder.

5
Transforming the Romance: the Murderous Worlds of Byron and Landon

Byron's early poem 'To Romance' (1806/7) offers an interesting countertone to Southey's address of 1792 that opened this volume. In it, the self-styled 'infant Bard' makes repeated attempts to 'break the fetters of my youth' and 'leave [Romance's] realms for those of Truth'.[1] Where Southey accusingly came to recognise Romance's 'true' character – 'Romance! I know thee well' – Byron presents himself as not only already fully aware of Romance's falseness, but eager to quit 'her' treacherous, hypocritical sway. 'Romance! disgusted with deceit,/ Far from thy motley court I fly' (33–4): the poet casts Romance as a romantic seductress, a villainess whose attractions still remain strangely compelling. Indeed, although the speaker declares his intention to quit Romance in stanza 1, as early as stanza 2 he admits his difficulty, even as he offers his first critique of 'her' powers: 'And, yet, 'tis hard to quit the dreams,/ Which haunt the unsuspicious soul,/ Where every nymph a goddess seems,/ Whose eyes through rays immortal roll;/ .... / When Virgins seem no longer vain,/ And even Woman's smiles are true' (9–12, 15–16). Romance commits the unforgivable sin of making women appear 'true': genuine, virtuous, virginal, and this, more than any of the images of falseness and disappointment that follow, most deeply indicates Romance's perfidy. And yet, true to Byronic stereotype, the attraction persists. It takes the poet 64 lines to succeed in bidding 'adieu ... a long adieu' to the 'fond race' (57) of romantic creations, but he is not satisfied with merely leaving Romance; interestingly, where Southey detected violence *in* Romance, Byron uses violence *against* Romance. Unable to walk away, he instead metaphorically destroys genre:

> The hour of fate is hov'ring nigh,
> Even now the gulph appears in view,
> Where unlamented you [nymphs of Romance] must lie;
> Oblivion's blackening lake is seen,
> Convuls'd by gales you cannot weather,
> Where you, and eke your gentle queen [Romance],
> Alas! must perish altogether.[2]
>
> (58–64)

Here, it is the poet's creative embrace that is fatal; Romance, reputation ruined, does not survive the poem she at first appeared to dominate. Byron thus dramatises the strength of Romance's attractions, his desire to escape them, the need for violent destruction, and, importantly, his association of Romance and female treachery. The suitability of violence to facilitate poetic wish-fulfilment is unquestioned, and functions as the expression of his ambivalence towards genre and its contents.[3]

Similarly, Letitia Landon's 'Six Songs of Love, Constancy, Romance, Inconstancy, Truth, and Marriage' (1821) offers a trenchant critique of the emotion she was criticised by Elizabeth Barrett Browning among others for concentrating on too exclusively: 'love and love'.[4] Embedded in these songs is Landon's version of 'To Romance', plotted as the inevitable link between Constancy and Inconstancy. The voice proclaiming Constancy resembles Byron's Romance-struck youngster, impressionable and trusting: 'Oh! Say not love was never made/ For heart so light as mine;/ .... / Oh! Say not, that for me more meet/ The revelry of youth;/ .... / Tho' mirth may many changes ring,/ 'Tis love that gilds the mirthful hour,/ That lights the smile for me,/ Those smiles would instant lose their power/ Did they not glance on Thee!'[5] Indeed, Landon insists on exactly the female 'truth' Byron's speaker rejects as romantic, that is, unreal; for her, joy is an outward expression of the deep river of love and the romance of constancy, and leads directly to the Eve of St Agnes-like ritual depicted in 'Romance': 'Oh! Come to my slumber/ Sweet dreams of my love,/ I have hung the charmed wreath / My soft pillow above' (1–4). 'Romance', associated with superstition, dreams, and desire for what is absent (alternate versions of the unreal), is also infused with sadness, as the speaker attempts to make her night-time vision of love recompense her for daily neglect: 'Let sleep bring the image/ Of him far away;/ 'Tis worth all the tears/ I shed for him by day' (21–4). Romance functions as a more pleasant substitute for Reality – it is Byron's world of 'golden dreams', but where Byron can only escape by consigning Romance to its own destruction, Landon is both more direct and more subtle. The 'sweet dreams of my love!' (28) are shattered by the opening lines of 'Inconstancy': 'How vain to cast my love away/ On bosom false as thine' (1–2). The fantasy of love, the assertion of (female) constancy, lead inevitably in Landon's 'Songs' to (male) inconstancy; no more sanguine than Byron that Romance makes for happy endings, Landon reverses the players: man seduces and abandons, leaving woman with a cold heart, a new-found distrust of the romantic ideology, and an abiding interest in self-advancement. 'Truth' follows 'Inconstancy' and concludes a romance-laden panegyric on the attractions of the 'hidden Eden of the heart' with this realisation: 'I thought thus of the flowers, the moon,/ This fairy isle for you and me;/ And then I thought how very soon/ How very tired we should be' (17–20). Landon ends her 'Songs' with a 'matrimonial creed' that sees the final overthrow of romance – the speaker declares 'He must be rich whom I could love' (1), and old, and generous to a young wife. Without the melodramatic conjuring of a 'gulph' in which to dispatch Romance, Landon as effectively as Byron kills it off.

In these short poems, both poets more forthrightly reveal the mistrust, unease and dislike with which they view the romance, attitudes that belie the frequency with which both returned to the genre. 'To Romance' and 'Six Songs' consolidate, moreover, the themes which both poets continually treat in their romances: the perfidy or general trouble embodied by the opposite sex, a cynical depreciation of the worth and value of romantic – that is, heterosexual – love, the impossibility of happiness or stability. As with the romances discussed in the last chapter, Landon's and Byron's rely heavily on the death of key players, although here it is the more familiar female corpse who provides the impetus for action or emotion.[6] However, Landon and Byron do not merely write and rewrite violent romances; instead, they infuse their poems with change and transformation, both in characterisation and in form. As Jacqueline Rose notes, 'the affinity between representation and sexuality is not confined to the visual image';[7] these poems offer representations of sexuality dependent on an eccentric realignment of the classic love triangle. Both poets tilt the romance; they swing their sympathies away from male–female pairing, and they push the boundaries of the romance itself until it assumes a new shape – that of the melodrama. Peter Brooks recognises that melodrama 'generally operates in the mode of romance, though with its own specific structures and characters';[8] as this chapter will argue, under Byron and Landon the romance completes its transformation into melodrama, and in so doing allows for, even depends on, murder, sexual realignment, and the erection of impassable barriers: the separate spheres of gender.

Although the melodrama is usually defined as a dramatic form, dating in Britain to Thomas Holcroft's 1802 *A Tale of Mystery*, its components are not confined to the stage. Judith Pascoe characterises the 1790s treason trials as melodramatic, for instance, asserting that 'the key features of melodrama – ... heightened emotiveness in acting style and female victimization as subject-matter – predate [Holcroft's] crystallizing work' (57). Despite Pascoe's emphasis on 'acting style', one can see, even in her parenthesis, how aspects of melodrama permeate Byron's and Landon's work. The Giaour's many lines of confession or self-justification, for instance, are certainly 'heightened', while all of Byron's Eastern Tales depend on female victimisation. Similarly, Landon's 'The Venetian Bracelet' finds its energy in the character of Amenaïde who combines in herself heightened emotion and female victimisation (not to mention pure villainy). Because 'the melodrama' is so closely identified as a dramatic subgenre, however, it is necessary to describe how its characteristics apply to the poetry of Byron and Landon. They are not simply melodramatic – that is, silly and extravagant – in their romances; they also employ melodrama as a guiding trope, utilising its theatrical flair if not its purely dramatic credentials. The common understanding of melodrama – that it 'deal[s] in vulgar extravagance, implausible motivation, meretricious sensation and spurious pathos'[9] – provides a useful starting-point. Value judgements aside, extravagance, implausibility, sensation and pathos are by now familiar catchwords. Throughout this study, we have seen human relations constructed around these notions; indeed, it is one of the defining aspects of the romance that it is somehow different from 'real life', whether through setting, event or characterisation. What we expect from the melodrama is that it somehow romanticises romance itself, heightens the already high, injects drama into what is already theatrical. Brooks summarises prevailing wisdom when he states the 'melodrama at heart represents the theatrical impulse itself: the impulse toward dramatization, heightening, expression, acting out' (xi). In this way it escapes its stage-bound existence, becomes a way of being, a trait, communicated through the theatricality of the dialogic exchanges in Byron's Tales or of the feeling, participative narrator in Landon's poems. The melodramatic mode, then, allows poetry, and poetic speakers, to act out their own distress, fears, and tendencies towards violence.[10]

William Morse sees melodrama as an 'essentialist discourse' of which 'romantic subjectivity might be considered the ultimate refinement'; it 'suggests the reality of a world beyond representation'.[11] This indicates that melodrama allows for the voicing of the normally unspeakable, the enacting of subterranean desires, the poetic staging of inadmissible scenes.[12] Melodrama encourages the simultaneous expression and suppression of the unlawful, and it raises expectations of order within, despite, or dependent on disorder. Its characters are motivated by single impulses, undiluted by the uncertainty or hesitation that characterises tragedy (Smith 7–17 *passim*). More forcefully than the romance, it is 'ideologically counterproductive' (Morse 28) in that it plays on the desires and conventions of ideology and apes its mannerisms and disguises, but it also mocks its customs; the very regularity with which good wins out over evil, the hero successfully woos the heroine, and 'dream justice' (Smith 34) prevails serves to emphasise the lack of such order in the 'real world'. When Byron or Landon portray stock melodramatic scenarios, they simultaneously play along (order is re-established, usually through death), and play *with*, the lines of melodrama: the order they allow at poem's end is superficially ideologically defensible but also melodramatically complex. It is both of, and beyond, the world of melodrama. Therefore, even as melodrama invites definition, it eludes its own confines. Brooks's expansive description of melodrama indicates its flexibility: melodrama sees 'the indulgence of strong emotionalism; moral polarization and schematization; extreme states of being, situations, actions; overt villainy, persecution of the good, and final reward of virtue; inflated and extravagant expression; dark plottings, suspense, breathtaking peripety' (11–12). The poetry of Byron and Landon makes use of all these elements except the happy ending, in common with their fellow romancers discussed in previous chapters, and they energise the devilry of melodrama through a consistent, and persistent, reliance on full frontal violence: that is, for both Byron and Landon violence is not only a narrative option but a romantic requirement, and it undermines the formation of subjectivity encouraged, in Morse's view, by melodrama.

As I have indicated, however, Byron and Landon do not simply rewrite romance as melodrama. Instead, they take advantage of the melodrama's 'extreme conflicts' and 'extreme conclusions' (Smith 8) to ask questions about the nature – the naturalness – of romantic relations. In this they demonstrate melodrama's 'structural malleability', its willingness 'to incorporate the discourse of ... gender conflict'; it is, as Michael Hays and Anastasia Nikolopoulou argue, a 'process-like genre, that is, a genre that does not come to rest in fulfillment but, rather, presents a continually renewed realization'.[13] Under their poetic management, melodrama not only takes over for romance but it also recalibrates the parameters of gendered interaction. Romance, as previous chapters have argued, is built around uncontested sites of gendered behaviour translated into generic roles: hero, heroine, villain, and it is one of the markers of Romantic iconoclasm that so many writers of the period manipulate these certainties, even as they exploit their familiar appeal. The Della Cruscans, with their literary harem; Coleridge and Keats, each pursuing the romantic quest, neither satisfied with generic conformity; Robinson and Hemans, unable to support, or even to compose, a romance that allows the hero to survive: all defamiliarise the romance but none open up or question the romance of heterosexuality to the extent that Landon and Byron do. For, bolstering their tales, one finds melodramas not merely of failed relationships, but of the impossibility of heterosexuality. Expressed through the heightened sensationalism of murder, betrayal and suicide, Byron's and Landon's poetry renders opposite-sex attraction violently destructive.

They present this differently, however; Byron teases his readers with repeated examples of fatal devotion, superficially romantic but in each case triggered by or leading to a necessary homosocial conjoining, while Landon conveys a despair with the irresistibility of heterosexual love and its attendant loss of life. In *Romanticism and Gender*, Anne Mellor remarks on the prevalence of unhappy love stories in Landon's poetry and concludes that Landon 'insists upon the absolute division of the male and female spheres. ... Her poetry can construct only the private realm of female affections' (118). Built into Mellor's assertion is an assumption of limitation and a reliance on a dichotomy based on the patterns of gendered behaviour Mellor sees Landon as celebrating. However, this chapter questions the construction of Landon as confined by her exploration of love and romantic relations; instead, even as Landon reiterates her stories of doomed lovers and thwarted love, she draws on a very unBurkean notion of feminine beauty as informed and supported by violence. Landon conflates the 'good girl' and the femme fatale, creating heroines who as often turn their despair outward as inward, as soon murder as die. Landon's poetry depends on love, but it also explodes romance, substituting a world of betrayal and loss. In this way she suggests a femininity that thrives on loss and goes down fighting. Landon reinvents romance as melo-

drama, and disrupts what will, in later decades, become stock characters and situations by her inclusion of a knowing, participatory
narrative voice, empowered through the paradox of disastrous love.
Where Landon's melodrama depends on the strength of feminine
weakness, Byron's emerges from the overwrought and sensational
worlds dominated by the Giaour and others. Byron's conflicted and
despairing men, like Landon's equally despairing women, require
death: in this case, the death not of love or of one's rival in love, but
of the love-object. This allows an identification of masculinity with
excessive and ceaseless suffering over love, but without the inconve-
nience of a lover. Moreover, that neither Landon nor Byron shy away
from the explicit and drawn-out depiction of violence allows for an
intriguing and suggestive scenario: the drama of the romance and
violence plays itself out amid the ruins of chivalry, romanticised
gender roles, and literary cohesion.

Byron, writing in the 1810s, constructs his melodramas around the
absent bodies of dead women: Leila, Zuleika, Medora and Parisina are
the putative love-objects for his strong, alienated, compromised
'heroes'. In each poem, murder figures, but it is in his engagement
with violence that Byron institutes change, for the battles and feuds
his male characters indulge in mask a deeper connection than ever the
hero has established with his female lover. The very marginality of the
women's deaths serves as a comment on their importance to plot: for
Byron, the love triangle is only resolved through the woman's death
followed or accompanied by violent clashes between the men. Hero
and villain are blurred categories, and chivalry a mechanical response,
only enlivened when called up in its martial guise. The focus, then, is
not on the heterosexual love relationship, but the hostile homosociality found between men. Melodrama serves to emphasise the
heightened emotions and extreme situations that accomplish the
displacements of 'love' and 'hate'. Landon, writing a decade later, is
no less shy than Byron when it comes to violent situations, and she
too focuses on the disastrous consequences of heterosexual triangles.
Her innovation is to recast the role of rival; where Byron's men fight
each other, Landon's women, with the possible exception of
Amenaïde,[14] fight masculinity itself – they find themselves in competition with the very public sphere held so enticingly open to the men.
Like Byron, however, she (melo)dramatises the incompatibility of the
feminine and masculine worlds and insists on the destructiveness of
love and heterosexual interaction. In 1814, the *New British Theatre*
proposed that 'in the melo-drama the catastrophe is the physical

result of mechanical stratagem' (in Cox 27). In the poems discussed in this chapter, catastrophe is the direct result of the characters' adherence to the strictures of gender and the mechanics of genre, but both Byron and Landon suggest an alternative world to that of star-crossed lovers. In Byron, this otherworld is only discernible through the violent dispatching of the principle players, an ironic foretaste of the paradox of unscripted homosocial desire; in Landon, the otherworld is one always already denied by the endemic, destructive presence of love itself, which, siren-like, beckons its victims to their deaths.

'The confusion and subversion of the natural order of things':[15] Byron

For Coleridge, the melodrama represented the topsy-turvy world of un-nature, especially in its privileging of the ordinary man and woman over established higher classes; he saw that the melodrama only superficially ratified real-world values and that, at heart, it valued the confusing and mixing of roles and classes. Coleridge's fears may have been based in a desire to preserve a class-bound *status quo*, but his perception is valid nonetheless, especially when applied to Byron's romantic melodramas;[16] in these Tales Byron explores an otherworldly, subversive landscape that allows, even encourages, the substitution of homosocial bonding for heterosexual love. Byron's Tales are, famously, about thwarted love, and the torment experienced by the hero over what is most often a hidden, unspoken grief. The 'Byronic' hero codified by Peter Thorslev and described in Chapter 3 is as much a product of the immensely successful romantic melodramas of 1813–16 as he is derived from the despondent, melancholic Childe Harold. In his Eastern Tales, Byron presents the verities of romance, violently disrupted to produce what James Smith calls the melodrama of defeat, where the requisite happy ending is exchanged for catastrophe; in this version, the good are inevitably hurt by the bad, and events conspire to thwart resolution (Smith 56 *passim*). From 'The Bride of Abydos' (1813) to 'Parisina' (1816), the weight of events and predetermined hatreds and prejudices effectively sabotage any hope of a happy ending; characters wilfully pursue paths littered with risk and failure, guided by the *deus ex machina* of the poet himself. When read as a cluster, these poems reiterate the single point of doomed subjectivity: in each, the seriously flawed hero and the semi-justified villain move inexorably towards a moment of violent confrontation, while the heroine occupies a deeply compromised, literally marginalised space. Indeed, Byron's technique exemplifies Brooks's notion of 'occult meanings', the 'transfer [of] significance into another context' (9), where metaphor inhabits image to the extent that things are always both what they seem and beyond appearances altogether. For Byron, the occult meanings of his Eastern Tales gesture towards a world outside expression, though not outside representation; shadowing, then, the certainties of romance is an order of things that depends on a melodramatic reappropriation of the categories of love and desire.

It is a truism of canonical Romanticism that 'the Romantic hero in effect *creates* his loved one as an author would a character; she has no existence apart from his narcissistic perception of her as an extension of himself'.[17] But as Atara Stein goes on to note, it is because she functions as little more than an emanation[18] that the beloved's 'sexuality is so threatening; the Romantic hero ... wishes to deny his own physicality, to achieve the ideal. Thus, he is repulsed by female sexuality, and he must avoid contact with it at all costs in order to maintain his transcendent, superhuman condition' (190). Stein makes a useful point: the discomfort and ambivalence that accompanies expressions of strong desire in Byron's Tales suggest that it is not the female version-of-Self who energises the hero, but rather the antagonist; the true Other is he who provokes conflict. Despite the easy blame so often assigned to, say, Leila for the disasters that permeate the Tales, strife arises between men: woman is tangential, a superfluity. Jacqueline Rose offers this formulation: 'it is in the normal image of the man that our certainties are invested and, by implication, in that of the woman that they constantly threaten collapse' (232). 'Meaning', stability, the Known is self-evident, defined by the male body, so that by pushing the female body to the margins, by ejecting heterosexual romance (a dangerous mix of meaning and disintegration) and focusing on the melodrama of homosocial attraction, Byron actually creates the melodramatic romance of Self and Other(Self), in a subversive rewriting of society's rules of attraction. In the Eastern Tales, then, the heterosexual economy of the romance suffers repeated assaults, signified by the battered female body, and transmutes into a homosocial exchange, cemented by male-on-male violence.[19] Even here, the theatricality of melodrama obtains; as Victor J. Seidler has argued, masculinity, proved and ratified through sex, is a public performance, carried on in the public arena and subject to external checks, yet 'split' and 'fragmented'.[20] Byron's Tales, in the melodrama of male/male attraction, seek to repair these splits, and yet, as the fragmentary nature of 'The Giaour' shows, for instance, such efforts are not fully successful.[21]

Melodrama, therefore, enacts what Brooks calls 'the saying of self' (38); through melodrama emerges self-expression, cloaked in extremity. Byron allows for a 'saying of self' that the romance cannot countenance: a realignment of the romantic relationship and an enlivening of relations between men, paradoxically founded in murder. Paraphrasing Luce Irigaray, Trevor Hope describes the 'apparent heterosexual economy of desire imperative within the laws of kinship and language [that] in fact reproduces itself though a profound sexual *in*difference'.[22] In other words, heterosexuality historically is a device by which men disguise their abiding interest in men – as Irigaray herself calls it, an 'alibi'.[23] In 'The Giaour', 'The Corsair', 'Lara', 'The Bride of Abydos', and 'Parisina', action hinges on male/male contact: plot is activated by encounters between men, while heterosexual love resides in the descriptive realm, a passive bystander in the clashes precipitated by men's violent emotion. This is not to say that Byron's female characters do not suffer violence – indeed, their role *is* to suffer and, in most cases, be still, immobilised by the emotion of their men. The poems persist in picturing not their presence, but their absence, on a variety of literal and metaphorical levels: they die, are murdered, are mute, or erased, or even regendered. While Caroline Franklin is right to say that Byron 'recast[s] ... courtly love as violent forbidden passion' (33), she misidentifies the players in this passion: the violence is present between men, not between man and woman. The heroines may desire to be the focus of the men's attentions,[24] but in each case they are tangential to the poems' primary concern: the confrontation of 'hero' and 'villain'.

In 'The Bride of Abydos' and 'The Giaour', both from 1813, Byron offers an interesting contrast in method, based around fragmentation, revision, and the unspoken/unspeakable. 'Bride' reads like a dry run – a dress rehearsal – for the more intense melodrama of 'Giaour'; its cast goes through the motions of transferral, exposure and violence carried off more subtly in 'Giaour'. By dividing 'Bride' into two cantos, Byron forces revelation: like the turn in a sonnet, the space between Cantos 1 and 2 carries the burden of information half-revealed, of secrets half-guessed: 'Tonight, Zuleika, thou shalt hear/ My tale, my purpose, and my fear – / I am not, love! What I appear!'[25] Selim's provocative declaration creates mystery but refuses explanation, putting it off until 'tonight'; it is a familiar melodramatic technique to create suspense through a partial confession, and Byron emphasises the theatrical nature of Selim's 'tale' with the long stretches of dialogue: Selim both is, and represents, the mysterious stranger whose vital information proves the key upon which action hinges. To Zuleika, Selim has become at once known and not-known; he has deconstructed his identity as 'brother' but has not erected a new persona in its place. Again, the space between cantos serves as a borderland – in dramatic terms, it allows the poet to change the set, to shift alliances, to lower a new backdrop. The device of cantos assumes an order the poem's content does not necessarily support, lending a veneer of structure very different from that found in 'Giaour' with its multiple speakers and confusing shifts of scene. Indeed, in 'Bride' the poet takes pains to make sense, opening the poem with a kind of fairy-tale invocation of a land far away and strange:

> Know ye the land where the cypress and myrtle
>   Are emblems of deeds that are done in their clime,
> Where the rage of the vulture – the love of the turtle –
>   Now melt into sorrow – now madden to crime? –
>   . . . .
>
> 'Tis the clime of the East – 'tis the land of the Sun –
> Can he smile on such deeds as his children have done?
> Oh! wild as the accents of lovers' farewell
> Are the hearts which they bear, and the tales which they tell.
>   (I:1–4,16–19)

The lilting, singsong meter reflects the languid description, and hurries the reader past the small signs – 'crime' (4), or 'revenge', for instance, relegated to a footnote – that this descriptive paradise of scent and colour might be troubled. The narrator is in character as bard, the teller of a tale already composed: the romance, always already in existence, shadows the tale and provides generic structure, while the faint hint of menace shows the presence, from the first, of a kind of whispered, gestured-towards, constitutional violence.

The story in 'Bride' follows the familiar melodramatic lines of mistaken identity, jealousy, love and revenge. It explores passion and its aggregates: violence and aggression. If, as Jenni Calder argues, for Byron poetry 'was a way of making passion acceptable', or at least voiceable, we might read Selim's partial revelation at the end of Canto I as his attempt to move his passion, with its putative object, Zuleika, into the realm of possibility.[26] Calder goes on to say, however, that 'passion described, even implied, is passion tamed. Language, particularly written language, has a defusing effect at the same time that it has an inflating, self-enhancing tendency' (113). 'Bride', in its dual position as written (poem) and oral (tale with internal dialogue) attempts the juggling act of representing inflamed passions while simultaneously interpreting them: Byron's juxtaposition of the innocent, almost simple Zuleika, ignorant of passions and unable to withstand their first onslaughts; and the conflicted, vengeful Selim, the embodied secret, the living evidence of Giaffir's treachery, bespeaks a poetry dependent on paradox and deception. The order promised structurally competes with the disorder brought on by plot, even as Selim's passion, once spoken, becomes wild rather than tamed, releasing the underwritten aggression between Selim and Giaffir. True to Calder's premise, the omnipresent narrator ensures the equal but opposite reaction of Giaffir's fear and jealousy, the only possible answer to Selim's desire (Zuleika remains silent). The romantic love story figured by Selim and Zuleika is always countered by the melodrama that simmers between Selim and Giaffir. Indeed, the poem opens with declarations, not of love, but of hatred and contempt, as Giaffir taunts Selim to 'assume the distaff' with his 'less than woman's hand', and Selim shoots 'glances even of more than ire' at his father, as we readers are encouraged to call Giaffir (I:100, 99, 113). Byron sets up, but seems immediately to disallow, the male–male–female love triangle; by maintaining the illusion that Giaffir, Selim and Zuleika form a family, he undermines the power of sexual and romantic love. That Zuleika is never able successfully to comprehend Selim's transformation from sibling to lover underscores her marginality in the poem: Selim professes concern and love for her, but fixes his attention on Giaffir; he deliberately misapplies Zuleika's promise never to leave him despite her complete incomprehension at his change. Zuleika bases her promise on the fear that the Sultan to whom Giaffir plans to marry her is 'some foe' of Selim's; her 'if so' shows that her vow not to marry 'without [Selim's] free consent' comes not from desire for Selim, but desire for his approval (I:311, 312, 315). Self-effacingly, she only wants to please her 'friend' and 'guide' (I:320), but Selim, following his own internalised plot of desire and revenge, translates sisterly affection into romantic love, and the desire to please into a plight of troth. Were 'Bride' a straightforward romance, Zuleika should find that Selim's protestations awaken in her wifely desires; instead, she feels only confusion, her inability to understand Selim's oblique speech proof of her *lack* of romantic desire:

'Think not thou art what thou appearest!
  My Selim, thou art sadly changed;
This morn I saw thee gentlest, dearest,
  But now thou'rt from thyself estranged.
My love thou surely knew'st before,
It ne'er was less, *nor can be more.*
      . . . .

Thy cheek, thine eyes, thy lips to kiss,
Like this – and this – *no more than this,*
For, Alla! Sure thy lips are flame,
  What fever in thy veins is flushing?
My own have nearly caught the same,
  At least I feel my cheek too blushing.
      . . . .

I meant that Giaffir should have heard
  The very vow I plighted thee;
      . . . .

  Can this fond wish seem strange in me,
To be what I have ever been?
      . . . .

  What other can [I] seek to see
Than thee, companion of [my] bower,
  The partner of [my] infancy?
  (I:383–8, 394–9, 418–19, 422–4, emphasis added)

Zuleika's words illustrate her abiding desire for things to remain as they are, for love to remain chaste and familial, and her repeated questioning – 'Say, why must I no more avow?' (I:426) – indicate her rejection of the mystery Selim has invoked. That he chooses, not to answer, but to send her back to her 'tower's retreat' (I:453), the same domestic space to which Giaffir consigned her, demonstrates his similarity, rather than contrast, to his 'father'. Readers have now arrived at the gap between cantos, seething with the unexplained, the very muteness of its text speaking volumes.

Byron uses Canto I to set up the antagonism between Selim and Giaffir and to sketch in the 'romance' between Selim and Zuleika; in its reliance on mysterious vows, misunderstandings, and secrecy, however, the romance is already flimsier than the as-yet-unrevealed cause of the Selim/Giaffir rivalry. Giaffir's fragmented 'I would not trust that look or tone – / No – nor the blood so near my own – / That blood – he hath not heard – no more – / I'll watch him closer than before –' (I:140–3) resonates with Selim's declaration 'I am not, love! What I appear' and implies what Canto II will make clear: the meaningful emotional bond is that between Selim and Giaffir. Zuleika functions as a symbol of their hatred; her position on the triangle is that described by Eve Sedgwick: she exists to embody desire between men, but where Sedgwick concentrates on love, the Byronic triangle focuses on hate.[27] As Selim reveals, Giaffir is not his father, but his father's brother, enemy and murderer; Selim himself signifies the violence of that past family disruption and symbolises its longevity. The verbose explanation he offers Zuleika returns repeatedly to this violence rather than his romance, now legitimate, with Zuleika; indeed, she too can see only its violent implications for herself, voiced in terms of loss and fear:

> 'Oh! Not my brother! – yet unsay –
> God! Am I left alone on earth?
> To mourn – I dare not curse – the day
> That saw my solitary birth!
> Oh! thou wilt love me now no more!
> My sinking heart forboded ill;
> But know *me* all I was before,
> Thy sister – friend – Zuleika still.
> Thou led'st me here perchance to kill;
> If thou hast cause for vengeance – See!
> My breast is offer'd – take thy fill![28]
> Far better with the dead to be
> Than live thus nothing now to thee –
> Perhaps far worse – for now I know
> Why Giaffir always seem'd thy foe;
> And I, alas! am Giaffir's child,
> For whom thou wert contemn'd – reviled –
> If not thy sister – wouldst thou save
> My life – oh! bid me be thy slave!'
> (II:165–83)

I have quoted this at length to demonstrate that Zuleika's concerns rest in family connections, asexual and unromantic; to her lament

Selim makes only the cursory response 'My slave, Zuleika! – nay, I'm thine:/ But, gentle love, this transport calm', and within eleven lines has reaffirmed 'thy Sire's my deadliest foe' (II:184–5, 196). This preoccupies Selim, and fills up nine stanzas, during which Zuleika, 'mute and motionless,/ Stood like that statue of distress – / When, her last hope for ever gone,/ The mother hardened into stone' (II:491–4). Despite Selim's vows of romantic love, Zuleika consistently thinks, and is presented, in terms of family love, and this, much more than inscription alone, defuses the passion of love in their 'romance'; in this poem, the romance of family transmutes into melodrama of rivalry, the body – the fact – of Zuleika furnishing both cause and effect. When Giaffir finally appears and battle begins, Zuleika remains in the grotto in which she had met Selim and heard his tale of family destruction. Selim, meanwhile, goes to fight and join his comrades, only to be killed by Giaffir in another meaningful pause: 'Ah! wherefore did he turn to look/ For her his eye but sought in vain?/ That pause – that fatal gaze he took – / Hath doomed his death – or fixed his chain' (II:563–6). The poem climaxes in death, Selim's and Zuleika's, whose heart 'burst[s]' and eye 'close[s] before his own'; unable to bear the revelations, she simply expires (II:619, 620). And yet her death is marginal, literally and figuratively: the action and the focus is on the death of Selim at Giaffir's hands, while Zuleika is reduced to parts, 'the only heart – the only eye –' (II:615) – unnamed, barely remarked. Even, then, as the poet allows us a glance at Zuleika, he drains her of significance in the text; the 'marble stone' laid to commemorate her death transports itself overnight to 'where Selim fell', so that Zuleika's final memorial recognises only Selim (II:717, 722). There meaning resides, melodramatic talisman marking not love, but death; not forgiveness, but rancour. The poem revolves around the struggle between Giaffir and Selim, fought around but ultimately unconcerned with Zuleika: she is incidental, a romantic footnote to the body of the text.[29]

'Bride' gestures towards the creation of full-blown melodramatic conflict, but has not yet relinquished the romance, hence Zuleika's odd status; she is there and not there, a catalyst yet inessential to the melo-romantic plot. In 'The Giaour' Byron presents a more coherent melodrama of violence, paradoxically accomplished through the rhetoric of fragments. Jerome McGann has called 'Giaour' an 'evident masquerade': 'masquerade is interpersonal and social',[30] taking place publicly, a means of facilitating social contact while maintaining the privacy of personal passions. The poem, with its changing speakers and points of view, allows for the constant intermingling of voices, playing parts and conforming to types, encouraged by the masquerade; it is a kind of costumed melodrama, a performance based on audience participation and on their willingness to gloss over the dramatically unromantic nature of the Giaour/Hassan/Leila love triangle. As with 'Bride', this relationship pivots on the woman, but unlike 'Bride', she is absent before the poem even begins. The well-known panegyric to Greece that opens the poem allows the poet to establish the ground rules of gender, filtered through politics: Greece is persistently feminised, a 'fair clime' that 'lend[s] to loneliness delight' (7, 11), comparable in sensations evoked to the romance of 'the attachment of the nightingale to the rose' (Byron's footnote). Overrun by the tyrants of Lust and Rapine, 'hers is the loveliness in death' (l. 94); Greece is now the equivalent of a fallen woman with an illustrious past betrayed by the sordid present. Considering the status of 'Giaour' as a romance, the speaker's avowal – 'no more her sorrows I bewail,/ Yet this will be a mournful tale' (164–5) – suggests that the 'her' that is Greece foreshadows the human female whose entrance in the poem coincides with her exit: fair Leila, the unnamed 'it' whose dispatching is accomplished in a single line. Greece, in part responsible for her own downfall, prefigures Leila, and the speaker's lengthy turn serves to introduce both the notion of female culpability, and the necessity to turn from it to another tale. 'Women', to quote Calder, 'enhance the hero, but are expendable' (120): hence Leila's equivocal position; she serves to bring together Hassan and the Giaour, but is never actually there herself – that is, she is only ever spoken of, always already absent.

Leila, then, not even named until line 444 (70 lines after her death), is the cipher by which Hassan and the Giaour encode their mutual attraction – although perhaps repulsion is the more suitable word. Her colour is white,[31] itself invisible and empty, whether she is the 'speck of white' sinking like a 'lessening pebble', or the post-humous memory with 'fair cheek', white feet, and 'whiter neck' (382, 381, 493, 501, 511). Leila lacks blood: she is all white flesh, insubstantial, a ghost even before her death, a 'bundle' after. The speaker links the recital of Leila's sinking with a warning to Beauty:

> So Beauty lures the full-grown child
> . . . .
> If won, to equal ills betrayed,
> Woe waits the insect and the maid,
> A life of pain, the loss of peace,

From infant's play, or man's caprice:
The lovely toy so fiercely sought
Has lost its charm by being caught,
For every touch that wooed its stay
Hath brush'd its brightest hues away
Till charm, and hue, and beauty gone,
'Tis left to fly or fall alone.

(396, 400–9)

Here, again, the speaker gestures towards Leila's insubstantiality in the plot; if we are to make any sense of this aside, we can only see it as a veiled indication of Leila's alternative storyline: to be discarded by the Giaour. She is instead killed by Hassan for her 'faithlessness',[32] at which point the romance necessarily concludes, at least that conducted by the heterosexual couple. It is Leila's death that fires the passionate hatred of the Giaour for Hassan, and Leila's life that focused Hassan's attention on the Giaour: 'Her mate – stern Hassan, who was he?/ Alas! that name was not for thee!' (517–18). Although Marlon Ross asserts that the Byronic hero requires 'the presence of the feminine',[33] it is plain that only Leila's absence will do, and that the Giaour substitutes vows of love for vows of violence, his attention settled on stern Hassan; in this way 'Giaour' enacts what Juliet Flower MacCannell calls 'the regime of the brother', the potent exchange of patriarchy for fraternity.[34] As much as Selim's rage against Giaffir is that of the dispossessed son against the usurping father, so too the hatred of the Giaour and Hassan rests on their footing as equals. Again, Leila is the absent signifier; she exists – or rather, ceases existing – to facilitate and instigate their contact. Once Hassan has proved his interest by depriving the Giaour of Leila, the Giaour responds by depriving Hassan of life. The Giaour and Hassan, seemingly so different, follow the same philosophy of violence and revenge, and in this way they function as brothers-in-arms, 'mutually complicating self and other in a contingency so radical as to elide claims to an autonomous subject or object', in Laura Claridge's words.[35] In the partnership cemented over Leila's missing body, neither Hassan nor the Giaour emerge vindicated; each fights in her name,[36] but both fight for themselves, provoked by '*mutual* wrong/ And fate and fury' (634–5, emphasis added). The mutual wrong plays out the mutual implication described by Claridge.

'Giaour', then, is ruled not by the romance of lost love, or even the thwarted and disrupted romance described in previous chapters, but by a melodramatic privileging of hate, vengeance, and subversive attraction. The poet performs the substitution of love for hate by emphasising the attractions of violent emotion:

> But Love itself could never pant
> For all that Beauty sighs to grant,
> With half the fervour Hate bestows
> Upon the last embrace of foes,
> When grappling in the fight they fold
> Those arms that ne'er shall lose their hold;
> Friends meet to part – Love laughs at faith –
> True foes, once met, are joined till death!
>
> (647–54)

Byron appropriates the marriage ideal for this meeting of enemies,[37] but he goes further; not only are the Gaiour and Hassan 'joined till death'; they also share attitudes and beliefs (religion aside). They are matched in an ideology of homosociality that can see woman only as an appendage. When the Giaour bends over the dead Hassan 'with brow/ As dark as his that bled below' (673–4), he mirrors Hassan physically; when he confesses to the monk, he echoes Hassan's philosophy:

> ... if it dares enough, 'twere hard
> If passion met not some reward –
> No matter how – or where – or why,
> I did not vainly seek – nor sigh:
> Yet sometimes with remorse in vain
> I wish she had not lov'd again.
> She died – I dare not tell thee how;
> But look! – tis written on my brow!
>   ....
>
> Still, ere thou dost condemn me – pause –
> Not mine the act, though I the cause;
> *Yet did he but what I had done*
> *Had she been false to more than one;*
> Faithless to him – he gave the blow,
> But true to me – I laid him low;
> Howe'er deserv'd her doom might be
> Her treachery was truth to me.
>
> (1050–7, 1060–7 emphasis added)

He is most haunted by the battle with Hassan, although he consistently regards it in the light of Leila's death:

> 'Much in his visions mutter he
> Of maiden 'whelmed beneath the sea;
> Of sabres clashing – foemen flying,
> Wrongs avenged – and Moslem dying.
> On cliff he hath been known to stand
> And rave as to some bloody hand
> Fresh sever'd from its parent limb,
> Invisible to all but him,
> Which beckons onward to his grave,
> And lures to leap into the wave.'
>
> (822–31)

It is significant that Leila's death merits only one line, while the vision haunting the Giaour is that of Hassan's severed hand – severed, of course, by the Giaour. What Butler calls 'the hero's terrible sense of sexual guilt and loss' (92) rests as much on the loss of Hassan as of Leila; the Giaour concentrates both fury and desire on his mirror image, as much villain-hero as he is himself. The wild battle, the curses, the cries, the tableaux of bloody violence – 'sabre shiver'd to the hilt,/ Yet dripping with the blood he spilt' (655–6) – the set scenes of mountain pass and monastery: all invoke the excesses of the melodrama, called into use to disguise and yet accentuate the fateful meeting of the Giaour and Hassan. Brooks says that 'the desire to express all seems a fundamental characteristic of the melodramatic mode' (4), and certainly the Giaour's more than 300 lines of confession attest to his powers of speech. He perhaps reveals more than he intends, or understands, however, when he casts himself and Hassan as from the same mould, and when he describes his vain search 'to find,/ The workings of a wounded mind' (1089–90). Though Hassan may not agree, the Giaour sees himself and Hassan as linked, and desires to find in Hassan the same 'wounded mind' he carries. His 'Leila – Each thought was only thine! –' (1181) rings less with conviction than with a certain hollow desire: Leila and Hassan are joined in the Giaour's imagination, so much so that the sight of her 'form' at the poem's end provokes the Giaour to assert immediately 'But *he* is dead – Within the dell/ I saw him buried where he fell;/ He comes not – for he cannot break/ From earth – why then are *thou* awake?' (1302–5, emphasis added). The reader recognises that for the Giaour, the heterosexual romantic bond and the homosocial bond are intimately linked. They draw, and define, each other, and both are predicated on moments of extreme brutality, the murder of the desired, and the plunge into sensation, violence and theatrical declarations of hatred and revenge. By blurring roles, by exploring the attraction of like to like filtered through the savage, yet silent, elimination of the female, Byron encourages a reading of 'The Giaour' as a romantic melodrama, 'cast[ing] [virtue's] very survival into question ... obscur[ing] its identity' (Brooks 29). The poem ends, paradoxically, by affirming 'He pass'd – nor of his name and race/ Hath left a token or a trace,/ Save what the father must not say/ Who shrived him on his dying day;/ This broken tale was all we knew/ Of her he lov'd, or him he slew' (1329–34). 'What the Father must not say' comprises exactly that which we have just finished reading: the oral and written clash again, producing the illogical situation that the poem's story, as related by the Giaour, is forbidden knowledge (as indeed it must be), and yet it is also common knowledge. The lines between the unspeakable, the unspoken, and the speechless waver, generating the melodramatic 'text of muteness' described by Brooks.

Attraction and repulsion thus join the congregation of the compelling taboo in Romantic poetry. In describing the parameters and uses of incest in Romanticism, for instance, Alan Richardson has noted that

> when the Romantics portray an erotic relationship ... the ideal they look towards is a total sympathetic fusion. Such sympathy cannot come about spontaneously, through an intuitive recognition of spiritual harmony, but must be developed through experience and shared associations.... The Romantic poet is drawn to mingle [erotic and sibling] love by a fascination with the power of sympathy, but that power is broken by the unconscious horror of incest, and the fascination turns to guilt or revulsion shortly before or shortly after the union is consummated.[38]

In 'The Giaour', all that Leila and the Giaour share is religious belief. They are both Christians, but even here the resemblance is only passing, as Byron emphasises when he colours Leila white and the Giaour black. The deepest shared experience – Richardson's 'sympathetic fusion' – is that between Hassan and the Giaour: as men, they share masculinity itself, and as the Gaiour makes plain, they both regard Leila as a possession, as a trophy, rather than as a true love;

both define love for a woman through images of ownership and of competition between men. 'Yet did he but what I had done/ Had she been false to more than one' (1062–3): the Giaour faults not Hassan's logic, but rather Hassan's choice of object for his violent revenge. As Daniel P. Watkins observes, 'it becomes apparent through the narrative that [Leila's] value depends exactly on [the Giaour's] ability to take her from Hassan for himself and to possess her entirely',[39] a formulation dependent not on Leila's centrality for the Giaour, but on Hassan's; the point, for the Gaiour, is what Hassan *has* rather than who Leila *is*. Leila stands in as the conveniently feminine, yet equally conveniently dead, substitute, an embodiment of the Hassan/Giaour relationship.[40] That relationship provides the *raison d'être* of the romantic melodrama energising the poem. Even as incestuous consummation – the heterosexual meeting of like with like – turns love to revulsion, so too homosocial consummation: expressed through violence and the hypermasculine activity of battle. The bloody dispatching of Hassan, the repellent picture of his 'lowering' 'unclos'd eye' (670, 669), and the transformation of body to corpse figure another version of the 'unconscious horror' described by Richardson. Thereafter, the Giaour's guilt, loss and melancholy revolve around Hassan as much as Leila, though articulated negatively (as they must be), and it is, finally, less surprising than fitting that, when confronting the vision of Leila at the poem's end, the Giaour looks around for stern Hassan as well, his partner in hate. To quote Watkins again, '"The Giaour" is excessively melodramatic and overtly escapist ... [and] in its final form it remains disturbingly fragmented' (874): in its attempt to escape the romance of compulsory heterosexuality, it turns instead to the melodrama, but even here the alternative to the romance remains unspeakable. The best that can be achieved is a fragmentary romantic melodrama, with no survivors, and with its secrets haltingly, yet effectively, maintained.

In 'The Giaour', then, Byron offers his most fully worked through, yet, with its competing narrators, obliquities of plot and sheer poetic density, most complexly fragmented alternative to romance; his subsequent Eastern tales – 'The Corsair', 'Lara', and 'Parisina', for example – are both more coherent as poems and less full as narratives of homosociality. And yet, each reiterates the 'Bride'/'Giaour' ethos that subordinates heterosexual romance to violent homosocial contact. The Eastern Tales portray women as little more than pawns, markers in the battle between men, Mellor's 'series of female corpses'.[41] It may be true that in 'The Corsair' (1814) 'love is one of the central fields of expression of the hero's personality', but it proceeds destructively: the semi-adulterous kiss with Gulnare inexorably means Medora's death: 'It was enough – she died – what recked it how?' (3:625).[42] Indeed, love and violence are intertwined in this poem – Gulnare proves hers, for instance, through the 'unsexing' act of murder. Again, however, the unremarked central relationship is that between Conrad and Seyd; Conrad rushes from Medora's arms to Seyd's more martial embrace and the consummation of their destructive feelings through battle. In this relationship, Seyd is the enigmatic odalisque, defined almost solely through his silences once the battle has begun, and waiting to die, although he does not know this: 'Within the Haram's secret chamber sate/ Stern Seyd, still pondering o'er his Captive's fate;/ His thoughts on love and hate alternate dwell,/ Now with Gulnare, and now in Conrad's cell' (3:131–4). Stern Seyd, like stern Hassan, conflates love and hate and, as his threatening response to Gulnare's pleas on Conrad's behalf show, elides the boundaries of enemy and friend. But it is Gulnare's murder of Seyd that focuses the poem's shifting sexual alliances, for this loss, more than that of liberty or of Medora's life, signals Conrad's transformation from active to passive: his hand 'had lost its firmness, and his voice its tone' (3:540). Byron extends his description of Conrad's turmoil to a distracting degree (it occupies stanzas 13–17), and certainly Conrad explains his change to himself in terms of Gulnare's betrayal of her femininity and his part in her crime, but nonetheless, even as Conrad has lived a life of violence and confrontation, he has required an object on which to focus, and it is his loss of Seyd, rather than Medora, that provokes his change. As in 'Lara', the unsexed (or cross-dressed) woman is tangential to the concentrated hatred between men, fuelled by melodramatic reliance on images of unnamed treachery, irrational violence, and 'dramatic confrontation and peripety' (Brooks 25). In 'Lara' (1814), Kaled's unmasking – itself a melodramatic development – is shunted to near the poem's end; the Lara/Otho quarrel dominates Canto Two (Canto One is used to establish character), from the men's mutual 'bar[ing]' of 'willing weapons' (II:iii:34) to their subsequent focused, mutual hatred and warring.[43] It is battle between men, not romantic love, that fuels these poems: repeatedly, men turn to, find their fullest existence in, the public sphere of violence, where they join like with like and progress to the expected denouement: violent death, the only permitted expression (or outcome?) of homosocial attraction.

'Parisina' (1816) completes the cycle, and adds only the twist of incest, not of blood but by law. By creating Parisina as Hugo's love initially before claimed by Azo ('thy bride/ ... / Thou know'st for me was destined long. / Thou saw'st, and coveted'st her charms' [253, 255–6], says Hugo), Byron redirects the conflict inward: incest signifies not irresistible romantic love but unchecked male–male aggression and rivalry.[44] Like Leila, Parisina exists to focus the hatred between Azo and Hugo; romance is submerged in the melodrama of revenge, sought both by Hugo on his mother's account and Azo on his own. Parisina's marginality is confirmed by her silence in the text: after her drama-inducing 'mutter' of 'a name she dare not breathe by day' (71, 72), her only other utterances are a 'low hollow groan', 'one long shriek', and a 'shrill', 'wild' 'woman's shriek' (344, 347, 489, 498). Significant in their wordlessness, Parisina's sounds highlight the extended speeches given to Azo, Hugo and the speaker himself; from the start, Parisina is 'still, and pale, and silen[t]', 'all pale and still', and puts up no resistance to the narrator's judgement that she is 'the living cause of Hugo's ill' (147, 326, 327). This nod to convention incompletely masks the true cause of Hugo's troubles – his father's inadequacies; Parisina's silence and hidden fate (she merely disappears) suggest she is purely functional. Incest, then, represents the unspeakable closeness of Azo and Hugo, a father–son pair whose most significant relationship is with each other. Ironically enough, although 'Parisina' signals the end of Byron's explorations of romantic melodrama, it is the least satisfying, the least coherent in its construction of the male–male bond. It is as if, by telling the story again and again, Byron's copies get fainter and fainter: the outline remains but the details have become blurred, distorted, almost obliterated. What Brooks calls the text of muteness is also invoked by James Soderholm's concept of 'active forgetfulness', the 'creation of new values or the transvaluation of old ones'. This allows for the creation of a 'new language (a new vocabulary) for reweaving one's web of beliefs and desires'.[45] In telling and retelling his Tale, Byron recasts the heterosexual romance as the melodrama of homosociality, and yet he relates it increasingly unsuccessfully. The Eastern Tales are an exercise in repeated forgetting: the same story repeatedly told, with much the same outcome. As an attempt to change the established narrative pattern of the romance, the Tales successfully redirect the attractions of the heterosexual love story, instituting the melodrama of shared experience, an exploration of homosocial bonding only voiceable through violence. For Byron, violence is both a useful narrative element and an essential structural device; what Laura Claridge calls his 'healthy appetite for his own fictions of total divestiture' (211) enforces the repeated exploration, and destruction, of sustained homosocial bonding, of desire between men. Because romance between men is not speakable, Byron turns to the melodrama and its potential for signifying silences.

'Grief, disappointment, the fallen leaf, the faded flower, the broken heart, the early grave':[46] Letitia Landon

Landon, contemporary of Hemans, died in 1838, and in her we find the ultimate Romantic Victorian,[47] romancer, melodramatist, biographer of love and violator of its softer comforts; she was 'deeply read in Byron' whose 'life and writings were the dominant influence on her own work and career. She inherited the scepticism for which his name would be the byword', and she directed her sceptical gaze on romance and its ramifications (McGann and Riess, 17, 18). Ironically enough for a poet criticised in her own time and now as a disciple of love,[48] Landon embeds in her poetry distrust and disillusion, and provokes repeated confrontations with the stereotype of Woman Writing Romance: like Hemans, she invests love with death, although where Hemans allows only the mother to invade the heterosexual binary, Landon utilises both same-sex rivals, and culture itself, as the melodramatic twist to her tale. Byron's interest lay in redirecting romantic energy from heterosexuality to homosociality; he adapted the melodrama to transformative ends, using its excesses, twinning them with violent and bloody deaths, merging attraction and repulsion in a compulsive meeting of like with like, a compulsive retelling of the tale of negative desire. Landon, however, uses melodrama not to allow the unlawful, but to dramatise the dark excesses of love on the female body, to release the violence of hatred in the otherwise properly feminine, and to encourage the destruction of romance. Heterosexual desire underpins her romances, but it acts implosively; when Landon declares that she has 'always sought to paint [love] as self-denying, devoted, and making an almost religion of its truth' (*Venetian Bracelet*, 'Preface', vi–vii), one sees the skill with words that has led Harriet Kramer Linkin to describe her as 'the controlling female poet who effects an aesthetic liminality that frees her from the limits imposed on the specularized body her [poetic] character[s] represen[t]'.[49] Landon uses reassuringly conventional diction, but it is the literal truth that her version of Love denies, even erases, the body (through death); is 'devoted' in its zealous, fanatical and purposefully destructive sense; and comprises a religion in its rituals, rites and superstitions. And yet, as is necessary for a poet who writes for a living and who must, like Hemans and Robinson before her, please a fickle audience, Landon veils her violent impulses: hostility is rendered as tragedy, and premeditation trivialised as hysteria. In so doing, Landon establishes the melodrama as the only possible genre for love: tales of mistaken identity, fatal mistakes and noble orphans abound, all in the service of the religion of love. Landon uses melodramatic situations and domesticised violence to ridicule human pretensions to romantic happiness; in her poems, successful love is as unattainable as masculine contentment is in Byron's.

To activate her tales, Landon draws on cultural stereotypes of gender; in Mellor's memorable phrase, she 'exhausts the beautiful', playing on expectations of femininity, female authorship and female responses to love, characterised (by Byron most famously) as central to women's existence.[50] Mellor, however, sees in Landon's technique a complicity with social mores; in her readings, Landon 'work[s] from *within* an essentialist construction of the female as beautiful and loving' (120). While it is undeniable that, as Mellor notes, Landon 'insists upon the absolute division of the male and female spheres' (118), she does so in a more active way than Mellor allows for: she works, not 'within', but *with* essentialist constructions, exploring the results of acculturation, exposing the risks of wholesale reliance on love. She portrays the spheres of masculine and feminine lifestyles not from the blinkered perspective of one trapped within 'the private realm of female affections' (Mellor 118), but from the omniscient position of narrator and poet, one aware enough to recognise the market value of romance even as she refutes its self-referentiality:

> with regard to the frequent application of my works to myself, considering that I sometimes portrayed love unrequited, then betrayed, and again destroyed by death – may I hint the conclusions are not quite logically drawn, as assuredly the same mind cannot have suffered such varied modes of misery. However, if I must have an unhappy passion, I can only console myself with my own perfect unconsciousness of so great a misfortune.
>
> (*Venetian Bracelet*, 'Preface', vii–viii)

In other words, Mellor's entrapped poetess represents simply a persona employed by Landon to demonstrate her poetic fitness – she writes what she knows (but don't believe all you read). However, accompanying her witty disclaimer to being the unfortunate victim of her own scenarios of failed love are her poems – tragic, romantic, melodramatic: accumulations of proof that Love itself 'necessitates' the separation of spheres, as I discuss below. '[D]arker strains ... [and the] haunting omnipresence of death' (Curran 189) freely roam her poetry, imagery correlated with the mixing of spheres; the violence that infiltrates all love relationships functions as an indication that the exaggeration of gender and the perceived need for separate spheres causes actual bodily harm. Landon's melodramatic romances culminate in moments of crossing over. Therefore, in her poems, she dramatises the ramifications of a cultural insistence on separate spheres by repeatedly showing the danger inherent in their joining. Melodrama resides in the excesses of emotion and plot contingent on declarations of love – declarations always doomed from the moment of utterance, since they signal the momentary meeting of spheres as well as of bodies. Her experienced and cynical narrator can conceive of no viable romantic attachments, and so continually constructs worlds wherein desire irresistibly invites violence, while love reveals itself as the mask for betrayal and destruction. In this way, violence replaces love, and by manipulating stereotypes of emotion Landon frees herself to reveal the inadequacies of gender. Where Byron, then, creates a melodrama of unspeakable passions, Landon wields the melodrama of defeat to expose the damage inherent in separating spheres, and she does so by allowing the violence intrinsic to a divided society to redound on its willing inhabitants. She poisons the spheres, renders them fatal to the opposite sex, and thereby hastens the demise of romance itself.

For Landon, gender is the worst enemy of love. Byron, although transformative and discontent, still worked within conventions of gender: he wrote men's men and men's women. Landon, too, populates her poems with stock characters, easily recognisable to a twentieth-century audience familiar with theatrical stereotypes, but she goes further than Byron: for her, gender is necessarily both self- and other-destructive. For Landon, poetry is the vehicle whereby she challenges society to justify its morals, and her disillusionment is evident in her repeated tragic outcomes. Landon's *narrator* is complicit with society, rather than the poet, who deploys the narrative voice as a participant in her romances. As McGann and Riess realise, 'Landon's greatest subject [was] *dis*satisfaction with her epoch's satieties and satisfactions' (*Selected Writings* 30): far from reiterating 'love, and love', she exposes it, accuses it of murder, and executes it in the courtroom drama underpinning her romances, each of which is further evidence of love's criminality. Backing love is the societal mandate for division, figured mainly by gender and symbolised by separate spheres. As Isobel Armstrong says, 'the simpler the surface of the poem, the more likely it is that a second and more difficult poem will exist beneath it'.[51] Landon uses conventional imagery to pillory convention; she borrows sensation from melodrama to rile her romances, and to irritate Love into giving up its secret: its destructiveness for women and men. But because she does not let her narrator in on this project, the poem seemingly pursues and replicates its plotted concerns, a centripetal narrative velocity leading readers ever further in. Landon reserves her prefatory space for her author's voice; she narrates the poem in her poetess's voice. The dedicated serial reader may come to understand that in the repeated scenes of despair, grief and death Landon builds up her 'more difficult poem'; the melodrama may contain meaning, or only house emotions. Landon challenged her culture to remedy the damage caused by an expedient acceptance of hierarchy and the false chivalry of separate spheres, and in this way she performs the most difficult task of romance: the doomed defence of the weakest. In the deaths suffered by her women and men, the issue of who loves who is in the end subordinated to a disquisition on Love itself, and the main witness called against its cultural monopoly is the melodrama.

In 'The Venetian Bracelet' (1829), Landon foregrounds her theme of the destructive nature of heterosexual love by contrasting the internal ravages of consuming violent emotion with its murderous outward expression. Devoting herself to love, Amenaïde, the young and beautiful heroine, plays out a role predestined to end in tragedy; as with all her romances, in 'Venetian Bracelet' Landon allows not surprise, but familiarity, to guide her plot, and in so doing exposes the truth of love's danger. Within the poem, characters, settings and plot are all subordinate to the intertextual preoccupation with the irresistibility of love and its automatic, unavoidable failure; as she says in 'Roland's Tower' (discussed below), 'they loved; – they were beloved' (93). But the sensation of being in love is, in Landon, the catalyst for catastrophe – something happens when a woman and a man feel and declare love, a kind of chemical reaction that adduces only, and ever, violence. In 'Venetian Bracelet', Landon begins her tale by apostrophising Italy, much as Byron treats Greece in 'The Giaour': 'Another tale of thine! Fair Italie – / What makes my lute, my heart, aye turn to thee?' (1–2). Italy is to Landon as Homer is to Keats: the unknown yet vital signifier, mediated through others' representations, omnipresent as the necessary corollary to a certain kind of poetry, a certain kind of plot. Not knowing the language or the cities of Italy does not prevent Landon from writing of them; indeed, the poem's first stanza contains a credible description of what Landon affirms she does not know, yet finds herself returning to. Italy functions as the unreal – 'Thou art not stamped with that reality/ Which makes our being's sadness, and its thrall!' (23–4) – and therefore gives licence to romance, yet it paradoxically provides the setting for a tale Landon portrays as all too real, and too frequently betrayed love. Authorising romance, Landon's fantasy Italy escapes its comforting identity as unreal and free from life's 'sadness' as soon as the narrator introduces the idea of sadness, 'for e'en on this bright soil/ Grief has its shadow, and care has its coil' (57–8). Despite Italy's initial status as the antidote to grief and care, Landon inexorably reveals its participation in sadness; if not already 'stamped with reality', Italy receives the impress by the narrator herself, who seems impelled to invade Eden. And yet, since Italy always already contained grief, it seems more to the point to note that Landon does not so much impose, as uncover grief, and in so doing reiterates the inescapabiity of love gone wrong. Moreover, she has a project, reminiscent of the value of the vicarious described by Anna Letitia Barbauld and discussed in Chapter 1: 'we rise up less selfish, having known/ Part in deep grief, yet that grief not our own' (73–4). Landon has manoeuvred violence and tragedy from 'real life' to the unreal, to record an object lesson in emotions untrammelled: the melodrama shortly to unfold, then, is part fable, part entertainment, part revelation; the Italy of 'Venetian Bracelet' serves as the backdrop to an exploration of female violence. The 'female Byron' directs our attention to a tale as dependent on, yet revelatory of, conventions of gender as any Eastern tale.[52]

In 'Venetian Bracelet', Landon offers an initial romantic tableau complete in all particulars: an attractive young pair, 'she with her eyes cast down, for tears were there,/ Glittering upon the eyelash, though unshed;/ He murmuring those sweet words so often said/ By parting lover' (76–9). Landon relies on readers steeped in romance to supply the dialogue; here, she is motivated by the visual suitability of the couple, whose youth, beauty and pathos mark them as the young lovers soon to be parted by circumstance. They are stock melodramatic characters,[53] and as such at this point are rendered completely visually, especially Amenaïde, whose description hints at another melodramatic convention:

The girl was beautiful; her forehead high
Was white as are the marbled fanes that lie
On Grecian lands, making a fitting shrine
Where the mind spoke; the arch'd and raven line
Was very proud ...

    ....

She wore the peasant dress, – the snowy lawn
Closer around her whiter throat was drawn,
A crimson bodice, and the skirt of blue
So short, the fairy ankle was in view;
The arm was hidden by the long loose sleeve,
    But the small hand was snow; around her hair
A crimson net, such as the peasants weave,
    Bound the rich curls, and left the temples bare.
She wore the rustic dress, but there was not
Aught else in her that mark'd the rustic's lot:
Her bearing seem'd too stately, though subdued
By all that makes a woman's gentlest mood –
The parting hour of love.

               (81–5, 88–99, emphasis added)

Landon encourages the specularisation of Amenaïde; she holds our attention, is the poem's focus, while Leoni, her lover, is little more than a prop, the necessary adjunct to Amenaïde's deep emotion. Love, too, is stereotyped, described by the experienced narrator in world-weary tones that bode ill for happy endings: 'They loved with such deep happiness and truth, –/ .... / They parted trustingly; they did not know/ The vanity of youthful trust and vow' (115, 123–4). Even as she introduces the lovers, the narrator invites sympathy for their inevitable lorn state, and shunts the romance to the past. Amenaïde and Leoni have already fallen in love, and that love is already fated to end, just as Leoni is fated to 'spring upon his snow-white steed' (133) and go to war, and Amenaïde is fated to suffer anxiety, fear, dread, and woe: 'And these, Amenaïde, were all for thee' (154). The speaker uses the poem's first lines to establish that her story is an old one, and to squeeze in the expected moments of love, loss, and restored identity, for no sooner does Leoni leave and Amenaïde reflect on her orphaned rustic status than her nurse thrusts her into a group of strangers who call her Countess and seemingly remove the only obstacle in her union with Leoni – her class-position. Landon is in a hurry: she compresses parting and revelation into Part I of the poem's 14,[54] gathering for her readers the necessary players, sketching the necessary events, and, importantly, combining Amenaïde's necessary depth of emotion with 'pride'. Glennis Stephenson notes that 'Love is, indeed, at the very center of Landon's poetic universe',[55] but she does not credit Landon with much finesse: while 'Venetian Bracelet' is 'about' love betrayed and the woman scorned, it is also about the clash between romance and reality, as suggested by the opening appeal to Italy. What we have read so far is romance, which Landon proceeds to complicate.

Part II opens with another portrait of Amenaïde, changed in rank but not in attractions. We learn that Leoni 'was return'd, with all war could confer/ Of honourable name, to home and her' – and yet not quite to her, as instead of rushing lover-like to her arms, 'Leoni would tonight be in the hall/ Where Count Arezzi held his festival' (223–4, 225–6). Amenaïde salves her 'moment's grief' that they should 'meet first in a careless crowd' with her pride 'that he should see how well she could beseem/ Her present rank, yet keep her early dream' (230, 229, 231–2). Landon at this point assumes Amenaïde's point of view so that readers see Amenaïde's sincerity, but she also foreshadows trouble in Leoni's strange absence, and sure enough, Part III balances another visual emphasis on Amenaïde's looks ('"How beautiful she looks this evening!" burst/ From every lip' [247–8]) with Leoni's corresponding betrayal: 'sudden came Arezzi to her side – / "Look there, the Count Leoni and his bride!"' (283–4). It has become evident that Landon intends each section to represent a tableau vivant, and each to advance the melodrama by touching only on the most visually telling scenes: I gives us a combination of Young Love/Parting/Virtue Rewarded, II presents Awaiting the Lover's Return, III sets up The Lover's Betrayal, while IV puts forward The Rival/The Lover Altered (these titles are my own rather than Landon's). Where Amenaïde uses pride to sustain her,[56] Leoni is simply thoughtless, 'alter'd' (329): changed inwardly though the same outwardly. Landon wants to dramatise sexual difference, among other things, and so Leoni's change causes him nothing other than 'a moment's awkwardness' (326), a superficial response to an emotional situation, while Amenaïde's grief inculcates 'an evil feeling … / …. / Part bitterness, part vanity, part woe' (347, 349) that spurs her to close the scene by Outshining the Rival.

Landon's approach is complex, for by invoking melodrama and theatrical situations she is not merely suggesting that such scenes are unreal, or that emotion is always necessarily feigned; instead, she indicates that love itself follows a preordained path, a theatricalised script familiar to readers and to the narrator, but not to the players – that lovers, especially women, are at the mercy of love's inevitable progression from pleasure to pain. In 'Venetian Bracelet' she uses the violence of Amenaïde's emotion to represent the harm love does: the struggle between an emotion sincerely felt and an abstract – Love – characterised by its own failure. Amenaïde undergoes torture because of its presence, conveyed in Part V's highly dramatic 'Alone!' scene:

> Corpse-like she lay, – her dark hair wildly thrown
> Far on the floor before her; white as stone,
> As rigid stretch'd each hand, – her face was press'd
> Close to the earth; and but the heaving vest
> Told of some pang the shuddering frame confess'd,
> She seem'd as stricken down by instant death. –
> Sudden she raised her head, and gasp'd for breath;
> And nature master'd misery. She sought,
> Panting, the air from yonder lattice brought.
> Ah, there is blood on that white lip and brow![57] –
> She struggles still – in vain – she must sleep now:
> She wept, childlike, till sleep began to press
> Upon her eyes, for very weariness.
> She sleeps! – so sleeps the wretch beside the stake:
> She sleeps! – how dreadful from such sleep to wake!
>
> (381–95)

Part VI functions as an Interlude where we are told again of Amenaïde's pride, of her faults, and of the value of her love – 'Her love was all her nature's better part' (428).[58] Like a scrim behind which the scene is changed, Part VI both hides and makes plain a transformation, the subject of Part VII: when Amenaïde awakes, the sight of herself in the mirror nearly provokes a scream. Still young, still beautiful, she is also, now, somehow monstrous: ' – that pale face, – / Why lip and brow are sullied by the trace/ Of blood; its stain is on her tangled hair,/ Which shroud-like hides the neck that else were bare' (442–5). Pictured in the terms of a revenant, Amenaïde returns to life transformed, determined to deny her feelings – '"Oh, never let Leoni know the worst:/ 'Tis well if he believe I changed the first. / Too much e'en to myself has been reveal'd' (480–2) – and thereby confirming her change from heroine to something darker. Again, melodramatic events are put in the service of a violent overthrow of romantic love, manifested physically on Amenaïde's marked face.

Landon eases violence into her text by way of Amenaïde's self-mutilation. The tableaux continue, giving us Leoni's English bride's story, itself a highly melodramatic tale of filial love and loss, and also a description of her beauty, fair 'like morning's' (508) to rival Amenaïde's 'midnight' (244), but it is Part VIII[59] that spurs the action. Amenaïde in her grove encounters the standard 'aged Jew' who offers her both a 'ruby cross' and a bracelet 'twisted as a serpent, whose lithe fold/ Curl'd round the arm' and which contains the 'subtlest poison' (557, 584, 572–3, 576). Amenaïde chooses the 'fatal band' and sin, and 'the solitude of crime': 'That night there was another saddest scene', and Edith 'convulsive[ly] sobs' her life away (585, 596, 597, 604).[60] Where Byron's triangles revolve around the dead body of the loved one, 'Venetian Bracelet' finds partial resolution in the conventional picture of woman scorned dispatching her rival. Having introduced murder, Landon piles event on event: in Part XI, tableau gives way to action, as Leoni is arrested, Amenaïde finds herself unable to own her 'shame' (654), Leoni is found guilty, Amenaïde sends in her confession, and then disappears. During Leoni's trial, Amenaïde had sat 'a very statue, with that cold set face,/ Save that red flushes came at each light sound,/ While the wild eyes glanced fearfully around' (656–8), drained of humanity even as Edith had been drained of life. Love torments Amenaïde, forcing physical, emotional, and moral changes, and finally killing her, for Part XII sees her in Leoni's cell, where she confesses, takes the bracelet's poison, and 'lies a ghastly corpse before his feet' (708). From love to death via hate and revenge, Amenaïde invites our gaze as a spectacular example of the violent effects of love and its inevitable deadly outcome. 'Venetian Bracelet' fetishises love as a poison, represented by the confining, sinful bracelet that imprisons Amenaïde, and offers the female body as the site of death and of moralising: first Edith, then Amenaïde, whose grave becomes a tourist attraction even as her identity fades. While the tomb embodies the crime – the serpent bracelet is prominently carved on its side – the crime outlives the individual – 'A few brief words, that passing pity craved – / "Pray for the wounded heart, the sinful deed";/ And, half effaced, a name – "AMENAÏDE"' (716–18). Dramatising the 'disruptive effect of passion' (Linkin 177), Landon externalises its violence, and we find in 'Venetian Bracelet' not so much a 'travestying of femininity' (Armstrong 325) as an exploration of its pains, a melodramatic rendering of romance that serves to underscore its failures and its dangers. When Amenaïde kills Edith and then herself, she embodies the destructive violence of love, staged and heightened for effect.

'Venetian Bracelet' asserts the impossibility of living happily ever after, but more than that it suggests a poet fully aware of the pitfalls and inadequacies of romance, with its fixations on the unreal.

'Venetian Bracelet' more than her other romances shows female activity: agency claimed through violence. It must be noted that although Amenaïde dies, she is not condemned for her crime; readers are asked to pity her, and she escapes the pages of self-morti-fication indulged in by the Giaour. In fact, although her run-in with Love is violent, the pain is short-lived – only two days pass between Leoni's return and Amenaïde's suicide. There is time enough for Landon to establish the 'Art of Disillusion' described by McGann and Riess: the literal dispelling of illusion that informs all her most highly-wrought poems of love, but she refrains from blame; no person is at fault, not even Leoni, but rather Love itself, cast as the only true villain in the melodrama. It is Love that makes Leoni false, Amenaïde too extreme, Edith a victim, and it is Love that focuses the tensions between Leoni and Amenaïde themselves. Melodrama 'comes into being in a world where the traditional imperatives of truth and ethics' and, I would add, of Love 'have been violently thrown into question' (Brooks 15). Landon is concerned not only with the imperative of women to love, but of men also; while 'Venetian Bracelet' concentrates on Amenaïde, Leoni is at least allowed to justify his own change of heart, albeit briefly, while his love for Edith is never in doubt. Landon is alive to the dependency on Love felt by both sexes, and to the rigid demarcation of experi-ence represented by the separate spheres – Leoni leaves Amenaïde to return to the masculine sphere of war. Women depend on men to love them, men depend on women to submit to their love, and to forget when they do, as Leoni shows: 'How much we give to other hearts our tone,/ And judge of others' feelings by our own!/ Himself was alter'd: – all he sought to do/ Was to believe that she was alter'd too' (327–30). Far from endorsing Byron's dictum that love is 'woman's whole existence', as Mellor suggests that she does (*Romanticism and Gender*, 114 *passim*), Landon pursues the far more complex course of dramatising that insistence though melodramatic overstatement, and in that way questioning its verity. She writes romances that aim to please, but like Hemans, like Robinson, she interweaves her stories with a problematic tendency to condemn that which she is believed to support so unquestioningly: romantic love. 'Venetian Bracelet' contained its violence in the home, whether castle or cottage (or prison), but something very interesting happens when Landon acknowledges the existence of the outside world. Love proves itself the enemy not only of woman's whole existence, but of man's as well.

In 'Roland's Tower', Landon melds romance with tragedy to produce a melodrama of masculine failure. Whereas 'Venetian Bracelet' played with convention in what may be called a conventional way – Amenaïde, though violent, nevertheless conforms to an extreme version of rejected womanhood, and wreaks her vengeance on her innocent rival rather than her faithless lover – 'Roland's Tower' skilfully manipulates conventional assumptions of the separate spheres and the behaviour and emotions thought appropriate for each. 'Roland's Tower' collapses on its own definition of love, first offered in the epigraph: 'Oh, Heaven! The deep fidelity of love!' Striking in its simplicity, this epigraph gives little away, but it is uncomfortably ambiguous: is it thankful? Admiring? Despairing? It certainly avoids overt praise, and the exclamation 'Oh, Heaven!' conveys more desperation than comfort. Landon follows this up by writing a narrator whose personal experience of love, although expressed obliquely, is far from encouraging. After comparing a ruined convent, picturesque in its covering ivy, to 'the so false exterior of the world' (11), she moves to a familiar *memento mori*, the grave; covered in violets, it reminds her not of the transitoriness of life, but of love:

> ...   I do love violets:
> They tell the history of woman's love;
> They open with the earliest breath of spring;
> Lead a sweet life of perfume, dew, and light;
> And, if they perish, perish with a sigh
> Delicious as that life. On the hot June
> They shed no perfume: the flowers may remain,
> But the rich breathing of their leaves is past; –
> Like woman, they have lost their loveliest gift,
> When yielding to the fiery hour of passion:
> The violet breath of love is purity.
>
> (18–28)

The narrator's warning is familiar, but out of place, since the poem to follow deals with other disasters than woman's lost honour; instead, these lines hint at a counter-story, the narrator's own, referred to again when, in describing the poem's young lovers, Roland and Isabelle, she bursts through their narrative with her own:

> I did love once –
> Loved as youth – woman – genius loves; though now
> My heart is chilled and seared, and taught to wear
> That falsest of false things – a mask of smiles;
> Yet every pulse throbs at the memory
> Of that which has been!
>
> (98–103)

'Roland's Tower', from the 1824 collection *The Improvisatrice*, predates 'Venetian Bracelet' by five years, and without that poem's prefatory disclaimer against reading the narrator as Landon, encourages readers to identify the tragic narrator with the bereft poet.[61] Once the narrator is designated as a tragic heroine, the love story the poem recounts is fatally coloured with the narrator's own loss: her personal experience ensures her authority in the matter of love's pain, bolstered by the by-now dark lamentation of the epigraph. In dramatic terms, the narrator acts as a chorus, the only player with clear sight and a grip on the narrative, and the only one able to pinpoint the moments of importance in the romance, to 'isolat[e the] moments of sensation' (Armstrong 326) on which melodrama depends.

Because of the narrator's gloomy tone, the reader is discouraged from associating young love with perfect happiness, and from rewarding female beauty with automatic approbation. Isabelle, blonde, blue-eyed,[62] lovely, musical, the daughter of Lord Herbert and therefore of the appropriate class for romance, entertains her father and guests with 'lute/ And song' and stories of 'young Roland's deeds' (64–5, 79). This is a new *chanson de Roland*, simultaneously past and present, for even as Isabelle finishes her song with the words 'I would give worlds ... to see this chief,/ This gallant Roland! I could deem him all/ A man must honour and a woman love!' (86–8), art (the song) transforms into reality (Isabelle's world), and a young, cloaked pilgrim reveals himself to be Roland: 'Lady! I pray thee not recall those words,/ For I am Roland!' (89–90). Seemingly sung into being by Isabelle, Roland immediately fulfils her expectations of his attractions, for within two lines 'They loved; – They were beloved' (93). As she will do in 'Venetian Bracelet', Landon skips over all romantic details: the mere appearance of the hero means the heroine loves him, while the beauty of the heroine automatically captures the hero's love. The romantic script, once activated, chugs along; the players, having met, *must* love, and having loved, *must* part. After the long digression wherein the narrator reveals her own failed love, the poem swiftly moves forward in time: 'spring/ Has wedded with summer' (119–20),[63] and Roland leaves Isabelle to 'raise his vassals' (124) in Lord Herbert's support ('Lord Herbert's towers/ Were menaced with a siege' [124–5]). Given Roland's legendary military prowess – he is already famous in song, as we have seen – there seems little to fear, were it not for the fatalistic narrator, but her experience prevails. First, Roland fails to appear at the battle: 'Lord Herbert's banner flies/ ... / But where is he who said that he would ride/ At his right hand to battle? – Roland! where – / Oh! Where is Roland?' (129, 131–3). The knightly hero, late for battle, thereby fails to fulfil his pledge to support Herbert, but he commits a far worse blunder.

> Isabelle stood upon her lonely tower;
> And, as the evening-star rose up, she saw
> An armed train bearing her father's banner
> In triumph to the castle. Down she flew
> To greet the visitors: – they had reached the hall
> Before herself. What saw the maiden there?
> A bier! – her father laid upon that bier!
> Roland was kneeling by the side, his face
> Bowed on his hands and hid; – but Isabelle
> Knew the dark curling hair and stately form,
> And threw her on his breast. He shrank away
> As she were death, or sickness, or despair.
> 'Isabelle! it was I who slew thy father!'
> She fell almost a corpse upon the body.
> It was too true! With all a lover's speed,
> Roland had sought the thickest of the fight;
> He gained the field just as the crush began; –
> Unwitting of his colours, he had slain
> The father of his worshipped Isabelle!
>
>   (138–56)

Roland's mistake is unbelievable – an experienced knight, famed for his skill, kills his lover's father by accident, 'unwitting of his colours', even though he has gone to 'raise his vassals' specifically to fight for those colours. What has gone wrong?

The clue lies buried in the romance itself. Isabelle and Roland occupy different worlds: she, the heroine, inhabits the house of her father, domesticated, ensconced, and waiting for love; he, the hero, lives in the outside world, identified with war, soldierly deeds, manly prowess. Drawn by love into Isabelle's realm, Roland is changed; the only explanation for his mistake is that, blinded by love, he is now a bad soldier, an inept knight, a disarmed hero. It is not the encounter with Isabelle, but the entry into Love's world and the concomitant sojourn in the domestic that unmans Roland, and once affected he never recovers. While Isabelle retires to a convent, Roland 'built/ A tower beside the Rhine' in sight of the convent, and each night watches for Isabelle's 'white scarf waved' to let him know she still lives (174–5, 176).[64] When she finally dies, her 'tomb/ Was Roland's death-bed!' (187–8), the final retreat. Roland, once he has crossed into the domestic sphere, is unable to return successfully to the world of war, of action; even as Amenaïde's foray into the world of violent action leads directly to her death, so too Roland – as knight – cannot survive his encounter with love. Once he 'worships' Isabelle, he has compromised his masculinity: he is violently stripped of the markers of heroism and knightly valour. The melodramatic moment of mistaken identity, the sensationalised force of lines like 'she fell almost a corpse upon the body', the irony inherent in 'with all a *lover's* speed' – surely Roland should enter battle with a soldier's speed? – reaffirm that to love is to invite tragedy. While it is often true that in Landon's poetry 'the woman who loves is rejected, abandoned, or merely forgotten by her cruel lover' (Mellor 115), the man who loves suffers as well; the villain in Landon's romances is not the faithless lover, or even the overly-passionate woman, but Love – Romance – itself, with its dangerous, unavoidable excesses.

Roland, marked by Love, cannot leave Isabelle, even after she has left him; unfitted for his appropriate sphere – war – he can only wait for death. In 'The Mountain Grave' (1829), Herman finds it easy to leave Agatha, with whom, we understand, he has only dallied; his 'I am not late tonight' (21) bespeaks that he has been late before. 'Mountain Grave' closes the collection introduced by 'Venetian Bracelet', and in it Landon sketches in shorthand the violence perpetrated by Love. 'What oppresses the young heart like love?' the narrator demands; 'O youth, and love, which is the light of youth,/ Why pass ye as the morning?' (14, 44–5). Again, love is doomed before the poem's romance commences, although Herman's question itself spells trouble: Agatha, the heroine, has 'cause' for sorrow, agrees the narrator. Like Leoni, Herman stays only long enough to affirm love, then he too mounts a 'snow-white steed' and goes off to war. Where Roland finds that love has disabled him, and Leoni forgets Amenaïde in Edith's arms, Herman does not return at all:

> Ambition took the place of Love, and Hope
> Fed upon fiery thoughts, aspiring aims;
> And the bold warrior, favourite of his king,
> If that he thought of his first tenderness,
> Thought if it but with scorn, or vain excuse,
> And in her uncomplaining silence read
> But what he wish'd, – oblivion; and at last
> Her very name had faded, like the flower
> Which we have laid upon our heart, and there
> Have suffer'd it to die.
>
> (112–21)

Herman exchanges Love for War; he successfully pursues the martial career that chimes with masculinity and the public sphere in Landon's poetry, while Agatha, fulfilling society's expectation that woman lives for love, dies without it, 'in silence, without sign or word/ That might betray the memory of her fate', except that she desires to be buried 'beneath the shade of the laburnum tree' where she used to meet Herman (145–6, 148). Agatha pathologically fulfils woman's destiny; her only speech describes Herman's leaving, and her total immersion in the feminine space – she watches, waits, despairs, and dies – necessitates her elimination. Landon shows the inevitable result of passivity, not to condone, but to condemn; Agatha's death is not celebrated, but instead rather flatly concludes a life of fetishised femininity. Herman's fate, too, is intimately tied to Love: when he returns to the valley 'upon warlike mission' (172) and sees Agatha's tomb, it forces him to recognise the strength of love.

> ... if he thought
> Of his once love, it was but how to shun
> The meek reproaching of her mournful eye,
> Or else to think she had like him forgot.
> But dead! – so young! – he had not dream'd of this. –
> He knelt him down, and like a child he wept: –
> Gentle affections struggled with, subdued –
> Tenderness, long forgotten, now burst forth
> Like rain drops from the summer sky. Those tears
> Pass'd, and their outward trace; but in his heart
> A fountain had sprung up which dried no more.
>
> (172–82)

As long as he rejected Love, Herman was safe: military violence, paradoxically, proves less threatening to him than love, for as soon as he truly feels love, Herman loses his nerve. 'He died early', and deputes 'the brother of his arms to take/ His heart, and lay it in the distant grave/ Where Agatha was sleeping' (185, 186–8). Love, denizen of the domestic sphere, kills the man who feels it (and who thereby crosses spheres) and the woman who loses it (and who thereby becomes like a man). The clash of spheres, the fatality of love: in Landon's melodramatic romances, violence is Love's guarantee.

Michael Hays and Anastasia Nikolopoulou note that the melodrama juxtaposes two competing discourses, 'two different "horizons" of understanding and desire': it both offers plot and comments on that plot's unsatisfactoriness (xiv), a point made also by Brooks when he describes melodrama's tendency to 'evok[e] meanings beyond its literal configuration' of plot (10–11). Melodrama therefore opens a space for the unsayable; in its exaggerations can be detected critiques of the values it so hyperbolically supports. Certainly, Landon's poems energetically plot romance, but they just as effectively plot to destroy it; her world of failed love, murderous women, suicide and unmanned men posits Love not as a blessing, but as a curse, a monstrous force for oppression leading inevitably to catastrophe.[65] Her many disillusioned narrators function to comment on love's violence and darkness even as they dutifully set up repeated scenarios of pseudo-romance – of melodramatic tragedy. It is difficult to tell if Landon supports the validity of separate spheres, but plainly she recognises their popular appeal, and just as plainly she recognises their inherent incompatibility. Her romances explore the disasters attendant on such insistence on separation; they point out the impossibility of love under such conditions. In 'Love's Last Lesson' (1827),[66] she creates a doubled voice to drive this point home: the initial narrator who craves 'forgetfulness' and whose apostrophe to her 'god on earth' leaves the reader uncertain if she means a lover, or Love itself (1, 3);[67] and the embedded narrator, who takes over for the first when bitterness chokes off her song. Love both silences the first speaker, and gives her a topic; and we easily recognise the weary, experienced tones of the second speaker. Love's *last* lesson reveals its true identity: 'Joys' are felt 'at first; but what is the result?'

> Hopes that lie mute in their own sullenness,
> For they have quarrell'd even with themselves;
> And joys indeed like birds of Paradise:

> And in their stead despair coils scorpion-like
> Stinging itself; and the heart, burnt and crush'd
> With passion's earthquake, scorch'd and wither'd up,
> Lies in its desolation, – this is love.
>
> (89, 91, 92–8)

Landon portrays Love generous enough to admit its own villainy – after it has enslaved.

For both Byron and Landon, the melodrama amplifies the falsities of romance: it allows for role-playing, for the overt adoption and covert dismissal of a script. Each enhances their reappraisals of romantic, heterosexual love by filtering this relationship through melodrama: Byron subsumes it to a prevailing interest in homosocial bonding, while Landon refuses to countenance its possibilities for success altogether. Neither is happy with the conventional wisdom of the romance: but both Byron's expressed aversion to and Landon's suggestively worded acceptance of its burdens indicate an interest in its attractions, a desire to explore its implications. Violence emerges as contingent on, a corollary to, the preoccupations of the romance, and while Byron and Landon construct contrasting personae to guide their readers through Love's landscape, both return repeatedly, in common with the writers discussed throughout this book. The pull of romance, the allure of violence, the snares of desire: when approached, employed and redeployed by poets during the Romantic period, the romance offers myriad opportunities for questioning, reordering and representing culture. For Landon and Byron, the blurring of the romance into melodrama allows for a focused rewriting of the conventions of heterosexual attraction. If, then, we find ourselves characterising the poetry of Byron and Landon as melodramatic, it is not because of the looseness of the term, but because they *are* melodramatic; they feature heightened, sensationalised, overwrought characters, storylines and conclusions. In each, we discern the generic trappings of the romance, not the least in the poems' overriding emphasis on love, but in each, the romance has given way before the powerful, unstoppable flow of the melodrama. The Victorian period will see the codification of melodrama into the familiar stagebound theatrical experience, but what the poetical melodramas of Byron and Landon confirm is a final transmutation, the violent overthrow of genre by genre: the death of the Romantic romance.

Notes

Introduction

1 Curran, *Poetic Form and British Romanticism* (New York: Oxford University Press, 1986), 129. Subsequent references will be made in the text.

2 Brownstein, *Becoming a Heroine: Reading About Women in Novels* (1982; New York: Columbia University Press, 1994), xxi.

3 Although the romances popular during the late seventeenth–early eighteenth centuries, most written or revised by Madeleine de Scudéry, often revolved around great queens – Cleopatra, Semiramis – they were concerned to subsume the queen's personal greatness to her love-life. The queen's importance served to show she was worthy to be romanced, rather than worthy to rule her domain.

4 Pinch, 'Learning What Hurts: Romanticism, Pedagogy, Violence', *Lessons of Romanticism: A Critical Companion*, ed. Thomas Pfau and Robert Gleckner (Durham: Duke University Press, 1998), 413. Subsequent references will be made in the text.

5 See Duff, *Romance and Revolution: Shelley and the Politics of a Genre* (Cambridge: Cambridge University Press, 1994) and Langbauer, *Women and Romance: The Consolations of Gender in the English Novel* (Ithaca: Cornell University Press, 1990). Both studies provide important information about and interesting readings of the Romantic/Victorian romance.

6 I borrow the image of the ghostly genre from Jerrold Hogle, 'The Gothic Ghost as Counterfeit and its Haunting of Romanticism: The Case of "Frost at Midnight"', *European Romantic Review* 9 (1998), 283–92.

7 My discussion of the Julia and Vaudracour episode is based on the 1805 version of *The Prelude*, found in *The Oxford Authors: William Wordsworth*, ed. Stephen Gill (Oxford: Oxford University Press, 1988). Subsequent references, to book and line numbers, will be made in the text.

8 Incidentally, Wordsworth also veers close to the Romantic habit of plagiarising; despite his intertextual citation of his 'patriot Friend' (IX: 554), he also draws on Helen Maria Williams's *Letters Written in France*, published in 1790. See Gill 735, n. to p. 522. As readers of this book will see, the Julia/Vaudracour plotline also resembles closely that of Mary Robinson's 'The Hermit of Mont-Blanc'; see Chapter 4.

9 Wordsworth 'sees' these images because of the romance he associates with the forests of France, but it is interesting that even in his fantasising, violence enters, not only the political violence associated with the ruined convent, but also the sexual violence of these lines: 'anon the din/ Of boisterous merriment and music's roar,/ With sudden Proclamation, burst from haunt/ Of Satyrs in some viewless glade, with dance/ Rejoicing o'er a Female in the midst,/ A mortal Beauty, their unhappy Thrall' (IX: 459–64).

10 Vaudracour is a type of the failed hero; see Chapters 3 and 4 for further discussions.

11 See Michael Gamer, 'Marketing a Masculine Romance: Scott, Antiquarianism and the Gothic', *Studies in Romanticism* 32 (1993), 523–49. See also Bruce Beiderwell, 'Scott's *Redgauntlet* as a Romance of Power', *Studies in Romanticism* 28 (1989), 273–89. Both of these articles recontextualise Scott's romancing along more acceptably masculine lines: 'history' and 'power'. Subsequent references to Gamer will be made in the text.

12 Daniel P. Watkins, *Sexual Power in British Romantic Poetry* (Gainesville, FL: University Press of Florida, 1996), 3.

13 Praz summarises this in his 'Note to the Second Edition' of his book. See Praz, *The Romantic Agony*, tr. Angus Davidson (Oxford: Oxford University Press, 1970), xxiv.

14 See Nancy Armstrong and Leonard Tennenhouse, *The Violence of Representation: Literature and the history of violence* (London: Routledge, 1989) for a revealing collection of essays attempting exactly to engage with the discourse of literary violence. Interestingly for the present study, *The Violence of Representation* deals with 'Early Modern Culture' (the seventeenth century), 'Modern Culture' (the nineteenth century and after) and 'Contemporary Culture', but skips the Romantic period. It is tempting to argue that Romantic-period literary violence has been shunted conveniently to the Gothic and otherwise rendered invisible. One of the aims of *The Romantic Paradox* is to allow the voicing of Romantic violence.

1   Reviving the Romance: What's Love Got to Do with It?

1 Robert Southey, 'Romance', from *Poems containing The Retrospect, Odes, Elegies, Sonnets, etc.*, with Robert Lovell (Bath: R. Cruttwell, 1795).

2 Many critics note the 'ambiguity' surrounding the romance; see, for example, Patricia Parker, *Inescapable Romance: Studies in the Poetics of a Mode* (Princeton: Princeton University Press, 1979); David Duff, *Romance and Revolution: Shelley and the Politics of a Genre* (Cambridge: Cambridge University Press, 1994); Fredric Jameson, 'Magical Narratives: Romance as Genre', *New Literary History* 7 (1975), 135–63; Miriam Allott, *Novelists on the Novel* (London: Routledge and Kegan Paul, 1959).

3 See especially 30–4 and 134–53 in *Romance and Revolution*.

4 Southey's gendering of love as masculine, while it conforms to the Greek ideal (Cupid being a boy), takes on a greater significance when one realises the extent to which his feminine Romance is concerned with the traditional masculine pursuits of war.

5 As Kate Davies argues, the American Revolution offered spectacles of extreme violence to its 'audience' back in Britain; some common subjects for prints were that of the king devouring his own children, and of Britannia dismembered and bleeding. Romance offered a comforting diversion from such horrors, with its ordered, balanced and streamlined ethos. See Davies, *Gender and Republicanism in Britain and America: The Meanings of Catherine Macauley* (unpublished D.Phil. thesis, University of York, England, 1999).

6 Eric Auerbach, *Mimesis*, tr. Willard R. Trask (Princeton: Princeton University Press, 1974), 132.

7 This becomes more troubling and much more difficult to maintain in the 1790s and into the nineteenth century.

8 Such a need will become even more apparent during the Regency; see Mark Girouard, *The Return to Camelot: Chivalry and the English Gentleman* (New Haven: Yale University Press, 1981), 26–7, for a description of George IV's elaborately courtly coronation ceremony.

9 Batty, *The Spirit and Influence of Chivalry* (London: Elliot Stock, 1890). Subsequent references will be made in the text.

10 Hurd, *Letters on Chivalry and Romance, with the Third Elizabethan Dialogue*, ed. Edith J. Morley (London: Henry Frowde, 1911), 83, 84. Subsequent references will be made in the text.

11 Arthur Johnston, *Enchanted Ground: The Study of Medieval Romance in the Eighteenth Century* (London: The Athlone Press, 1964), 87.

12 *The Percy Letters*, eds David Nichol Smith and Cleanth Brooks (6 vols; Baton Rouge: Louisiana State University Press, 1944–61), vol. 2, 7.

13 I will discuss Dobson later in this chapter; she is rather unusual in that she continues to produce studies of the romance, rather than stopping at one.

14 Frye, *The Secular Scripture, A Study of the Structure of Romance* (Cambridge, MA: Harvard University Press, 1976), 76.

15 Reeve, *The Progress of Romance* (Dublin: Price, Exshaw, White, Cash, Colbert, Marchbank and Porter, 1785), 1. Subsequent references will be made in the text.

16 One remembers that for the more ambivalent Hurd, it is in Elizabeth's court that the romance became 'absurd'; what for Reeve is a profitable association between a female ruler and a feminised genre is, for Hurd, an uncomfortable instance of gender imbalance.

17 By this time (Volume II), Euphrasia has taken on the novel, which, in its debilitating and depressing realism, seems a stronger adversary than even Hortensius' scepticism.

18 As if to underscore her point, Reeve earlier has Euphrasia herself (ironically?) try out Hortentius' politesse:

> *Euphrasia.* You know your advantages, and that a woman is your opponent.
> *Hortentius.* Whether you mean me a compliment or a reproof, is not clear' (11).

In this exchange, Reeve seems to be signalling her own authorial disregard for such patronising codes.

19 The reader notes that devotion to the opposite sex does not feature in Euphrasia's list of heroic qualities.

20 'Dialogue XXVIII', from *Dialogues of the Dead*, in *Novel and Romance 1700–1800, A Documentary*, ed. Ioan Williams (London: Routledge and Kegan Paul, 1970), 226. Subsequent references, to 'Montagu, *Novel and Romance*', will be made in the text.

21 By the 1790s, the dilemma is between an ideal that ennobles, and an exaggeration that debases, the mind.

22 From *On Fable and Romance*, in *Novel and Romance*, 319. Subsequent refer-

ences, to 'Beattie, *Novel and Romance'*, will be made in the text.

23   *The Literary History of the Troubadours. Containing their Lives, Extracts from the Works, And many Particulars relative to the Customs, Morals, and History of the Twelfth and Thirteenth Centuries. Collected and Abridged from the French of Mr. De Saint-Pelaie, By the Author of the Life of Plutarch* (London: T. Cadell, 1779), v, vi. Subsequent references, to *History*, will be made in the text.

24   Dobson here anticipates the language that will be used against the French Revolution by those disillusioned by Robespierre's Reign of Terror; they, too, will see the romance of liberty, fraternity and equality degenerate into bloody scenes.

25   In light of the argument this book advances – that the romance pervades this period as an organising, as well as a vexed, metaphor – the standard female-authored prefatory disclaimer takes on a new resonance, but a thorough investigation of this aspect is beyond the scope of this book.

26   *Memoirs of Ancient Chivalry. To Which are Added, The Anecdotes of the Times, from the Romance Writers and Historians of those Ages. Translated from the French of Monsieur de St.Palaye, by the Translator of the Life of Plutarch* (London: J. Dodsley, 1784), vii, viii. Subsequent references, to *Memoirs*, will be made in the text. As her use of 'rescue' shows, Dobson continues to appeal to the language of chivalry despite herself.

27   Dobson refers to medieval France, but the ramifications for her own time are clear.

28   Hugh Murray, *The Morality of Fiction; or, An Inquiry into the Tendency of Fictitious Narratives, with Observations on Some of the Most Eminent* (Edinburgh: Mundell and Son, 1805), 20; and *The Works of Tobias Smollett, M.D. with Memoirs of his Life; to which is prefixed A View of the Commencement and Progress of Romance, by John Moore, M.D.* (London: B. Law *et al.*, 1797), xv. Subsequent references to these works will be made in the text.

29   Robinson, *Hubert de Sevrac* (London: Hookham and Carpenter, 1796), 5. Subsequent references will be made in the text.

30   See Mark Girouard, *The Return to Camelot: Chivalry and the English Gentleman.*

31   Burke's language throughout his lamentation is determinedly romantic:

> It is now sixteen or seventeen years since I saw the queen of France, then the dauphiness, at Versaille; and surely never lighted on this orb, which she hardly seemed to touch, a more delightful vision. I saw her just above the horizon, decorating and cheering the elevated sphere she just began to move in, – glittering like the morning-star, full of life, and splendour, and joy. Oh! What ... an heart must I have, to contemplate without emotion that elevation and that fall! Little did I dream ... that I should have lived to see such disasters fallen upon her in a nation of gallant men, in a nation of men of honour and of cavaliers. I thought ten thousand swords must have leapt from their scabbards to avenge even a look that threatened her with insult. – But the age of chivalry is gone. – That of sophisters, oeconomists, and calculators, has succeeded; and the glory of Europe is extinguished for ever.

See *Reflections on the Revolution in France, and on the Proceedings in Certain Societies in London Relative to that Event*, ed. Conor Cruise O'Brien (Harmondsworth: Penguin, 1969), 169–70.

32 See my book *Romantic Visualities: Landscape, Gender and Romanticism* (Basingstoke: Macmillan, 1998) for a discussion of the gendered and cultural significance of disinterestedness and abstract thought.

33 In light of this discussion, Burke's sustained argument against the need for a written constitution is telling; for Burke, chivalry was exactly, and the only, constitution Britain needed.

34 From *The Tea-Table, or a Conversation between some Polite Persons of both sexes at a Lady's Visiting Day*, in *Novel and Romance*, 83.

35 From *The History of Romances, An Enquiry into their Origin; Instructions for composing them; An Account of the most Eminent Authors; With Characters amd Curious Observations upon the Best Performances of that Kind*, tr. Stephen Lewis (1715), in *Novel and Romance*, 54. Subsequent references, to 'Huet, *Novel and Romance*', will be made in the text.

36 The number and scale of alternatives, however, proves the instability and riskiness of this enterprise.

37 From 'On Fictitious History', in *Lectures on Rhetoric and Poetry* (1762), in *Novel and Romance*, 247.

38 One could describe this paradox as a type of the returned repressed; in Gillian Beer's words, the romance represents 'not simply [what is] unreal or artificial. Rather, it expresses the lost or repressed emotional forces of the imagination, which they sought to release' (*The Romance* [London: Methuen and Co. Ltd, 1970], 60–1). The tension between expression and repression is the nexus of violence.

39 From *Miscellaneous Pieces in Prose and Verse* (1773), in *Novel and Romance*, 281. Subsequent references, to 'Barbauld, *Novel and Romance*', will be made in the text.

40 From *The Microcosm* 26 (14 May 1787), in *Novel and Romance*, 341.

41 From Vicessimus Knox, 'On Novel Reading', no. XIV, *Essays Moral and Literary* (1778), in *Novel and Romance*, 305.

42 Barbauld's language anticipates contemporary arguments against the deadening effect of ever-more-horrific slasher films and explicit visual and textual violence. In terms of the period under discussion here, it is also conceivable that the immersion in romanticised violence made many liberal thinkers fear that the violence of their society would not affect the young deeply enough to make them want to change society for the better.

2 Sexing the Romance: the Erotic Violence of the Della Cruscans

1 William Gifford, *The Baviad, The Baviad and Maeviad* (London, 1800), 41.

2 As McGann says, 'If we want to reacquire an understanding of Della Cruscan poetry, Gifford's fustian points us in the right direction'. See *The Poetics of Sensibility: A Revolution in Literary Style* (Oxford: Clarendon Press, 1996), Chapter 9: 'The Literal World of the English Della Cruscans', 75. Subsequent references to McGann will be made in the text.

3 Otherwise known as Robert Merry and Hannah Cowley. When discussing Della Cruscan poetry, I will use their Della Cruscan names; much of the romance of Della Cruscanism depends on the personae created by these two poets. Their readers saw them as Della Crusca and Anna Matilda; their true identities were unimportant to the emotive relationship they built up. Similarly, Mary Robinson becomes Laura; and, later, Charlotte Dacre (itself a pseudonym, according to Adrianna Craciun and Kim Ian Michasiw) 'is' Rosa Matilda. For an engaging discussion of the theatricality of Della Cruscan names, see Judith Pascoe, *Romantic Theatricality: Gender, Poetry, and Spectatorship* (Ithaca: Cornell University Press, 1997), Chapter 3: '"That fluttering, tinselled crew": Women Poets and Della Cruscanism'. Pascoe also supplies a useful brief history of the trend. Subsequent references to Pascoe will be made in the text.

4 The nineteenth-century flavour of this process – hook readers through the ephemeral medium of the newspaper, and then allow them the full enjoyment of the story in the expensive permanency of a book – goes some way towards inflecting the Della Crusca/Anna Matilda romance with another sort of eroticism: that of commerce.

5 Some novels made it their express aim to challenge this stereotype; see, for instance, *Amelia* by Henry Fielding (1751/52), *Agreeable Ugliness* by Sarah Scott (1754), *Camilla* by Frances Burney (1796), and *Something New* by Anne Plumptre (1801). Here, inner beauty is matched with outer ugliness, which tests and ultimately defeats the morally upright suitors – the romantic necessity of beauty is upheld even as the beauty/goodness paradigm is challenged. In the nineteenth century, sensation fiction capitalised on this assumption by allying beauty, not with goodness, but with evil; see, especially, M.E. Braddon, *Lady Audley's Secret* (1862).

6 See Bostetter, 'The Original Della Cruscans and the Florence Miscellany', *Huntingdon Library Quarterly* 19 (1956), 277–300; Hargreaves-Mawdsley, *The English Della Cruscans and Their Time, 1783–1828* (The Hague: Martinus Nijhoff, 1967).

7 Indeed, for a short time Merry himself wondered if Anna Matilda was Seward. See Hargreaves-Mawdsley, 175.

   Susan Wolfson, in '"Romantic Ideology" and the Values of Aesthetic Form', quotes from a 1796 essay in the *Monthly Magazine*, 'Is Verse essential to Poetry?', in which the author asserts that metre 'confin[es] the productions of the muses within the enclosure of measured lines' and that poetry itself is 'confin[ed] within the narrow inclosure of metre'. For this author, poetic formality performs exactly the function I am suggesting: it serves to imprison the power and energy poetry might otherwise unleash. Wolfson's excellent essay is found in *Aesthetics and Ideology*, ed. George Levine (New Brunswick, NJ: Rutgers University Press, 1994), 188–218. Subsequent references will be made in the text.

8 These engravings offer further evidence of the rote nature of the romance followed by Anna Maria and Della Crusca. While the two are represented in differing poses – Della Crusca has his head on his right hand and looks at his viewer, and Anna Matilda holds a book open in her left hand, holds her right hand at her waist, and looks off to the left with a half-smile on her face – both are set within an oval inscribed at its base with the sitter's

name. More importantly, the background to Della Crusca's portrait (a Muse-figure above him; billing doves under him; bow, arrows and torch to his lower left; lyre, flute and quill to his lower right) is reused in reverse in Anna Matilda's: the two portraits function as mirror-images, even as their likenesses reflect each other's passion.

9　Eagleton, *The Ideology of the Aesthetic* (Oxford: Basil Blackwell, 1990), 28.

10　Brooks, 'Aesthetics and Ideology – What Happened to Poetics?', in *Aesthetics and Ideology*, ed. Levine, 155. Subsequent references will be made in the text.

11　Maria Dibattista, '"Sabbath Eyes": Ideology and the Writer's Gaze', in *Aesthetics and Ideology*, ed. Levine, 169. Subsequent references will be made in the text.

12　The most significant romantic exchange in the text, the Anna Matilda/Della Crusca correspondence, will be discussed in the next section of the chapter.

13　'Ode to Mrs. Siddons', *The British Album, In Two Volumes* (London: John Bell, 1792), 1, 18, 22, 25, 29, 33. Subsequent references to poems from *The British Album* will be to line numbers and made in the text. The power of Siddons' voice is such that Madness itself is driven mad: 'Dancing upon the flinty plain/ *As tho' 'twere gay to suffer pain,*/ That sees his tyrant Moon, and raving runs to woo' (34–6).

14　Wells's artlessness can, of course, like Siddons' pathos, be seen as artful – as derived from her artistic prowess. Della Crusca wants his readers to see Wells as sincere, activated by genuine emotions rather than the artifice of acting. In this way she is a more suitable romantic object.

15　See Wolfson, 194.

16　Anna Matilda also promotes this doctrine; it is what allows her to see through Della Crusca's disguise as 'Leonardo'. See the discussion of their romance, below.

17　The slightly threatening tone of Emma's verse – the promise of eternal clinging – anticipates the suffocating grasp of some of Felicia Hemans's heroines in *Records of Woman*; see Chapter 4.

18　In *The British Album*, the gaze always focuses on the female body, with the exception of Emma's Henry.

19　This phrasing – 'produced by the pen of Della Crusca' – allows Della Crusca to occupy a passive position, as if his pen has more volition than he does, and is liable to go off on romantic tangents. It also enhances the artifice of Della Crusca himself, who is, as I have noted, no more than a name.

20　See Chapter 5 for a discussion of Letitia Landon's version of 'unhappily ever after'.

21　William Keach, '"Words Are Things": Romantic Ideology and the Matter of Poetic Language', in *Aesthetics and Ideology*, ed. Levine, 228.

22　Indeed, in her clever combining of youth and age in her poem (we see auburn hair and the slim form as clearly as the 'snow' and 'warped' body), Anna Matilda maintains her physical attractiveness as well.

23　Pascoe asserts that 'the ongoing and primary preoccupation of each pseudonymous poet [in *The British Album*] is not the other's physical body but rather the other's body of verse' (76). While certainly the corpus comes into it, I argue instead that the physical body and the body of verse are identical in Della Cruscan poetry, and are made so by the poets' firm conflation of sensation and style.

24 At this point, the Della Cruscan romance reifies 'the discursively constructed values of male authority and female contingency'. However, the plot will thicken: neither player willingly occupies their standard romance role for long. The quotation is from Laura Runge, *Gender and Language in British Literary Criticism, 1660–1790* (Cambridge: Cambridge University Press, 1997), 211.

25 In addition, Anna Matilda embeds in this poem a critique of Della Crusca's stuffy poetic style:

> And be thy lines irregular and free,
> Poetic chains should fall before such Bards as thee.
> Scorn the dull laws that pinch thee round,
> Raising about thy verse a mound,
> O'er which thy muse, so lofty! dares not bound.
> Bid her in verse meand'ring sport;
> Her footsteps quick, or long, or short
> Just as her various impulse wills –
> Scorning the frigid square, which her fine fervour chills.
>   (13–21)

Anna Matilda schools Della Crusca in a more lively style, allowing her poetic structure to exemplify her advice.

26 In this Anna Matilda anticipates Letitia Landon, whose narrators and heroines always suffer at the hands of Love; see Chapter 5.

27 This contrasts with Anna Matilda's first response to Della Crusca's power. It is part of Anna Matilda's – or rather, Hannah Cowley's – subtlety as a poet that Della Crusca's poetic power is rendered as a form of penetration, thus underpinning the eroticism of the Della Cruscan romance.

28 Della Crusca counters Anna Matilda's frequent penetration imagery with images of swelling and bursting – clearly, both poets understood and exploited the sexuality of their romance.

29 Even as she sends him away, Anna Matilda reveals her feelings for Della Crusca, calling him 'my Della Crusca' and worrying that Florence, his putative destination, might tempt him away from her memory.

30 One remembers Anna Matilda's initial description of her *auburn* locks sprinkled with snow.

31 One can also speculate that hiding behind Anna Matilda's sorrow is a mischievous Cowley.

32 Arley's poems are the bane of *The British Album*, although also the most overtly sexual. They are concerned with sexual conquest and with warning susceptible young women about the lascivious world and the consequences of lost virtue. In poems about ravished maids and premarital sex, both implicit and explicit ('Tho' I boast not the name, I've the Truth of a Wife'; 'and does she hold her Spoiler dear?'), Arley consistently casts himself as a doomed romantic hero. He also writes 'Love Renew'd. A Sonnett', which consists of nine 4-line stanzas.

33 It is significant that Mary Robinson's posthumously published *Poetical Works* contain a poem entitled 'To Leonardo', which, as its repetition of key words and direct responses to key sentences from 'To Laura' show,

originally directly followed Leonardo/Della Crusca's offering. This poem's opening lines show Laura's suspicion of Leonardo's motives: 'And dost thou hope to fan my flame/ With the soft breath of FRIENDSHIP's name?' (1–2). The romance in *The British Album*, however, depends upon a constant Della Crusca, and omits a poem that calls into question his disinterested offer of 'friendship'. Even Laura – that is, Robinson (or perhaps Robinson's editor) – colludes in the cover-up, as 'To Leonardo' is hidden without comment or context deep in Volume III of the collected poems. See Robinson, *The Poetical Works of the Late Mrs. Mary Robinson: including Many Pieces Never Before Published* (3 vols; London: Richard Phillips, 1806).

34 Anna Matilda is subtle, but the implication remains: Man's sagacious Art could just as easily be the ability to tell plausible lies as it is poetic skill.

35 These lines further the artifice of the poem: although spoken in Della Crusca's voice, the lines are italicised, and hence, in the typography of the poem, actually written by Anna Matilda. She, then, ventriloquises Della Crusca at the moment of her own dissolution: '*MATILDA fled! the closing Night pursued,/ And the cold INGRATE scarce I longer view'd;/ Her form grew indistinct – each step more dim,/ And now a distant vapour seems to swim,/ Her white robe glistens on my eye no more,/ Its strainings all are vain – the fond delusion's o'er*' (96–101). He, conversely, takes over at the moment she disappears: 'MY SONG subsides' begins the next (unitalicised) line (102).

36 Considering that all along Anna Matilda has allowed her mind to stand in for her body, that 'another' will now claim her mind is simply a way of saying that her body has been claimed: contact is inevitably sexualised.

37 This poem contains lines that may have worked upon a reader whose own early poetry was susceptible to the Della Cruscan influence, Coleridge:

> *How* would I write of dear PHILANDER dead!
> O! I would weave such verse, that round my head
> The Demons of the Night,
> Arrested in their wheeling flight,
> Should learn to pity and to mourn,
> And curse their *bounded* pow'r,
> Which would not let them say RETURN! RETURN!
> (38–44)

The rhythmic resonances of 'Kubla Khan' are suggestive.

38 This poem appends a note that both admits Della Crusca's philandering and implicitly confesses to Della Cruscan playacting: 'A FURIOUS modern SATIRIST [Gifford?], who cannot in any manner moderate his rage at the success which Mr. MERRY's Poetry has met with, under the signature of DELLA CRUSCA, falls foul on him in DESPERATION, and ACTUALLY charges him with the HEINOUS OFFENCE of POETICAL INCONSTANCY, for having addressed LOVE-VERSES to a VARIETY of WOMEN. The justice of the accusation cannot SERIOUSLY be denied!! All that we can say is, that we hope Mr. MERRY's MUSE will behave with more fidelity in future!'

3 Failing the Romance: Coleridge, Keats and the Wilted Hero

1 As Stuart Curran emphasises, 'the aim of most quest-romances is ... inner fulfillment' (*Poetic Form and British Romanticism* [New York: Oxford University Press, 1986], 142). Because the conversation poems offer such an intriguing rewriting of the heroic quest, I have chosen to focus on them rather than the more obvious romances written by Coleridge such as *Christabel*, 'Alice du Clos', 'Love', 'The Ballad of the Dark Ladie', etc. Unmistakably, these romances turn to violence to resolve narrative uncertainty, most especially 'Alice du Clos', where masculine jealousy leads directly to the murder of the heroine. In addition, the fragmentary nature of the poems, and the speaker's frequent inability to describe what he sees (as in *Christabel*: 'a sight to dream of, not to tell'), point to a narrative difficulty: even when he is not the target of his own constructs of poetic violence, Coleridge its unable to complete the act. Violence is thus created through its deflection, a technique also evident in Mary Robinson; see Chapter 4. Despite Coleridge's self-proclaimed dedication to love – 'Love is the vital air of my Genius' (see *Letters*, vol. I, p. 471), in his poems it is rendered as fruitless and failed, fragmentary and aborted. See, for instance, Anthony Harding, *Coleridge and the Idea of Love* (Cambridge: Cambridge University Press, 1974); Edward Bostetter, *The Romantic Ventriloquists* (Seattle: University of Washington Press, 1963), Chapter 3; and Jeanie Watson, *Risking Enchantment: Coleridge's Symbolic World of Faery* (London: University of Nebraska Press, 1990).

2 Claudine Herrmann, *Les Voleuses de langue*, in Nancy K. Miller, 'The Text's Heroine: A Feminist Critic and Her Fictions' (*Feminist Literary Criticism*, ed. Mary Eagleton [New York: Longman Inc., 1991], 62. Translation by Miller). Although Miller's essay focuses on female subjectivity, the romance vocabulary both in her essay's title and in the quotation from Herrmann indicate the infusion of romance ideology in the construction of sexual relations and gender identity. Herrmann's quotation points to the expected heroic behavioural paradigms of masculinity.

3 And, of course, by genre; Keats's unabashed writing of romances conformed to critical expectations of his abilities, as informed by his class, but also marked him as a writer of feminine verse. Hazlitt's well-known judgement that 'the fault of Mr Keats's poems was a deficiency in masculine energy of style' serves as one example (from Essay XXV in *Table-Talk: or, Original Essays*, 1822; found in *Keats: The Narrative Poems, A Casebook*, ed. John Spencer Hill [Basingstoke: Macmillan, 1983], 48).

4 Beer, *The Romance* (London: Methuen and Co., 1970), 10. Subsequent references will be made in the text.

5 Levy, *The Sword from the Rock* (London: Faber and Faber, 1953), 211.

6 Bowra, *Heroic Poetry* (London: Macmillan Press, 1966), 91, 97. Subsequent references will be made in the text.

7 Reed, *Meditations on the Hero* (1974; New Haven: Yale University Press, 1978), 10. Subsequent references will be made in the text.

8 Bishop, *The Romantic Hero and his Heirs in French Literature* (New York: Peter Lang, 1984), 2, 4, 5. Subsequent references will be made in the text.

Although Bishop studies mainly French literature, in his general comments on the heroic identity he draws on English and American literature as well.

9 See, for instance, Anne Mellor, *Romanticism and Gender* (London: Routledge, 1993); Marlon Ross, *The Contours of Masculine Desire* (New York: Oxford University Press, 1989); Jacqueline M. Labbe, *Romantic Visualities: Landscape, Gender and Romanticism* (Basingstoke: Macmillan, 1998); Tim Fulford, *Romanticism and Masculinity: Gender, Politics and Poetics in the Writings of Burke, Coleridge, Cobbett, Wordsworth, De Quincey, and Hazlitt* (Basingstoke: Macmillan, 1999).

10 Marlon Ross, 'Romantic Quest and Conquest: Troping Masculine Power in the Crisis of Poetic Identity', *Romanticism and Feminism*, ed. Anne K. Mellor (Bloomington: Indiana University Press, 1988), 48. Subsequent references will be made in the text.

11 A spectacular example of an attempt to get around this difficulty is Wordsworth's *Prelude*, an epic romance of the self that is determinedly heroic but also, in its focus on a single subjectivity, determinedly detached from culture. At least, that would seem to be Wordsworth's quest.

12 Robinson, *The Current of Romantic Passion* (Madison, WI: The University of Wisconsin Press, 1991), 74, emphasis added. Subsequent references will be made in the text.

13 Mellor, *Romanticism and Gender*, 20. Subsequent references will be made in the text.

14 Edward E. Bostetter, *The Romantic Ventriloquists*, 93.

15 Gerald Enscoe, *Eros and the Romantics* (The Hague: Mouton, 1967), 166.

16 Hoxie Neale Fairchild, *The Romantic Quest* (New York: Columbia University Press, 1931), 335.

17 Ironically, this staccato style is mirrored in some work on Coleridge; specifically, Richard Holmes's biography, the second part of which did not appear until nine years after the first, but which has been hailed as a work of deep intelligence. See Holmes, *Coleridge: Early Visions* (London: Hodder and Stoughton, 1989), and *Coleridge: Darker Reflections* (New York: HarperCollins, 1998).

18 This is more openly displayed in what Jeanie Watson calls his tales of Faery; see *Risking Enchantment*.

19 This frailty is used poetically in 'The Lime-Tree Bower my Prison', but it is also evinced in Coleridge's well-documented nightmares, addictions and emotional excesses, all of which further underscore his tendency towards sensibility.

20 For further discussions of these hero-types, see Thorslev, *The Byronic Hero* (Minneapolis: University of Minnesota Press, 1962), 27–50 *passim*. The Gothic finds more play, of course, in a poem like *Christabel*, but it also makes its appearance in, for instance, the unearthly quiet and fluttering 'stranger' in 'Frost at Midnight'.

21 Tellingly, Coleridge begins his quest having already apparently gained one of the main rewards offered by the romance – the love of a fair maid; however, as Kelvin Everest notes, the love union in Coleridge's handling is idealised into impossibility. See Everest, *Coleridge's Secret Ministry* (Sussex: Harvester Press, 1979), 46 *passim*. Subsequent references to Everest will be made in the text.

22 'The Eolian Harp', *The Oxford Authors: Samuel Taylor Coleridge*, ed. H.J. Jackson (Oxford: Oxford University Press, 1985), 1 1, 7, 2, 3. Subsequent references, to line numbers, are to this edition and will be made in the text.

23 With its emphasis on stillness, 'Harp' institutes a trope common to all the poems.

24 This image, with its echoes of Marvell and 'Kubla Khan', indicates the eroticism that Coleridge mingles freely with his romanticising. See, for instance, Harding, *Coleridge and the Idea of Love*; and Everest, *Coleridge's Secret Ministry*. Jerome McGann notes that the young Coleridge was influenced by the Della Cruscans, whose eroticism was discussed in Chapter 2: see 'Mary Robinson and the Myth of Sappho' (*Modern Language Quarterly* 56 [1995]), 56, n. 3; and *The Poetics of Sensibility* (Oxford: Clarendon Press, 1996).

25 Bygrave, *Coleridge and the Self* (Basingstoke: Macmillan, 1986), 109; and see 108 *passim*. Subsequent references will be made in the text.

26 In both 'Harp' and 'Reflections' Coleridge constructs the cot as a kind of Sleeping Beauty's palace, covered over with vines, and impenetrable.

27 For a full discussion of the ramifications of the prospect view during the Romantic period, see my book, *Romantic Visualities*.

28   Oh! What a goodly scene! Here the bleak mount,
            The bare bleak mountain speckled thin with sheep;
            Grey clouds, that shadowing spot the sunny fields;
            And river, now with bushy rocks o'er-browed,
            Now winding bright and full, with naked banks;
            And seats, *and* lawns, the Abbey *and* the wood,
            And cots, *and* hamlets, *and* faint city-spire;
            The Channel there, *and* Islands *and* white sails,
            Dim coasts, *and* cloud-like hills, *and* shoreless Ocean —
                            (29–37, emphasis added)
    The repetition of 'and' enhances the biblical tone; this is Coleridge the visionary.

29 The matter-of-fact tone of the headnote is in contrast to the overwrought claims in the poem's first lines of loss and isolation; it seems more melodrama than romance to exclaim that he 'never more may meet again' his visiting friends. Indeed, what stands out in the first stanza is not the speaker's imprisonment but his relative freedom to roam.

30 An alternative reading would argue that Charles continues to stand in for Coleridge, and therefore the closing turn to him represents a coded turn to Coleridge's own sensibility. This displacement loses its force, however, as soon as Coleridge returns to his own perspective in the last stanza.

31 The speaker's designation of his family as 'the inmates of my cottage' heightens the suggestion of imprisonment; even during Coleridge's time, 'inmate' carried negative connotations. See the *OED*'s secondary definition of the word: 'one not originally or properly belonging to the place where he dwells; a foreigner, stranger. Often fig.'. The figurative nature of this definition makes it particularly suitable for Coleridge's poem, which relies so heavily on metaphor, while the synonym 'stranger' chimes with the image of the fluttering ash that transfixes the speaker.

32 Bygrave says that the 'satisfying "return upon itself" [that closes] the poem . . . reveal[s] itself as continuation rather than closure of the circle' (129). In this

way, it resembles a maze or labyrinth in which the hero, trapped, repeatedly returns upon himself rather than finding (or making) resolution.

33 In all six poems, but especially in the last two, Coleridge concentrates the imagery of quietness to the point that it seems marvellous he can say anything at all. Given the nature of his quest and its almost-eager failure, one might say that the imagery indicates an awareness that what he is saying must be nearly inaudible if it's even to be said. This echoes Coleridge's strategy in *Christabel*, previously noted, where the fragmentary nature of the poem, matched with speaker's carefully chosen moments of speechlessness, allow Coleridge both to write and not to write his Gothic horrors.

34 One could read the introduction of the lord's deserted castle as somehow an example of the nightingale's song, but this requires a stretch and at any rate only further establishes the vexed nature of that song.

35 It is tempting to read the absent lord as another speaker-proxy, one who has escaped the confines of a failed and circular quest.

36 Although it is, of course, 'a Poetic Romance', *Endymion* does not form a part of this chapter. In this poem Keats is still working through a devotion to 'old romance', and *Endymion* itself offers few challenges to the form. See Nancy Moore Goslee, 'The Envisioning of Women: from *Endymion* to the Later Romantics', *Approaches to Teaching Keats's Poetry*, eds Walter H. Evert and Jack W. Rhodes (New York: Modern Language Association of America, 1991), 112–19; Ronald A. Sharp, 'Keats's *Endymion*', *Explicator* 37 (1979), 24; Miriam Allott, 'Keats's *Endymion* and Shelley's "Alastor"', *Literature of the Romantic Period, 1750–1850*, eds R. T. Davies and Bernard G. Beatty (New York: Barnes and Noble, 1976), 151–70; Stuart M. Sperry, Jr, 'The Allegory of *Endymion*', *Studies in Romanticism* 2 (1962), 38–53.

37 Stillinger, *The Hoodwinking of Madeline* (Urbana: University of Illinois Press, 1971), 31. 'Detested moods' and 'new Romance' come from Keats, *The Letters of John Keats, 1814–1821*, ed. Hyder E. Rollins (2 vols; Cambridge, MA: Harvard University Press, 1958), I, 262–3, and are found in Stillinger, 31. Subsequent references to Stillinger will be made in the text.

38 In this way Stillinger positions himself as hero, rescuing the text from obscurity. *Isabella* is still under-regarded; without by any means regarding it as a failure, I too seek to rescue it from its usual position as 'just a romance'.

39 Levinson, *Keats's Life of Allegory* (Oxford: Blackwells Ltd, 1988), 5. Subsequent references will be made in the text.

40 Fischer, *Romantic Verse Narrative* , tr. Sue Bollans (Cambridge: Cambridge University Press, 1991), 30.

41 See *Romanticism and Gender*, Part III, pp. 171–186.

42 Letter to John Taylor, 27 February 1818, in *Keats: The Narrative Poems, A Casebook*, ed. John Spencer Hill, 27. Subsequent references to materials found in Spencer Hill will be made in the text.

43 This can be compared with Coleridge's interest in Christabel's well-being: 'Jesu, Maria, shield her well!' and 'O shield her! shield sweet Christabel!' (I:54, 254).

44 van Ghent, *Keats: The Myth of the Hero*, rev. and ed. Jeffrey Cane Robinson (Princeton: Princeton University Press, 1983). Subsequent references will be made in the text.

45 There are also competing explanations of the versions; Elizabeth Cook's 1990 *Oxford Authors* edition states that 'The alterations made in the *Indicator* versions may have been made by Hunt. If they are Keats's own revisions they were made at a time of serious ill health which may well have led to a failure of nerve and loss of confidence in earlier judgements'. H.W. Garrod's 1956 edition, however, declares 'that its variants go back to Keats himself, and are not the work of Hunt, [which] seems sufficiently indicated by the fact that John Jeffry had a manuscript of the poem, in Keats's autograph, in which the first line was given as its appears in the *Indicator'*. See Cook, *The Oxford Authors: John Keats* (Oxford: Oxford University Press, 1990), 601, and Garrod, *Keats: The Poetical Works* (1956; Oxford: Oxford University Press, 1992), 465.

    For discussions of the Knight's culpability, see Karen Swann, 'Harassing the Muse', *Romanticism and Feminism*, ed. Anne K. Mellor (Bloomington: Indiana University Press, 1988), 81–92; and Labbe, *Romantic Visualities*, 107–12.

46 The persistent undervaluing of the romance as unworthy of a mature poet's consideration is reflected in such attempts to import philosophy – a 'higher' intellectual pursuit – into the poem. While such approaches can be illuminating, they all depend on the assumption that any meaning in the romance is self-evident and plot-led; that is, once recognised *as* a romance, the romance itself has been thoroughly explicated, and it is time to start allegorising the players.

47 See Swann, 88, 87.

48 'La Belle Dame Sans Merci', *The Oxford Authors: John Keats*, ed. Elizabeth Cook, 15, 16. Subsequent references to Keats's poetry will be to this edition and will be made in the text.

49 This dismissal functions overtly, but in his oppression of the Dame, the Knight/wight actually embodies the dark side of chivalry. See Chapter 1.

50 Enscoe, 135. The Wasserman quote is drawn from *The Finer Tone* (Baltimore: Johns Hopkins University Press, 1953), 74.

51 In this way Keats can be said to vampirise his poetic creations: they become useful only for what they have to offer.

52 I will discuss the romances in the order in which they appeared in the 1820 volume; as with Coleridge's conversation poems, they make up a sequence of violence that surges, peaks, and then falls back: detumescence. For a discussion of the 1820 romances as paradoxically supporting and rejecting romance values, see Tilottama Rajan, *Dark Interpreter: The Discourse of Romanticism* (Ithaca: Cornell University Press, 1980).

53 Paradoxically, of course, this results in increased desire; the Odes perform a kind of tease with their pictures of lush sensuality held in stasis.

54 David Perkins is thoroughly unimpressed: Lycius 'has little to characterize him except an extraordinary capacity for wish-fulfillment, a desire to retreat with his vision, and a lack of flexibility' (*The Quest for Permanence: The Symbolism of Wordsworth, Shelley and Keats* [Cambridge, MA: Harvard University Press, 1959], 265). For most critics, it seems, Lycius is a strangely uncompelling hero; the implied question is, what does Lamia see in him?

55 In this opening non-encounter Lamia claims the masculine sense of vision; Lycius is the objectified sexual attraction.

56 See Spencer Hill, 31, n. 1.

57   And last, pointing to Corinth, ask'd her sweet,
      If 'twas too far that night for her soft feet.
      The way was short, for Lamia's eagerness
      Made, by a spell, the triple league decrease
      To a few paces; not at all surmised
      By blinded Lycius, so in her comprized.
      They pass'd the city gates, he knew not how,
      So noiseless, and he never thought to know.
               (I:342–9)
    Lycius' concern for Lamia is undercut by the narrator's switch to Lamia's
    'eagerness' and her ability to shorten the distance home without Lycius'
    even noticing. Again, he is 'blind', bereft of his masculine vision, while
    Lamia directs and controls their course and destination.
58 Lycius' habitual shrinking functions descriptively; he personifies the
    detumescence that Keats uses to compromise his heroes' status.
59 See Chapter 4 for a thorough discussion of the trope of the dead man in
    the romances of Mary Robinson and Felicia Hemans. This chapter offers
    the corollary vision of the disempowered hero.
60 Even as Lycius plays the part of the tyrant, he lacks the necessary equip-
    ment for 'swelling'; that is, he continues to be associated with shrinkage.
61 This scene implies that, for Lorenzo and Isabella, love lives in the head, not
    the body or the heart; one remembers how it originally entered through
    the eyes and ears, with fond gazes and sighs. But it also connotes a phallic
    dismemberment, especially in the fertility the head comes to symbolise. It
    is not so much 'head' as 'member', and in its decay Keats suggests another
    form of detumescence.
62 Boccaccio is more restrained: 'having brought a keen Razor with her, by
    help of the nurse, she divided the Head from the Body, [and] wrapped it
    up in a Napkin'. See Stillinger, 40 *passim*.
63 In this way Keats once again indicates the association between romance
    heroism and the culture of gender. For a fuller discussion of Porphyro's
    perfidy, see Stillinger, 67–93. In addition, 'melting' continues the associa-
    tion of heroic action with softness; where the Knight/wight withered,
    Lycius shrank, and Lorenzo decayed, Porphyro melts. In all four romances,
    the hero simply cannot remain whole and hard.
64 *Concise Oxford Dictionary* (Oxford: Clarendon Press, 1964), 946.

4 Interrupting the Romance: Robinson, Hemans and Dead Men

1 Although by no means its only centre: she also relies on satire, comedy and
    autobiography, as critics such as Judith Pascoe, Stuart Curran, Lisa Vargo
    and others have shown. See Pascoe, 'Mary Robinson and the Literary
    Marketplace', *Romantic Women Writers: Voices and Countervoices*, eds Paula
    Feldman and Theresa Kelley (Hanover, NH: University Press of New
    England, 1995), 252–68; Curran, 'Mary Robinson's *Lyrical Tales* in
    Context', *Re-Visioning Romanticism: British Women Writers 1776–1837*, eds
    Carol Shiner Wilson and Joel Haefner (Philadelphia: University of

190 *Notes*

Pennsylvania Press, 1994), 7–35; and Vargo, 'The Claims of "real life and manners": Coleridge and Mary Robinson', *The Wordsworth Circle* 26 (1995), 134–7.

2 Clery's original phrase is 'Romance recognises that the gentlewoman is bound by the metaphorics of appearance, that her mind is of necessity given over to superstition'. See 'The Politics of the Gothic Heroine in the 1790s', *Reviewing Romanticism*, eds Philip Martin and Robin Jarvis (Basingstoke: Macmillan, 1992), 73. Subsequent references will be made in the text.

3 See Stone, *The Family, Sex, and Marriage in England, 1500–1800* (New York: Harper and Row, 1977). This shift is, of course, almost completely class-bound, but so, too, is the world of the romance (and its readers); with only a few exceptions, it is populated by an incongruous number of Ladies, Barons, disguised princes and princesses, and so on. See also Leonore Davidoff and Catherine Hall, *Family Fortunes: Men and Women of the English Middle Class, 1780–1850* (London: Hutchinson, 1987).

4 Niklas Luhmann, *Love as Passion: the Codification of Intimacy*, tr. Jeremy Gaines and Doris L. Jones (Cambridge: Polity Press, 1986), 122, 127, original emphasis. Subsequent references will be made in the text.

5 Penelope Harvey and Peter Gow, *Sex and Violence: Issues in representation and experience* (London: Routledge, 1994), 2. Subsequent references will be made in the text.

6 For instance, the refusal by the villagers of Racedown to believe that William and Dorothy Wordsworth really were brother and sister and not illicit lovers posing as brother and sister relies on a romantic reconstruction of reality as informed by transgression and violence against social codes and mores.

7 One such target was Mary Robinson; see this chapter, below. Also see Pascoe, '"The Spectacular Flâneuse": Mary Robinson and the City of London', *The Wordsworth Circle* 23 (1992), 165–71; Jan Fergus and Janice Farrar Thaddeus, 'Women, Publishers, and Money, 1790–1820', *Studies in Eighteenth-Century Culture* 17 (1987), 191–207; Robert Bass, *The Green Dragoon: The Lives of Banastre Tarleton and Mary Robinson* (London: Redman, 1957).

8 Deborah Cameron and Elizabeth Frazer, 'Cultural difference and the lust to kill', in *Sex and Violence*, eds Harvey and Gow, 160. Subsequent references will be made in the text.

9 Letitia Landon also explores this connection, presenting female violence as an inevitable result of thwarted love; see Chapter 5.

10 Although the woman, it must be noted, does not always survive, she often does, while the man seldom does.

11 The romantic world of Robinson and Hemans is determinedly heterosexual.

12 Curran, 31. Curran sees Robinson's romantic poetry as reflecting her own condition of powerlessness and victimisation; as if she is a character of her own making, she personifies the ceaseless loop of romantic desire and rejection found in her poems. My reading sees Robinson as more active, a creator of poetry rather than a passive mirror of her life's events.

13 For biographical information on Robinson, see Robert Bass, *The Green*

Dragoon; M. J. Levy, *Perdita: The Memoirs of Mary Robinson (1758–1800)* (London: Peter Owen, 1994); Judith Pascoe, 'Mary Robinson and the Literary Marketplace'; and Stuart Curran, 'Mary Robinson's *Lyrical Tales* in Context'.

14 See Jan Fergus and Janice Farrar Thaddeus, 'Women, Publishers, and Money, 1790–1820', for a reproduction of this print; like Curran, they emphasise the personal effect on Robinson of this kind of representation.

15 For more discussions of Robinson's habitual self-fashioning, see Judith Pascoe; Eleanor Ty, 'Engendering a Female Subject: Mary Robinson's (Re)Presentations of the Self' (*English Studies in Canada* 21 [1995], 407–31); and Sharon Setzer, 'Mary Robinson's Sylphid Self: The End of Feminine Self-Fashioning' (*Philological Quarterly* 75 [1996], 501–20).

16 An attitude that persisted after her death, as Arthur Aikin shows in his admonishing comment to any young lady readers of Robinson's poetry of sensibility: 'Before a tender-hearted young lady has committed to memory the invocation to "Apathy", or learned to recite with tragic emphasis the "Ode to Ingratitude", let her at least be aware from *what reflections* the author wished to take shelter in insensibility, and for *what favours* her lovers had proved ungrateful' (in Lonsdale, *Eighteenth-Century Women Poets* [Oxford: Oxford University Press, 1990], 470).

17 Interestingly, 'Golfre' redirects the female-on-female violence of Coleridge's then-unpublished 'Christabel' to a more complicated male-on-male-via-female triangle. Where Coleridge's narrator in 'Christabel', for instance, retreats to piety and meaningful silence in the face of violence, Robinson's in 'Golfre' moves her readers closest to direct representations of bloody murder, only to fall back on 'Rime'-ish platitudes at the climax.

18 Robinson's *Lyrical Tales* are built around a series of poetic 'tales' deriving from competing genres; one also finds 'A Sanctified Tale', 'A Domestic Tale', and 'A Gypsy Tale', for instance. For further discussion of the structural nature of the *Lyrical Tales*, see Pascoe; Curran; and Vargo, 'The Implications of Desire: Tabitha Bramble and the *Lyrical Tales*', paper delivered at '1798 and Its Implications', joint conference of the British Association for Romantic Studies and the North American Society for the Study of Romanticism, 6–10 July 1998, St Mary's University College, Strawberry Hill, London.

19 Later readers of both Keats's 'Isabella' and Charlotte Dacre's *Zofloya* would find this murderous scene familiar.

20 Ty notes that Robinson's novel *The False Friend* (1799) 'is the only one by Robinson that involves an incestuous relationship between a father and his daughter' (422 n. 26), but she does not mention 'Golfre' and its violent contribution to the incest plot.

21 As is usual in poetry of the period, 'fond' is ambiguous: carrying the meaning of 'silly' as well as 'affectionate', its use allows the poet to imply criticism even as she applauds the hermit's sensibility.

22 In 'The Doublet of Grey', Robinson again uses the theme of parental opposition to galvanise her romance, while also reusing elements of 'Golfre': in this poem, a young heiress's love for the penniless peasant's son Theodore is thwarted when her father attempts his murder in the manner of Golfre with Zorietto's lover. The unnamed heroine dresses as a squire in a doublet

of grey in an attempt to save Theodore, and at the moment her father meets Theodore, she throws a spear which, directed by Fate, finds its target in 'her foe'. In the morning she sees that both her father and Theodore are 'cover'd with wounds' and, despairing, embraces first her father and then Theodore, and determines to be his bride in the grave. The poem ends with accounts of a ghostly Theodore who calls for his love, while the castle site is haunted by a bloody, shrieking maid 'in her doublet of grey'. In this poem, Robinson relocates both romance and violence in the distant past – in legend.

23   As I noted in the Introduction, the Hermit's behaviour largely anticipates that of Wordsworth's Vaudracour.

24   This line acts as a piece of false suspense, as the 'peril' which awaits the hermit is rather far away at this point, and does not actually threaten him at all.

25   Robinson's collected poems were published after her death, so it is possible that her editor, her daughter Maria Elizabeth, removed the explicit lines. This would transform an authorial revision to an editorial bowdlerisation.

26   Freud, *The interpretation of Dreams*, tr. James Strachey (1911; New York: Avon, 1965), 194; Anzieu, *Freud's Self-Analysis*, tr. Peter Graham (1975; London: The Hogarth Press and The Institute of Psycho-Analysis, 1986), 244. See also Susan Stafford Friedman, 'Scenes of a Crime: Genesis, Freud's *Interpretation of Dreams, Dora*, and Originary Narratives', *Genders* 17 (1993), 71–96.

27   Darwin, *Zoonomia, or The Laws of Organic Life* (London: Joseph Johnson, 1794), I, 204. See also David S. Miall, 'The Meaning of Dreams: Coleridge's Ambivalence', *Studies in Romanticism* 21 (1982), 57–71.

28   Robinson's mixing of hallucination and reality presents an intriguing hybrid scene: the monks the Lady sees are 'real', but the corpse she sees them carry is not. The Lady, it seems, is not creating a visionary world, but merging fantasy and reality: dressing up the romantic mundane.

29   For the majority of Robinson's readers, Catholicism itself was 'superstition', so that to move from religious to Gothic visions would be to move from one superstitious milieu to another.

30   Although the voice has said that the lover 'hastes' to the Lady, instead she 'hastens' to him, again unheroine-like in her claiming of agency, of activity.

31   It is here that the holy land is revealed clearly as a crypt.

32   It could be said, however, that the changes to the dream figured by Part Two bespeak a subconscious dissatisfaction with what she has dreamed in Part One; considering the subversiveness of the message to 'forget' and the injunction to cease mourning, Part Two's changes both answer the Lady's doubts and punish her for having had them.

33   It is also the only poem where the hero survives. It is particularly telling that the threat lies in the heroine's suppressed desire that he die.

34   *Records of Woman* (1828; Oxford: Woodstock Books, 1991), 11–12, 21–2. By placing her speaker in the feminised space of the bower, and associating her with children (as the end of the poem shows), Hemans encourages the reader to see the speaker as a woman, probably Hemans herself.

35   The critical consensus on Hemans is that she exemplified for her readers

the domestic affections, although they arrive at this conclusion via differing assumptions; see, for instance, Anthony Harding, 'Felicia Hemans and the Effacement of Woman', *Romantic Women Writers*, eds Feldman and Kelley, 138–49; Anne Mellor, *Romanticism and Gender* (New York: Routledge, 1993), esp. 123–43; Marlon Ross, *The Contours of Masculine Desire: Romanticism and the Rise of Women's Poetry* (New York: Oxford University Press, 1989); and Kevin Eubanks, 'Minerva's Veil: Hemans, Critics, and the Construction of Gender', *European Romantic Review* 8 (1997), 341–59. Subsequent references to Harding, Mellor, and Eubanks will be made in the text.

36 Francis Jeffrey uses this phrase approvingly to describe the content and subject-matter of Hemans's *Records of Woman* and *The Forest Sanctuary* in his review of 1829: *Edinburgh Review* 50 (October 1829), 32–47; 34.

37 H.T. Tuckerman, 'Mrs. Hemans', *Southern Literary Messenger* 7 (1841), 382; found in Kevin Eubanks, 'Minerva's Veil: Hemans, Criticism and the Construction of Gender', 342.

38 Feldman, 'The Poet and the Profits: Felicia Hemans and the Literary Marketplace', *Keats–Shelley Journal* 46 (1997), 167–8.

39 Henry F. Chorley, *Memorials of Mrs. Hemans. With Illustrations of her Literary Character from Her Private Correspondence* (2 vols; London: Saunders and Otley, 1836), I:137.

40 See Eubanks for a useful discussion of critical reactions to Hemans and their possible affect on her output.

41 Dugald Stewart in *The Poetical Works of Felicia Hemans*, ed. W.M. Rossetti (London: Ward Lock and Co., 1878), 375n.

42 After a six-year marriage and four sons, Hemans's husband left her in 1818 when she was pregnant with their fifth son; he went to Italy and she never saw him again. Hemans's contemporaries often praised her powers of endurance: Wordsworth, for instance, noted approvingly that although 'she was sorely tried ... a beautiful trait in her character was, that she never uttered a complaint of her husband' (*Letters of William and Dorothy Wordsworth*, ed. Alan G. Hill, Vol. VI [Oxford: Clarendon Press, 1982], 314). For a full discussion of this aspect of Hemans's life, see Norma Clarke, *Ambitious Heights: Writing, Friendship and Love* (London: Routledge, 1990). Subsequent references to Clarke will be made in the text.

43 Kanneh, 'Love, mourning and metaphor: terms of identity', *New Feminist Discourses: Critical Essays on Theories and Texts*, ed. Isobel Armstrong (London: Routledge, 1992), 135.

44 In the dream that opens the poem, Arabella sees 'the stag leap free' and connects its escape from death with her reunion with Seymour: '*thou* wert there'. That she now envisions the stricken deer cut off from healing waters shows both the continuing currency of the dream, and its reconfiguration as a nightmare.

45 In imagining 'the crimson flood/ [That] sinks thro' the greensward', Arabella also foreshadows the dominant image of *Records of Woman*; Hemans gives her despairing heroine the voice of prophecy.

46 Indeed, so much does her name suggest this virtue that Mellor even mistakenly calls her 'Constanzia' (*Romanticism and Gender*, 132).

47 Here, the reader is reminded of the similarly confused hermit in 'The

Hermit of Mont Blanc'; like the hermit, Costanza is in danger of substituting the worship of her lost love for the worship of God. As this discussion will suggest, however, it is in her very single-mindedness – her monomania – that Hemans suggests the futility of commitment to enduring, unrequited, love.

48 Hemans, like Robinson, makes use of poetic placement to underline the significance of her alterations to the romance, although she is less strict in her application.

49 Comparing Ianthis's lifeblood to a child's tears has the perhaps inadvertent effect of trivialising his death; even as a child's 'hour' of woe quickly passes, so too does Ianthis's life – and we, like the child, turn to fresh amusements.

50 Lootens, 'Hemans and Home: Victorianism, Feminine "Internal Enemies," and the Domestication of National Identity', *PMLA* 109 (1994), 243.

51 Eudora's meaningless sacrifice on the burning deck parallels the Boy's in 'Casabianca': both die fiery deaths for their belief in ideals Hemans cannot fully support.

52 Hemans avoids the far more sexualised image of Imelda either impaling herself or sucking the poison from the sword itself, but she cannot resist the vampiric picture of Imelda draining Azzo, though her goal is not continued life in the face of relentless death, but rather the opposite.

53 Emphasis added. This image reminds one of Eudora's ivy-clasp, so loving and so deadly, in 'Bride'.

54 Gertrude's commonsensical approach to fidelity contrasts strongly with Juana's mad devotion and Imelda's fatal constancy, for instance.

55 Hemans ends 'Pauline' by noting 'the tender and the true/ Left [the miniature] alone her sacrifice to prove,/ Hallowing the spot where mirth once lightly flew,/ To deep, lone, chasten'd thoughts of grief and love'. That the spot requires 'hallowing' and 'chastened thoughts' emphasises the lightness of the mirth that had characterised the manor and Pauline, still proud of her appearance, and living a life of merriment. Pauline is a flawed mother, and her unsuccessful rescue and death acts as a punishment for too much 'mirth' and self-regard.

56 Langbauer, *Women and Romance; The Consolations of Gender in the English Novel* (Ithaca: Cornell University Press, 1990), 103.

57 Terri Doughty, 'Sarah Grand's *The Beth Book*: The New Woman and the Ideology of the Romance Ending', in *Anxious Power: Reading, Writing, and Ambivalence in Narrative by Women*, eds Carol J. Singley and Susan Elizabeth Sweeney (Albany, NY: State University of New York Press, 1993), 193.

5 Transforming the Romance: the Murderous Worlds of Byron and Landon

1 Byron, 'To Romance', from *Hours of Idleness*. *The Complete Poetical Works: Vol. I*, ed. Jerome J. McGann (Oxford: Clarendon Press, 1980), 55, 6, 8. Subsequent references to Byron's poetry will be to this edition and will be made in the text.

2 Byron here achieves a double feint: the 'alas' implies the speaker's regret at

Romance's demise, but this is obviated by the speaker's simultaneous satisfaction, evident in the relish with which he describes Romance's fate.

3 See Ronald Schreiber, 'The Rejection and Redefinition of Romance in Byron's Early Poetry', *University of Mississippi Studies in English* 2 (1981), 43–63, for a similar view, although Schreiber's 'redefinition' is focused on the turn to natural description in Byron's romances.

4 See 'L.E.L.'s Last Question' by Elizabeth Barrett Browning: 'Love-learnèd she had sung of love and love/. . . . / All sounds of life assumed one tune of love' (*Victorian Women Poets*, ed. Angela Leighton [Oxford: Blackwell, 1995], 15, 21).

5 Landon, 'Six Songs', *Letitia Elizabeth Landon: Selected Writings*, eds Jerome McGann and Daniel Riess (Peterborough: Broadview Literary Texts, 1997), 1–2, 5–6, 9–12, 17–20. Subsequent references to this edition will be made in the text.

6 For a discussion of the performative aspects of Landon's dead women, see Judith Pascoe, *Romantic Theatricality: Gender, Poetry, and Spectatorship* (Ithaca: Cornell University Press, 1997), 'Coda: Letitia Landon and the Deathly Pose', 229–43. Subsequent references will be made in the text.

7 Rose, *Sexuality in the Field of Vision* (London: Verso, 1986), 228.

8 Brooks, *The Melodramatic Imagination: Balzac, James, Melodrama, and the Mode of Excess* (New Haven: Yale University Press, 1976), 30. Subsequent references will be made in the text.

9 James Smith, *Melodrama* (London: Methuen, 1973), 6. Subsequent references will be made in the text.

10 Byron's *Manfred* also invites readers to analyse its melodramatic content, for instance in the extended and none-too-convincing scene on the Jungfrau, where Manfred is rescued from suicide by the Chamois-Hunter. In its reiterated appeals to its own visuality and Manfred's patience in waiting for the Chamois-Hunter to approach near enough to save him from himself, this scene announces its theatricality – its self-conscious performativity. *Manfred* allows Byron to cram into one work a myriad of dramatic forms: epic, farce, romance, melodrama. See Philip Cox, *Gender, Genre and the Romantic Poets* (Manchester: Manchester University Press, 1996), Chapter 5: 'Lord Byron: *Manfred* and the Closet Drama' (107–30) for an illuminating discussion of some of the other dramatic aspects of the poem.

11 Morse, 'Desire and the limits of melodrama', in *Melodrama*, ed. James Redmond (Cambridge: Cambridge University Press, 1992), 24. Subsequent references will be made in the text.

12 Under this rubric the poetry of Hemans and Robinson, discussed in the previous chapter, could also be said to be melodramatic, although in character it is less heightened, less overtly dramatic than that of Landon and Byron.

13 Hays and Nikolopoulou, 'Introduction', *Melodrama: The Cultural Emergence of a Genre*, eds Hays and Nikolopoulou (New York: St. Martin's Press, 1996), x, xi. They borrow the phrase 'process-like genre' from Hans Robert Jauss. Subsequent references will be made in the text.

14 Even Amenaïde's tragedy has its basic cause in her lover's departure to the masculine world of war, but she wreaks her revenge on the trophy he

returns with, as I discuss below.

15   The epigram is Coleridge, found in Morse, 27.

16   I borrow this term from Elaine Handley, who uses it in her book *Melodramatic Tactics: Theatricalized Dissent in the English Marketplace, 1800–1885* (Stanford: Stanford University Press, 1995) to designate 'the overall significance of melodrama in terms of the more prominent and more exhaustively discussed doctrines of English romanticism' (13). As her use of lower-case 'romanticism' shows, however, Handley confuses romance and Romanticism, leading her, as Pascoe has also noticed, to oppose the melodrama to the romance. What I propose by the term is more a fusion, a recognition that the melodrama and the romance are linked forms, the melodrama dependent on and growing from the romance, as this chapter argues.

17   Atara Stein, '"I Loved Her and Destroyed Her": Love and Narcissism in Byron's *Manfred*', *Philological Quarterly* 69 (1990), 190. Subsequent references will be made in the text.

18   Caroline Franklin argues that the Byronic heroine is an ever-evolving, independent and resourceful figure in her book *Byron's Heroines* (Oxford: Clarendon Press, 1992). While her approach is provocative, it does not seem convincing in light of the actual experiences Byron creates for his female characters; my argument in the following pages challenges Franklin's on several points, and is more in line with Stuart Curran's: 'the role of women in [the *Tales*'] world is to be abused by masculine dominance' (*Poetic Form and British Romanticism* [New York: Oxford University Press, 1986], 143).

19   In this way Byron, like Hemans and Robinson, uses violence to express desire; for all, the end result is death.

20   See Seidler, *Rediscovering Masculinity: Reason, Language and Sexuality* (London: Routledge, 1989), 23, 18.

21   It should be noted that I by no means intend to imply that homosociality itself is unnatural or melodramatic; instead, I am arguing that Byron takes advantage of a cultural assumption to embed a challenge to culture in his very popular Tales. He is subversive in that he disguises his challenge in the robes of romance: like the other poets under discussion in this book, he *uses* romance to convey anticonventional sentiments. He engages in what Curran calls, referring to Jerome McGann's work on Byron, a 'critique of the masculine mystique'. See Curran, *Poetic Form and British Romanticism*, 143, and McGann, *Fiery Dust: Byron's Poetic Development* (Chicago: University of Chicago Press, 1968), esp. 141–64. For a discussion of Byron's own homo- or bisexuality, see L. Crompton, *Byron and Greek Love* (London: Faber, 1985); for a discussion of Byron's textual representations of homosexuality, see Jonathan David Gross, '"One Half What I Should Say": Byron's Gay Narrator in *Don Juan*', *European Romantic Review* 9 (1998), 323–50.

22   Hope, 'Melancholic Modernity: the Hom(m)osexual Symptom and the Homosocial Corpse', *differences* 6 (1994), 174.

23   Irigaray, *This Sex Which is Not One*, tr. Catherine Porter (Ithaca: Cornell University Press, 1985), 172.

24   See Franklin, 32 *passim*, for the key aspects of her argument.

25 'Bride', *The Complete Poetical Works*, ed. McGann, vol. III (Oxford: Clarendon Press, 1981): I:480–2. These lines introduce what Brooks calls the 'text of muteness', a reliance on non-speaking signs: 'melodrama so often has recourse to non-verbal means of expressing meaning' (56). The silence figured by the gap between cantos takes the place of the confused questioning an announcement like Selim's should logically provoke.

26 Calder, 'The Hero as Lover: Byron and Women', *Byron: Wrath and Rhyme*, ed. Alan Bold (London: Vision Press Ltd, 1983), 113. Subsequent references will be made in the text.

27 See Eve Kosofsky Sedgwick, *Between Men: English Literature and Male Homosocial Desire* (New York: Columbia University Press, 1985). See also Paul Hammond, *Love Between Men in English Literature* (Basingstoke: Macmillan, 1996): besides offering a stimulating and comprehensive discussion of literary homosociality and homosexuality, this book also contains a thorough and indispensable annotated bibliography.

28 One suspects Byron of slyly resexualising the heterosexual romance at the very moment Zuleika denies it; it seems impossible not to read this line as a pun.

29 Giaffir, for instance, never even knows of Selim's love for Zuleika; he kills Selim because of their quarrel over Selim's father, not to save Zuleika for himself or his proxy, the Sultan.

30 McGann, 'Hero With a Thousand Faces: The Rhetoric of Byronism', *Studies in Romanticism* 31 (1992), 313, 308.

31 Hassan and the Giaour also have their identifying epithets: Hassan is 'stern', the Giaour 'black'. The superficiality of their designations is itself melodramatic, remembering that the melodrama relies on easily digested, one-dimensional characterisation.

32 Byron uses this word both in its religious and its social sense: Leila is of the Giaour's faith, Christianity, so that by loving the Giaour she proves her fidelity to religion as well. In this way, she could never be anything but faithless to Hassan, whose religion she does not share.

33 Ross, 'Romantic Quest and Conquest: Troping Masculine Power in the Crisis of Poetic Identity', *Romanticism and Feminism*, ed. Anne K. Mellor (Bloomington: Indiana University Press, 1988), 45.

34 See *The Regime of the Brother: After the Patriarchy* (London: Routledge, 1991).

35 Laura Claridge, *Romantic Potency: The Paradox of Desire* (Ithaca: Cornell University Press, 1992), 242. Marilyn Butler calls the Giaour and Hassan 'opposites'; see 'The Orientalism of Byron's *Giaour*', *Byron and the Limits of Fiction*, eds Bernard Beatty and Vincent Newey (Liverpool: Liverpool University Press, 1988), 86. Subsequent references will be made in the text.

36 For instance, Hassan: '"Tis he! Well met in any hour,/ Lost Leila's love – accursèd Giaour!"' (618–19); the Giaour: '"Yes, Leila sleeps beneath the wave,/ But his shall be a redder grave;/ Her spirit pointed well the steel/ Which taught that felon heart to feel"' (675–8). It is only in her loss that the men find agreement.

37 Sonia Hofkosh writes of the 'ambivalent love affair' conducted between Byron and Scott; she says 'Taking the place of Lady Byron and the poet's other disaffected admirers, Scott in his review of *Childe Harold* takes the

poet for better and for worse'. This, she notes, constitutes a 'marriage of minds, if not of bodies'. Such an account, derived from Scott/Byron correspondence, demonstrates the viability, both then and now, of the notion of male 'romantic friendships'. See Hofkosh, 'The Writer's Ravishment: Women and the Romantic Author – The Example of Byron', *Romanticism and Feminism*, 101.

38 Richardson, 'The Dangers of Sympathy: Sibling Incest in English Romantic Poetry', *SEL* 25 (1985), 744.

39 Watkins, 'Social Relations in Byron's *The Giaour*', *ELH* 52 (1985), 883. Subsequent references will be made in the text.

40 Leila's problematic there/not-there position further vexes the Hassan/Giaour bond.

41 *Romanticism and Gender* (New York: Routledge, 1993), 26. Mellor argues that the 'most famous Romantic love poems may thus propound a sexism of a most seductive and insidious kind, for the poet claims to cherish his beloved, bright star that she is, above all else. But the love he feels is but self-love: he ignores her human otherness in order to impose his own metaphors, his own identity, upon her, to render her but a clone (or soul mate) of himself' (27). If, however, the 'Romantic poet' yearns for a 'clone', an Other whose boundaries have been collapsed into Self-sameness, then it suggests the need for sex-sameness as well, to coin a term.

42 The narrator nonetheless arraigns Conrad: his choice not to explore 'the reason why' suggests he understands very clearly his responsibility, and also indicates his refusal to accept that responsibility. The quotation is found in Marina Vitale, 'The Domesticated Heroine in Byron's *Corsair* and William Hone's Prose Adaptation', *Literature and History* 10 (1984), 74.

43 Although both Kaled and Gulnare survive the poems' violence, they are both unsexed females, existing on the margins of identity, if not of plot.

44 'Parisina' revisits the incest plot of 'Bride', but its emphasis on merely legal incest is as deflating of the potential taboo as Selim's transformation from Zuleika's brother to her cousin.

45 See Soderholm, 'Byron, Nietzsche, and the Mystery of Forgetting', *CLIO* 23 (1993), 60–1 *passim*.

46 'Preface' to *The Venetian Bracelet*, vol. IV of *The Poetical Works of Letitia Elizabeth Landon, in Four Volumes* (London: Longman, Orme, Brown, Green, and Longmans, 1839), v. Subsequent references, to 'Venetian Bracelet', will be made in the text.

47 Indeed, Stuart Curran says of Landon (and Hemans) that in their work 'we can discern ... an actual transition into the characteristic preoccupations of Victorian verse'. Curran, 'The "I" Altered', *Romanticism and Feminism*, 188.

48 For instance, almost all of Landon's recent critics focus on this aspect of her poetry: Glennis Stephenson asserts that Landon 'focuses exclusively and obsessively on romantic love', Virginia Blain considers that her 'characteristic subject-matter' was 'thwarted romantic love', and Anne Mellor argues that 'Landon's poems repetitively construct the narrative of female love', while Daniel Riese maintains that 'the doomed love story' 'always' subsumes Landon's surface subjects. See Stephenson, 'Poet Construction: Mrs. Hemans, L.E.L., and the Image of the Nineteenth-Century Woman

Poet', *ReImagining Women: Representations of Women in Culture*, eds Shirley
Neuman and Stephenson (Toronto: University of Toronto Press, 1993), 69,
and also 'Letitia Landon and the Victorian Improvisatrice: The
Construction of L.E.L.', *Victorian Poetry* 30 (1992), 1–17; Blain, 'Letitia
Elizabeth Landon, Eliza Mary Hamilton, and the Genealogy of the
Victorian Poetess', *Victorian Poetry* 33 (1995), 39; Mellor, *Romanticism and
Gender*, Chapter 6 (New York: Routledge, 1993), 113; Riess, 'Laetitia
Landon and the Dawn of English Post-Romanticism', *SEL* 36 (1996), 816.
In addition, Landon's life, by 1928, itself appeared fodder for melodrama;
see D.E. Enfield, *L.E.L., A Mystery of the Thirties* (London: Hogarth Press,
1928).

49 Linkin, 'Romantic Aesthetics in Mary Tighe and Letitia Landon: How
Women Poets Recuperate the Gaze', *European Romantic Review* 7 (1997),
174.

50 See *Romanticism and Gender*, 107–23, for Mellor's discussion of Landon's
poetry.

51 Armstrong, *Victorian Poetry: Poetry, Poetics, and Politics* (London: Routledge,
1993), 324.

52 Lionel Stevenson calls Landon a 'female Byron' in 'Miss Landon, "The
Milk-and-Watery Moon of our Darkness", 1824–30', *Modern Language
Quarterly* 8 (1947), 358.

53 Brooks notes that in melodrama, 'good and evil can be named as persons
are named – and melodramas tend in fact to move toward a clear nomina-
tion of the moral universe' (17). It is a mark of Landon's originality that
even as she presents her readers with stock characters, she complicates and
enlarges their roles; initial characterisations are inevitably reworked and
represented.

54 Although 'Venetian Bracelet' seems only to comprise thirteen parts, the
original printing uses the heading 'VII' twice in a row.

55 Stephenson, 'Letitia Landon and the Victorian Improvisatrice: The
Construction of L.E.L.', 11.

56 Landon consistently reminds us of Amenaïde's pride, suggesting another
underlying melodramatic trope: pride goeth before a fall. Here, Amenaïde
uses her pride to mask her grief: 'Oh, misery, how much she had to hide!'
(302)

57 Amenaïde's first act of violence is internalised: love itself bleeds her.

58 In its echoes of 'better half', the line suggests that Amenaïde is wed more
to Love than to her desire for Leoni.

59 The repeated Part VIIs have the inadvertent effect of linking Amenaïde's
despair at her loss and Edith's (Leoni's bride) triumph at her gain; both are
dealt with in Part 'VII'.

60 In another link, Landon allows both Amenaïde's grief and Edith's death to
figure as 'saddest scenes'; her use of superlatives is both ironic and melodramatic. Edith's death scene 'grafts a ... celebration of female loveliness
on to a scene of violent death': 'Life passing in convulsive sobs away./ Still
mid her hair the red rose wreath was hung,/ Mocking her cheek with the
rich dye it flung;/ The festal robe still sparkled as it flow'd;/ Still on her
neck a few fresh flowers glow'd...' (604–8). The quotation is from Clare R.
Kinney, 'Chivalry Unmasked: Courtly Spectacle and the Abuses of

Romance in Sidney's *New Arcadia*', *SEL* 35 (1995), 46.

61 Many readers, of course, did just that, leading to the construction of L.E.L. as a fallen woman; both Mellor and Stephenson record William Macready's 1835 diary indictment: 'She is fallen!' (Stephenson 71; Mellor 122; Macready, *The Diaries of William Charles Macready, 1833–1851*, ed. William Toynbee [London: Chapman and Hall, 1912], I, 262). However, it is much easier to read Landon's narrators as the speaker in a dramatic monologue, whose own story is subsumed to the narration at hand, but who cannot refrain from hints and suggestions. This, of course, is in line with Landon's creative exploration of the improvisatrice, and in many of her poems she relies on the figure of the female bard: Isabelle in 'Roland's Tower' is introduced to readers as just such a figure. Isobel Armstrong contends in *Victorian Poetry* that the genre of the dramatic monologue was in fact 'invented' by women poets, commenting on the many female poets who spoke in another's voice in their work years before Browning and Tennyson took up the form; see Armstrong, 325 *passim*.

62 Even as Amenaïde's flaw is pride, so too Isabelle has hers: her eyes 'were too passionate for happiness' (75). And yet, despite the narrator's warning against indulging in passion, and Isabelle's 'too passionate' eyes, the poem's catastrophe proceeds rather from Roland's defect, as I will discuss.

63 We are first introduced to Isabelle when she is 'in the April hour of life'. Landon uses the imagery of the seasons to anchor her plot and suggest its developments, but this also associates the love story with the cycle of the seasons, always inexorably leading to winter.

64 There is a mystery surrounding this scarf. It is the same one that Isabelle gives to Roland 'for his colours': 'he snatched the scarf/ That Isabelle had tied around his neck,/ And gave it her' (123, 168–70). And yet, when Isabelle gives it to Roland it is *blue*. Although this may simply be a mistake on Landon's part, it is interesting to note that Isabelle's eyes, 'too passionate for happiness', also undergo a change of colour; just before she enters the convent we are told that 'her dim eye/ Had wept away its luxury of blue' (159–60). Somehow, Roland's error has drained the colour from Isabelle – she has moved from blue to white, from summer to winter. As much as Isabelle's love has undone Roland, his love has vampirised her: Love, plainly, is bad for you.

65 In this way Landon's version of Love functions like the dark version of chivalry described in Chapter 1.

66 From *The Golden Violet, with its Tales of Romance and Chivalry: and Other Poems* (London: Longman, Rees, Orme, Brown, and Green, 1827).

67 The speaker uses 'you' throughout, allowing lover and Love to conflate.

Bibliography

Aesthetics and Ideology. Ed. George Levine. New Brunswick, NJ: Rutgers University Press, 1994.

Allott, Miriam. *Novelists on the Novel.* London: Routledge and Kegan Paul, 1959.

Anzieu, Didier. *Freud's Self-Analysis.* Tr. Peter Graham. London: The Hogarth Press and The Institute of Psycho-Analysis, 1986.

Armstrong, Isobel. *Victorian Poetry: Poetry, Poetics, and Politics.* London: Routledge, 1993.

Armstrong, Nancy and Leonard Tennenhouse. *The Violence of Representation: Literature and the history of violence.* London: Routledge, 1989.

Auerbach, Eric. *Mimesis.* Tr. Willard R. Trask. Princeton: Princeton University Press, 1974.

Barbauld, Anna Letitia Aikin and John Aikin. *Miscellaneous Pieces in Prose and Verse. Novel and Romance 1700–1800, A Documentary.* Ed. Ioan Williams. London: Routledge and Kegan Paul, 1970. 280–90.

Bass, Robert. *The Green Dragoon: The Lives of Banastre Tarleton and Mary Robinson.* London: Redman, 1957.

Batty, John. *The Spirit and Influence of Chivalry.* London: Elliot Stock, 1890.

Beattie, James. *On Fable and Romance. Novel and Romance 1700–1800, A Documentary.* Ed. Ioan Williams. London: Routledge and Kegan Paul, 1970. 309–27.

Beer, Gillian. *The Romance.* London: Methuen and Co. Ltd, 1970.

Beiderwell, Bruce. 'Scott's *Redgauntlet* as a Romance of Power'. *Studies in Romanticism* 28 (1989): 273–89.

Bishop, Lloyd. *The Romantic Hero and his Heirs in French Literature.* New York: Peter Lang, 1984.

Blain, Virginia. 'Letitia Elizabeth Landon, Eliza Mary Hamilton, and the Genealogy of the Victorian Poetess'. *Victorian Poetry* 33 (1995): 31–52.

—. '"Thou with Earth's Music Answerest to the Sky": Felicia Hemans, Mary Ann Browne, and the myth of poetic sisterhood'. *Women's Writing* 2 (1995): 251–69.

Blair, Hugh. 'On Fictitious History'. *Lectures on Rhetoric and Poetry. Novel and Romance 1700–1800, A Documentary.* Ed. Ioan Williams. London: Routledge and Kegan Paul, 1970. 247–51.

Bostetter, Edward. *The Romantic Ventriloquists.* Seattle: University of Washington Press, 1963.

—. 'The Original Della Cruscans and the Florence Miscellany'. *Huntingdon Library Quarterly* 19 (1956): 277–300.

Bowra, C.M. *Heroic Poetry.* London: Macmillan Press, 1966.

The British Album, In Two Volumes. London: John Bell, 1792.

Brooks, Peter. *The Melodramatic Imagination: Balzac, James, Melodrama, and the Mode of Excess.* New Haven: Yale University Press, 1976.

—. 'Aesthetics and Ideology – What Happened to Poetics?' *Aesthetics and Ideology.* Ed. George Levine. New Brunswick, NJ: Rutgers University Press, 1994. 153–67.

Brownstein, Rachel. *Becoming a Heroine: Reading About Women in Novels*. New York: Columbia University Press, 1994.

Burke, Edmund. *Reflections on the Revolution in France, and on the Proceedings in Certain Societies in London Relative to that Event*. Ed. Conor Cruise O'Brien. Harmondsworth: Penguin, 1969.

Butler, Marilyn. 'The Orientalism of Byron's *Giaour*'. *Byron and the Limits of Fiction*. Eds. Bernard Beatty and Vincent Newey. Liverpool: Liverpool University Press, 1988. 78–96.

Bygrave, Stephen. *Coleridge and the Self*. Basingstoke: Macmillan, 1986.

Byron, Lord. *The Complete Poetical Works*. Ed. Jerome J. McGann. 7 vols. Oxford: Clarendon Press, 1980–93.

Calder, Jenni. 'The Hero as Lover: Byron and Women'. *Byron: Wrath and Rhyme*. Ed. Alan Bold. London: Vision Press Ltd, 1983. 103–24.

Cameron, Deborah and Elizabeth Frazer. 'Cultural difference and the lust to kill'. *Sex and Violence: Issues in representation and experience*. Eds Penelope Harvey and Peter Gow. London: Routledge, 1994. 156–71.

Canning, George. *The Microcosm* 26 (14 May 1787). *Novel and Romance 1700–1800, A Documentary*. Ed. Ioan Williams. London: Routledge and Kegan Paul, 1970. 341–6.

Chorley, Henry F. *Memorials of Mrs. Hemans. With Illustrations of her Literary Character from Her Private Correspondence*. 2 vols. London: Saunders and Otley, 1836.

Claridge, Laura. *Romantic Potency: The Paradox of Desire*. Ithaca: Cornell University Press, 1992.

Clarke, Norma. *Ambitious Heights: Writing, Friendship and Love*. London: Routledge, 1990.

Clery, E.J. 'The Politics of the Gothic Heroine in the 1790s'. *Reviewing Romanticism*. Eds Philip Martin and Robin Jarvis. Basingstoke: Macmillan, 1992. 69–85.

Coleridge, Samuel Taylor. *The Oxford Authors: Samuel Taylor Coleridge*. Ed. H.J. Jackson. Oxford: Oxford University Press, 1985.

Cox, Philip. *Gender, Genre and the Romantic Poets*. Manchester: Manchester University Press, 1996.

Craciun, Adriana. 'Introduction'. *Zofloya*, by Charlotte Dacre. Peterborough: Broadview Press, 1997. 9–32.

Curran, Stuart. *Poetic Form and British Romanticism*. New York: Oxford University Press, 1986.

—. 'Mary Robinson's *Lyrical Tales* in Context'. *Re-Visioning Romanticism: British Women Writers 1776–1837*. Eds. Carol Shiner Wilson and Joel Haefner. Philadelphia: University of Pennsylvania Press, 1994. 7–35.

—. 'The "I" Altered'. *Romanticism and Feminism*. Ed. Anne K. Mellor. Bloomington: Indiana University Press, 1988. 185–207.

Darwin, Erasmus. *Zoonomia, or The Laws of Organic Life*. London: Joseph Johnson, 1794.

Davidoff, Leonore and Catherine Hall. *Family Fortunes: Men and Women of the English Middle Class, 1780–1850*. London: Hutchinson, 1987.

Davies, Kate. *Gender and Republicanism in Britain and America: The Meanings of Catherine Macauley*. Unpublished D.Phil. thesis. University of York, England, 1999.

Dibattista, Maria. '"Sabbath Eyes": Ideology and the Writer's Gaze'. *Aesthetics and Ideology*. Ed. George Levine. New Brunswick, NJ: Rutgers University Press, 1994. 168–87.

Dobson, Susannah. *The Literary History of the Troubadours. Containing their Lives, Extracts from the Works, And many Particulars relative to the Customs, Morals, and History of the Twelfth and Thirteenth Centuries. Collected and Abridged from the French of Mr. De Saint-Pelaie, By the Author of the Life of Plutarch.* London: T. Cadell, 1779.

—. *Memoirs of Ancient Chivalry. To Which are Added, The Anecdotes of the Times, from the Romance Writers and Historians of those Ages. Translated from the French of Monsieur de St. Palaye, by the Translator of the Life of Plutarch.* London: J. Dodsley, 1784.

Doughty, Terri. 'Sarah Grand's *The Beth Book*: The New Woman and the Ideology of the Romance Ending'. *Anxious Power: Reading, Writing, and Ambivalence in Narrative by Women.* Eds. Carol J. Singley and Susan Elizabeth Sweeney. Albany, NY: State University of New York Press, 1993. 185–96.

Duff, David. *Romance and Revolution: Shelley and the Politics of a Genre.* Cambridge: Cambridge University Press, 1994.

Eagleton, Terry. *The Ideology of the Aesthetic.* Oxford: Basil Blackwell, 1990.

Enfield, D.E. *L.E.L., A Mystery of the Thirties.* London: Hogarth Press, 1928.

Enscoe, Gerald. *Eros and the Romantics.* The Hague: Mouton, 1967.

Eubanks, Kevin. 'Minerva's Veil: Hemans, Critics, and the Construction of Gender'. *European Romantic Review* 8 (1997): 341–59.

Everest, Kelvin. *Coleridge's Secret Ministry.* Sussex: The Harvester Press, 1979.

Fairchild, Hoxie Neale. *The Romantic Quest.* New York: Columbia University Press, 1931.

Feldman, Paula R. 'The Poet and the Profits: Felicia Hemans and the Literary Marketplace'. *Keats–Shelley Journal* 46 (1997): 148–76.

Fergus, Jan and Janice Farrar Thaddeus. 'Women, Publishers, and Money, 1790–1820'. *Studies in Eighteenth-Century Culture* 17 (1987): 191–207.

Fischer, Hermann. *Romantic Verse Narrative* . Tr. Sue Bollans. Cambridge: Cambridge University Press, 1991.

Franklin, Caroline. *Byron's Heroines.* Oxford: Clarendon Press, 1992.

Freud, Sigmund. *The Interpretation of Dreams.* Tr. James Strachey. New York: Avon, 1965.

Friedman, Susan Stafford. 'Scenes of a Crime: Genesis, Freud's *Interpretation of Dreams, Dora,* and Originary Narratives'. *Genders* 17 (1993): 71–96.

Frye, Northrop. *The Secular Scripture: A Study of the Structure of Romance.* Cambridge, MA: Harvard University Press, 1976.

Gamer, Michael. 'Marketing a Masculine Romance: Scott, Antiquarianism, and the Gothic'. *Studies in Romanticism* 32 (1993): 523–49.

Gifford, William. *The Baviad and Maeviad.* London: Becket and Porter, 1800.

Girouard, Mark. *The Return to Camelot: Chivalry and the English Gentleman.* New Haven: Yale University Press, 1981.

Handley, Elaine. *Melodramatic Tactics: Theatricalized Dissent in the English Marketplace, 1800–1885.* Stanford: Stanford University Press, 1995.

Harding, Anthony. *Coleridge and the Idea of Love.* Cambridge: Cambridge University Press, 1974.

—. 'Felicia Hemans and the Effacement of Woman'. *Romantic Women Writers:*

Voices and Countervoices. Eds Paula R. Feldman and Theresa Kelley. Hanover, NH: University Press of New England, 1995. 138–49.

Hargreaves-Mawdsley, W.N. *The English Della Cruscans and Their Time, 1783–1828*. The Hague: Martinus Nijhoff, 1967.

Harvey, Penelope and Peter Gow. *Sex and Violence: issues in representation and experience*. London: Routledge, 1994.

Haywood, Eliza. *The Tea-Table, or a Conversation between some Polite Persons of both sexes at a Lady's Visiting Day. Novel and Romance 1700–1800, A Documentary*. Ed. Ioan Williams. London: Routledge and Kegan Paul, 1970. 82–4.

Hemans, Felicia. *Records of Woman*. Oxford: Woodstock Books, 1991.

—. *The Poetical Works of Felicia Hemans*. Ed. W.M. Rossetti. London: Ward Lock and Co., 1878.

Hofkosh, Sonia. 'The Writer's Ravishment: Women and the Romantic Author – The Example of Byron'. *Romanticism and Feminism*. Ed. Anne K. Mellor. Bloomington: Indiana University Press, 1988. 93–114.

Hogle, Jerrold. 'The Gothic Ghost as Counterfeit and its Haunting of Romanticism: The Case of "Frost at Midnight"'. *European Romantic Review* 9 (1998): 283–92.

Hope, Trevor. 'Melancholic Modernity: the Hom(m)osexual Symptom and the Homosocial Corpse'. *differences* 6 (1994): 174–98.

Huet, Pierre Daniel. *The History of Romances, An Enquiry into their Origin; Instructions for composing them; An Account of the most Eminent Authors; With Characters and Curious Observations upon the Best Performances of that Kind*. Tr. Stephen Lewis. *Novel and Romance 1700–1800, A Documentary*. Ed. Ioan Williams. London: Routledge and Kegan Paul, 1970. 43–55.

Hurd, Bishop. *Letters on Chivalry and Romance, with the Third Elizabethan Dialogue*. Ed. Edith J. Morley. London: Henry Frowde, 1911.

Irigaray, Luce. *This Sex Which is Not One*. Tr. Catherine Porter. Ithaca: Cornell University Press, 1985.

Jameson, Fredric. 'Magical Narratives: Romance as Genre'. *New Literary History* 7 (1975): 135–63.

Jeffrey, Francis. *Edinburgh Review* 50 (October 1829): 32–47.

Johnston, Arthur. *Enchanted Ground: The Study of Medieval Romance in the Eighteenth Century*. London: The Athlone Press, 1964.

Kanneh, Kadiatu. 'Love, mourning and metaphor: terms of identity'. *New Feminist Discourses: Critical Essays on Theories and Texts*. Ed. Isobel Armstrong. London: Routledge, 1992. 135–53.

Keach, William. '"Words Are Things": Romantic Ideology and the Matter of Poetic Language'. *Aesthetics and Ideology*. Ed. George Levine. New Brunswick, NJ: Rutgers University Press, 1994. 219–39.

Keats, John. *The Poetical Works*. Ed. H.W. Garrod. Oxford: Oxford University Press, 1956; repr.1992.

—. *The Oxford Authors: John Keats*. Ed. Elizabeth Cook. Oxford: Oxford University Press, 1990.

—. *The Letters of John Keats, 1814–1821*. Ed. Hyder E. Rollins. 2 vols. Cambridge, MA: Harvard University Press, 1958.

Keats: The Narrative Poems, A Casebook. Ed. John Spencer Hill. Basingstoke: Macmillan, 1983.

Kinney, Clare R. 'Chivalry Unmasked: Courtly Spectacle and the Abuses of Romance in Sidney's *New Arcadia'. SEL* 35 (1995): 35–52.

Knox, Vicessimus. 'On Novel Reading'. *Essays Moral and Literary: No. XIV. Novel and Romance 1700–1800, A Documentary.* Ed. Ioan Williams. London: Routledge and Kegan Paul, 1970. 304–7.

Labbe, Jacqueline M. *Romantic Visualities: Landscape, Gender, and Romanticism.* Basingstoke: Macmillan, 1998.

—. 'A Family Romance; Mary Wollstonecraft, Mary Godwin, and Travel'. *Genre* 25 (1992): 211–28.

Landon, Letitia Elizabeth. *Letitia Elizabeth Landon: Selected Writings.* Eds. Jerome McGann and Daniel Riess. Peterborough: Broadview Press, 1997.

—. *The Golden Violet, with its Tales of Romance and Chivalry: and Other Poems.* London: Longman, Rees, Orme, Brown, and Green, 1827.

—. *The Poetical Works of Letitia Elizabeth Landon, in Four Volumes.* London: Longman, Orme, Brown, Green, and Longmans, 1839.

Langbauer, Laurie. *Women and Romance: The Consolations of Gender in the English Novel.* Ithaca: Cornell University Press, 1990.

Leighton, Angela. *Victorian Women Poets: Writing Against the Heart.* New York: Harvester–Wheatsheaf, 1992.

Levinson, Marjorie. *Keats's Life of Allegory.* Oxford: Blackwells Ltd, 1988.

Levy, G.R. *The Sword from the Rock.* London: Faber and Faber, 1953.

Levy, M.J. *Perdita: The Memoirs of Mary Robinson (1758–1800): Poet, novelist, feminist, first mistress of George IV.* London: Peter Owen, 1994.

Linkin, Harriet K. 'Romantic Aesthetics in Mary Tighe and Letitia Landon: How Women Poets Recuperate the Gaze'. *European Romantic Review* 7 (1997): 159–88.

Lonsdale, Roger. *Eighteenth-Century Women Poets.* Oxford: Oxford University Press, 1990.

Lootens, Tricia. 'Hemans and Home: Victorianism, Feminine "Internal Enemies," and the Domestication of National Identity'. *PMLA* 109 (1994): 238–53.

Luhmann, Niklas. *Love as Passion: the Codification of Intimacy.* Tr. Jeremy Gaines and Doris L. Jones. Cambridge: Polity Press, 1986.

MacCannell, Juliet Flower. *The Regime of the Brother: After the Patriarchy.* London: Routledge, 1991.

Macready, William. *The Diaries of William Charles Macready, 1833–1851.* Ed. William Toynbee. London: Chapman and Hall, 1912.

McGann, Jerome. *Fiery Dust: Byron's Poetic Development.* Chicago: University of Chicago Press, 1968.

—. *The Poetics of Sensibility: A Revolution in Literary Style.* Oxford: Clarendon Press, 1996.

—. 'Hero With a Thousand Faces: The Rhetoric of Byronism'. *Studies in Romanticism* 31 (1992): 295–314.

—. 'Mary Robinson and the Myth of Sappho'. *Modern Language Quarterly* 56 (1995): 55–76.

Mellor, Anne. *Romanticism and Gender.* London: Routledge, 1993.

Melodrama: The Cultural Emergence of a Genre. Eds. Michael Hays and Anastasia Nikolopoulou. New York: St. Martin's Press, 1996.

Melodrama. Ed. James Redmond. Cambridge: Cambridge University Press, 1992.

Miall, David S. 'The Meaning of Dreams: Coleridge's Ambivalence'. *Studies in Romanticism* 21 (1982): 57–71.

Michasiw, Kim Ian. 'Introduction'. *Zofloya, or The Moor*, by Charlotte Dacre. Oxford: Oxford University Press, 1977. vii–xxx.

Miller, Nancy K. 'The Text's Heroine: A Feminist Critic and Her Fictions'. *Feminist Literary Criticism*. Ed. Mary Eagleton. New York: Longman Inc., 1991. 61–9.

Montagu, Elizabeth. 'Dialogue XXVIII'. *Dialogues of the Dead. Novel and Romance 1700–1800, A Documentary*. Ed. Ioan Williams. London: Routledge and Kegan Paul, 1970. 222–9.

Morse, William. 'Desire and the limits of melodrama'. *Melodrama*. Ed. James Redmond. Cambridge: Cambridge University Press, 1992. 17–30.

Murray, Hugh. *The Morality of Fiction; or, An Inquiry into the Tendency of Fictitious Narratives, with Observations on Some of the Most Eminent*. Edinburgh: Mundell and Son, 1805.

Novel and Romance 1700–1800, A Documentary. Ed. Ioan Williams. London: Routledge and Kegan Paul, 1970.

Parker, Patricia. *Inescapable Romance: Studies in the Poetics of a Mode*. Princeton: Princeton University Press, 1979.

Pascoe, Judith. *Romantic Theatricality: Gender, Poetry, and Spectatorship*. Ithaca: Cornell University Press, 1997.

—. 'Mary Robinson and the Literary Marketplace'. *Romantic Women Writers: Voices and Countervoices*. Eds. Paula Feldman and Theresa Kelley. Hanover, NH: University Press of New England, 1995. 252–68.

—. '"The Spectacular Flâneuse": Mary Robinson and the City of London'. *The Wordsworth Circle* 23 (1992): 165–71.

The Percy Letters: The Correspondence of Thomas Percy and Richard Farmer. Ed. Cleanth Brooks. 2 vols. Baton Rouge: Louisiana State University Press, 1946.

Perkins, David. *The Quest for Permanence: The Symbolism of Wordsworth, Shelley and Keats*. Cambridge, MA: Harvard University Press, 1959.

Pinch, Adela. 'Learning What Hurts: Romanticism, Pedagogy, Violence'. *Lessons of Romanticism: A Critical Companion*. Ed. Thomas Pfau and Robert Gleckner. Durham: Duke University Press, 1998. 413–28.

Praz, Mario. *The Romantic Agony*. Tr. Angus Davidson. Oxford: Oxford University Press, 1970.

Rajan, Tilottama. *Dark Interpreter: The Discourse of Romanticism*. Ithaca: Cornell University Press, 1980.

Reed, Walter. *Meditations on the Hero*. New Haven: Yale University Press, 1978.

Reeve, Clara. *The Progress of Romance*. Dublin: Price, Exshaw, White, Cash, Colbert, Marchbank and Porter, 1785.

Re-Visioning Romanticism: British Women Writers 1776–1837. Eds Carol Shiner Wilson and Joel Haefner. Philadelphia: University of Pennsylvania Press, 1994.

Richardson, Alan. 'The Dangers of Sympathy: Sibling Incest in English Romantic Poetry'. *SEL* 25 (1985): 737–54.

Riess, Daniel. 'Laetitia Landon and the Dawn of English Post-Romanticism'. *SEL* 36 (1996): 807–27.

Robinson, Jeffrey. *The Current of Romantic Passion*. Madison, WI: The University of Wisconsin Press, 1991.

Robinson, Mary. *Hubert de Sevrac*. London: Hookham and Carpenter, 1796.
—. *Lyrical Tales*. London: Longman, 1800.
—. *The Poetical Works of the Late Mrs. Mary Robinson: including Many Pieces Never Before Published*. 3 vols. London: Richard Phillips, 1806.
—. *Complete Poetry*. Providence, RI: Brown University/ National Endowment for the Humanities Women Writers Project, 1990.
Romantic Women Writers: Voices and Countervoices. Eds. Paula R. Feldman and Theresa Kelley. Hanover, NH: University Press of New England, 1995.
Romanticism and Feminism. Ed. Anne K. Mellor. Bloomington: Indiana University Press, 1988.
Rose, Jacqueline. *Sexuality in the Field of Vision*. London: Verso, 1986.
Ross, Marlon. *The Contours of Masculine Desire*. New York: Oxford University Press, 1989.
—. 'Romantic Quest and Conquest: Troping Masculine Power in the Crisis of Poetic Identity'. *Romanticism and Feminism*. Ed. Anne K. Mellor. Bloomington: Indiana University Press, 1988. 26–51.
Runge, Laura. *Gender and Language in British Literary Criticism, 1660–1790*. Cambridge: Cambridge University Press, 1997.
Schreiber, Ronald. 'The Rejection and Redefinition of Romance in Byron's Early Poetry'. *University of Mississippi Studies in English* 2 (1981): 43–63.
Seidler, Victor J. *Rediscovering Masculinity: Reason, Language and Sexuality*. London: Routledge, 1989.
Setzer, Sharon. 'Mary Robinson's Sylphid Self: The End of Feminine Self-Fashioning'. *Philological Quarterly* 75 (1996): 501–20.
Smith, James. *Melodrama*. London: Methuen, 1973.
Soderholm, James. 'Byron, Nietzsche, and the Mystery of Forgetting'. *CLIO* 23 (1993): 51–62.
Southey, Robert and Robert Lovell. *Poems containing The Retrospect, Odes, Elegies, Sonnets, etc.*. Bath: R. Cruttwell, 1795.
Stein, Atara. '"I Loved Her and Destroyed Her": Love and Narcissism in Byron's *Manfred*'. *Philological Quarterly* 69 (1990): 189–216.
Stephenson, Glennis. 'Poet Construction: Mrs. Hemans, L.E.L., and the Image of the Nineteenth-Century Woman Poet'. *ReImagining Women: Representations of Women in Culture*. Eds Shirley Neuman and Stephenson. Toronto: University of Toronto Press, 1993. 61–73.
—. 'Letitia Landon and the Victorian Improvisatrice: The Construction of L.E.L.'. *Victorian Poetry* 30 (1992): 1–17.
Stevenson, Lionel. 'Miss Landon, "The Milk-and-Watery Moon of our Darkness", 1824–30'. *Modern Language Quarterly* 8 (1947): 355–63.
Stillinger, Jack. *The Hoodwinking of Madeline*. Urbana: University of Illinois Press, 1971.
Stone, Lawrence. *The Family, Sex, and Marriage in England, 1500–1800*. New York: Harper and Row, 1977.
Swann, Karen. 'Harassing the Muse'. *Romanticism and Feminism*. Ed. Anne K. Mellor. Bloomington: Indiana University Press, 1988. 81–92.
Thorslev, Peter. *The Byronic Hero*. Minneapolis: University of Minnesota Press, 1962.
Tuckerman, H.T. 'Mrs. Hemans'. *Southern Literary Messenger* 7 (1841): 382.
Ty, Eleanor. 'Engendering a Female Subject: Mary Robinson's (Re)Presentations

of the Self'. *English Studies in Canada* 21 (1995): 407–31.

van Ghent, Dorothy. *Keats: The Myth of the Hero*. Rev. and ed. Jeffrey Cane Robinson. Princeton: Princeton University Press, 1983.

Vargo, Lisa. 'The Claims of "real life and manners": Coleridge and Mary Robinson'. *The Wordsworth Circle* 26 (1995): 134–37.

—. 'The Implications of Desire: Tabitha Bramble and the *Lyrical Tales*'. British Association for Romantic Studies and the North American Society for the Study of Romanticism Joint International Conference: '1798 and Its Implications'. St Mary's University College, July 1998.

Vitale, Marina. 'The Domesticated Heroine in Byron's *Corsair* and William Hone's Prose Adaptation'. *Literature and History* 10 (1984): 72–94.

Wasserman, Earl. *The Finer Tone*. Baltimore: Johns Hopkins University Press, 1953.

Watkins, Daniel P. *Sexual Power in British Romantic Poetry*. Gainesville, FL: University Press of Florida, 1996.

—. 'Social Relations in Byron's *The Giaour*'. *ELH* 52 (1985): 873–92.

Watson, Jeannie. *Risking Enchantment: Coleridge's Symbolic World of Faery*. London: University of Nebraska Press, 1990.

Wolfson, Susan. '"Romantic Ideology" and the Values of Aesthetic Form'. *Aesthetics and Ideology*. Ed. George Levine. New Brunswick, NJ: Rutgers University Press, 1994. 188–218.

—. 'Keats's *Isabella* and the "Digressions" of "Romance"'. *Criticism* 27 (1985): 247–61.

Wordsworth, William. *The Oxford Authors: William Wordsworth*. Ed. Stephen Gill. Oxford: Oxford University Press, 1988.

— and Dorothy. *Letters of William and Dorothy Wordsworth*. 3 vols. Ed. Alan G. Hill. Oxford: Clarendon Press, 1982.

The Works of Tobias Smollett, M.D. with Memoirs of his Life; to which is prefixed A View of the Commencement and Progress of Romance, by John Moore, M.D.. London: B. Law *et al.*, 1797.

Index